# Building Embedded Systems with Raspberry Pi, Linux and ELBE

KRISHNA PATTABIRAMAN

ISBN: 978-3-9828344-0-5

Cover design by Germancreative
Interior formatting by @jenny_ebooks

# DEDICATION

To my dear wife Sumona and my dear son Kratu

# ACKNOWLEDGMENTS

I would like to express my sincere gratitude to the following individuals for taking the time to review this book and share their valuable insights. Their feedback, perspectives, and encouragement have contributed meaningfully to improving the clarity, accuracy, and overall quality of this work.

- Balamurugan Selvaraj
- Balemarthy Vamsi Krishna
- Chris Simmonds
- Erik Lundh
- Gareth Bult
- John Ogness
- Josef Holzmayr
- Karthikeyan Rukmangathan
- Manikandan Pattabiraman
- Manuel Traut
- Dr Simon Monk
- Toby Roberts

# INDUSTRY SPONSOR: AFRA GMBH

**AFRA GmbH** founded in 1989 in Erlangen, Germany, is a software engineering company with over three decades of experience in the development of embedded and automation systems. The company specializes in the design of reliable, maintainable, and long-lived software solutions for technically demanding environments. AFRA's longstanding focus on quality and structured system design reflects its commitment to disciplined and sustainable engineering practices. Further information about the company and its activities can be found at https://www.afra.de.

A central aspect of AFRA's work is embedded Linux system development, including system architecture, build environments, customization, and testing. The company advocates treating the operating system as a controlled and reproducible component of the product rather than as a static image. This approach aligns closely with Debian-based embedded Linux systems and the ELBE build environment. AFRA's engineers apply these principles in projects across multiple industries where stability and long-term maintainability are critical.

By sponsoring this book, AFRA GmbH supports the dissemination of practical engineering knowledge and the promotion of best practices in embedded Linux development. The company's commitment to open technologies, disciplined system engineering, and continuous learning reflects its focus on building production-ready embedded systems based on Raspberry Pi, Linux, and ELBE.

# FORWORD

In 2008, we at Linutronix set out to develop a free software tool (ELBE) to replace our pile of custom scripts for creating Debian root filesystems. Over the years it has been a joy not only developing and using ELBE but also participating in the ELBE community. I was particularly taken back when Krishna approached me during 2025 embedded world trade fair and presented an early draft of his ELBE cookbook. I was impressed by the clear, technical, and friendly tone of his writing. And I am thrilled that someone from the community with such an obvious passion for the Raspberry Pi and ELBE would find the time and motivation to write such a book.

Today it is easier than ever to get involved in embedded Linux. But often new embedded developers treat the operating system as a black box, neither understanding the fundamental components nor knowing how to modify them to fit their needs. This book does an excellent job introducing these fundamentals while providing the necessary hints to allow a reader to dig deeper on their own. But the real strength of this

book is the well thought out practical use cases and ELBE solutions it presents. They give the reader clean examples ranging from simple minimal systems and SDKs to systems utilizing advanced security, virtualization and storage management features, all tuned for specific use case requirements.

I believe this book is a solid stepping stone for embedded newbies and ELBE experts alike. The joy of embedded Linux is not only in tinkering with devices, but also about fine-tuning and streamlining your system to be exactly what you need it to be. Enjoy your journey into learning about the Raspberry Pi, Linux root filesystems, the powerful Debian distribution, and how it all comes together using the ELBE tool.

John Ogness,
Core Developer and Original Contributor to ELBE at Linutronix

# ABOUT THE AUTHOR

Krishna Pattabiraman is an embedded systems technologist with nearly two decades of professional experience in Linux-based product development. His journey with Linux began in his school years and has evolved into a career centered on embedded Linux, electronics, and building production-ready systems.

Over the years, Krishna has contributed to the design and development of a wide range of real-world products, including telephones, set-top boxes, thermostats, vehicle diagnostic tools, and medical X-ray devices. His work spans the full product lifecycle—from low-level Linux bring-up and kernel customization to system integration, deployment, and maintenance.

Beyond his professional work, Krishna is an avid tinkerer who enjoys experimenting with single-board computers (such as the Raspberry Pi), 3D design and printing, and electronic prototyping. He is passionate about creating educational tools and sharing practical, hands-on knowledge. As a technical writer, he focuses on making complex engineering concepts clear, approachable, and immediately applicable for engineers, developers, and learners alike.

# TRADEMARKS AND COPYRIGHTS

**Raspberry Pi** is a registered trademark of Raspberry Pi Foundation.

**Linux** is a registered trademark of Linus Torvalds in the U.S. and other countries.

**Debian** is a registered trademark of Software in the Public Interest, Inc.

**ELBE** (Embedded Linux Build Environment) is developed and maintained by Linutronix GmbH. It is part of the open-source community and is distributed under its applicable open-source license.

All product names, logos, and brands mentioned in this book are the property of their respective owners. All companies, products, and service names used in this book are for identification purposes only. Use of these names, trademarks, and brands does not imply endorsement.

TABLE OF CONTENTS

# 1 Introduction

**Abstract:** This opening chapter sets the stage for the book by outlining its goals: to equip readers with practical skills for building reproducible, maintainable embedded Linux systems on Raspberry Pi using ELBE. It covers expected learning outcomes, the book's structured recipe-based approach, target audience (engineers, developers, hobbyists), prerequisites, and tips for effective use—including setting up a development environment and accessing source code. Readers gain a clear roadmap for transforming from manual tinkering to automated, professional-grade embedded development.

In today's world, electronic gadgets are everywhere, and it's amazing to see how even unexpected places are becoming smarter thanks to advancements in technology. The ever-shrinking size of silicon chips and the flexibility of software have made it possible for intelligent edge devices to permeate every corner of our lives.

A significant turning point in this technological evolution was the arrival of the Linux operating system. Linux, with its open-source nature and robust capabilities, set the stage for an explosion in the use of edge devices. Its widespread adoption was greatly facilitated by Debian, a long-term, stable, and secure distribution that helped spread Linux across the globe.

In more recent times, the emergence of Raspberry Pi has played a pivotal role in bringing Linux and Debian into schools, educational institutions, and various industries. This compact, affordable computing device has made it easier than ever for people to explore, learn, and innovate with technology, driving further adoption of Linux and expanding its impact across diverse fields.

This book delves into the integration of the Debian Linux distribution with Raspberry Pi, using the industry-standard ELBE build system. It offers a comprehensive guide for creating various use cases that leverage the combined strengths of Linux, Debian, Raspberry Pi, and ELBE to achieve optimal results.

Whether you're a hobbyist, developer, or engineer, mastering these tools will empower you to craft efficient and scalable embedded solutions. The practical approach of this book ensures hands-on experience with the scenarios you'll encounter during embedded Linux development, equipping you with the skills needed to navigate and excel in this dynamic field.

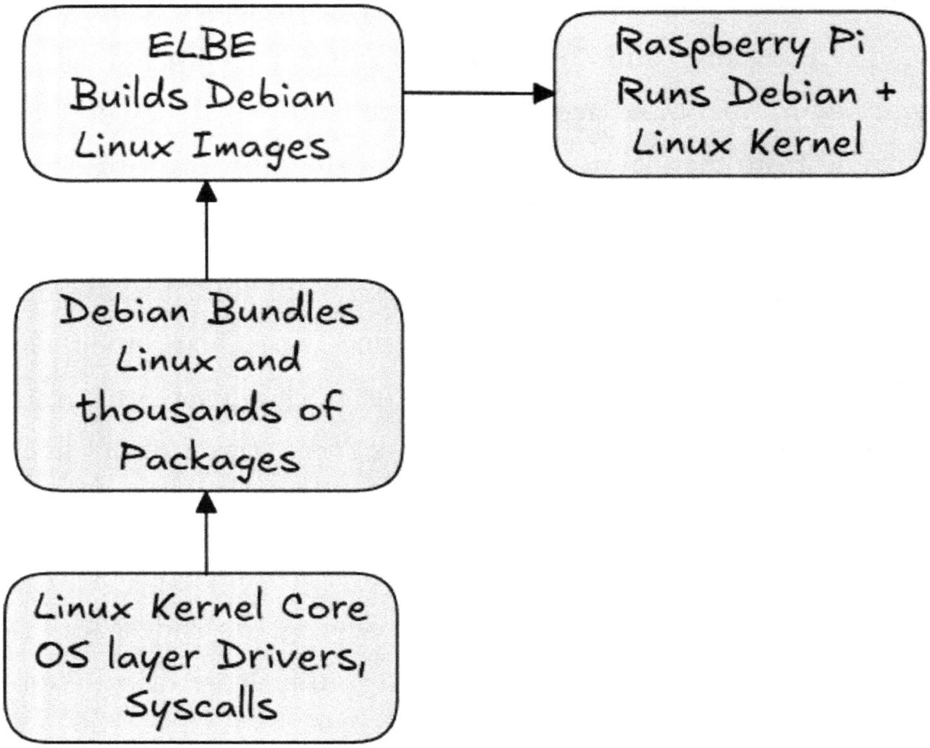


*Figure 1:Relationship between Linux, Debian, Raspberry Pi and ELBE*

## 1.1 Goals and Objectives

The primary goal of this book is to provide a comprehensive guide to building Debian-based embedded systems for Raspberry Pi using ELBE. By the end of this book, you will have achieved the following objectives:

**Linux Fundamentals**: Gain an understanding of Linux, including its core principles and application in embedded systems. Explore the Linux boot process, how to compile the Linux kernel, modify boot parameters, and review various boot methods.

**Debian Insights:** Delve into the architecture of Debian and uncover its advantages. Examine Debian's operational principles, how to tailor and optimize it for various applications, and how to leverage its package management system for effective software management and system maintenance.

**Raspberry Pi Overview:** Gain familiarity with Raspberry Pi hardware, including setup and integration with Debian-based systems. Learn about the booting process, differences among hardware versions, and practical tips for leveraging Raspberry Pi's capabilities in embedded projects.

**ELBE Mastery:** Discover the architecture and functionality of ELBE for creating custom Debian images. Learn how to manage builds and optimize embedded Linux systems using ELBE's features. Explore various options and techniques through numerous recipes tailored to different use cases.

## 1.2 Expected Outcomes

By following this book, you will be able to:

**Build Custom Debian Images**: Design and create customized Debian-based systems for Raspberry Pi using ELBE, tailored to meet specific project needs and constraints.

**Solve Real-World Problems**: Utilize your skills to address practical challenges, from setting up development environments to configuring advanced system settings.

**Update Strategies:** Develop and implement tailored update strategies for systems requiring unique solutions.

**Rapid Development:** Leverage ELBE to quickly develop solutions for urgent problems, focusing more on application needs than on infrastructure.

**Execute Practical Projects:** Complete a range of projects and recipes that showcase your ability to effectively apply the concepts and tools covered in the book.

## 1.3 Structure and Approach

**Chapter Organization:** The book is divided into two main types of chapters: thematic chapters and recipe chapters. The thematic chapters cover foundational topics such as Linux, Debian, Raspberry Pi, and ELBE. The recipe chapters focus on various use cases, providing detailed instructions on how to build and customize Debian images for different scenarios.

**Practical Recipes:** Each recipe chapter offers step-by-step instructions for creating Debian images tailored to specific needs. These recipes are designed to help you apply the concepts learned in the thematic chapters to practical, real-world situations.

## 1.4 Navigating the Content

**Read in Order of Familiarity:** The thematic chapters are organized to be read in sequence according to your existing knowledge. If you're familiar with all topics except ELBE, you can jump directly to the ELBE chapters. For those new to these subjects, reading all the thematic chapters is recommended to build a solid foundational understanding.

**Revisit When Needed:** Each recipe chapter is self-contained, offering all the necessary instructions and commands. Although detailed explanations are not repeated in every recipe, this design allows you to work through each recipe independently without needing to revisit the thematic chapters.

**Hands-On Practice:** Actively engage with hands-on projects and recipes. Experiment with the presented techniques and solutions to solidify your understanding and gain practical experience.

## 1.5 Who Should Read This Book

This book is intended for anyone interested in creating custom embedded Linux systems with Debian on a Raspberry Pi. Whether you're a student working on an academic project, a hobbyist enhancing your personal projects, a developer crafting specialized embedded solution, an engineer tackling complex system configurations, or an innovator with a groundbreaking idea needing a Raspberry Pi-based solution, this book provides valuable insights and practical guidance. It is especially useful for those who want to harness the power of ELBE (Embedded Linux Build Environment) to simplify and accelerate their development process

## 1.6 Accessing the Recipe Source Code

All the recipe examples, configuration files, and supporting scripts discussed throughout this book are available on github.com. This repository serves as a practical companion to each chapter, allowing you to explore, clone, modify, and build the images on your own system.

You can access the source code here:

```
https://github.com/rootfx-io/elbe-cookbook-recipes
```

Each recipe chapter in the book corresponds to a specific directory in the repository. The folder structure is organized by chapter and recipe type for easy navigation:

```
/
├── 01-docker
├── 02-desktop
├── 03-qemu-arm
├── 04-raspberrypi-basic
├── 05-raspberrypi-btrfs
├── 06-raspberrypi-overlayfs
├── 07-raspberrypi-encrypt
├── 08-raspberrypi-container-inside
├── 09-raspberrypi-custom-kernel
├── 10-raspberrypi-llm
└── 11-raspberrypi-ros2-ubuntu
```

You're welcome to contribute, suggest improvements, or report issues via GitHub to help enhance the recipes.

## 1.7 Prerequisites

### 1.7.1 Basic Knowledge Assumed

To effectively use this book, readers should have a basic understanding of the following:

- **Linux Basics:** Familiarity with Linux commands, filesystems, and user management will be helpful.
- **Debian Fundamentals:** While having prior experience with Debian is advantageous, it is not necessary, as the book will cover the essential concepts.
- **Raspberry Pi Basic:** Basic knowledge of Raspberry Pi hardware and setup, including connecting peripherals will assist you in getting started quickly.

### 1.7.2 Tools and Resources Needed

To follow along with this book, you will need:

- **Hardware:** A Raspberry Pi (preferably a recent model), along with essential peripherals such as a microSD card, a microSD card reader, a USB serial cable, and a power supply. For building images with ELBE, ensure your development machine has at least a dual core x86 CPU, 2 GB of RAM (4 GB recommended), and 20 GB of free disk space.
- **Software:** A development environment set up on a machine running Debian (Bookworm/Trixie) Linux, with sufficient disk space for compiling the Linux kernel and building images using ELBE.
- **Resources:** Continuous internet access for downloading Debian packages. Additionally, access to online documentation, forums, and community resources will be helpful for troubleshooting and expanding your knowledge.

## 1.8 How to Get the Most Out of This Book

### 1.8.1 Tips for Effective Learning

For the best learning experience, follow these tips:

- **Study Strategy:** Approach the thematic chapters in sequence based on your prior knowledge You may skip chapters covering topics you're already familiar with and focus on those that require deeper understanding.
- **Active Engagement:** Take notes, work through exercises, and experiment with the techniques presented in the recipes to reinforce your understanding. Engage with online communities or forums for additional support and discussion.

### 1.8.2 Setting Up a Development Environment

To set up your development environment:

- **Environment Setup:** Install the necessary software tools and ELBE on your development machine. Ensure compatibility with your Raspberry Pi model and other hardware.
- **Configuration:** Follow the configuration steps provided in the book to set up a smooth and efficient workflow. Make sure your environment is properly configured to avoid common pitfalls and streamline your development process.

# Basics of ELBE, Debian, Raspberry Pi, and Linux

Before we dive into building custom images and working with recipes, it's important to understand the foundational technologies that make this entire process possible. This chapter serves as a guided overview of the key components that underpin everything, we'll be doing in the chapters ahead.

We'll begin with a brief introduction to Linux, the open-source operating system at the core of almost all embedded systems today. Then we'll take a closer look at Raspberry Pi, a popular and versatile hardware platform that we'll be targeting throughout this book.

Next, we'll explore Debian, one of the most stable and widely used Linux distributions, known for its robustness, package ecosystem, and community support. Since ELBE is designed to build Debian-based embedded systems, understanding Debian's philosophy and structure is crucial.

Finally, we'll focus in detail on ELBE, the central tool used in this cookbook. ELBE provides a powerful and reproducible way to generate Debian-based images tailored for embedded systems. You'll learn how it works, what makes it unique, and why it's well-suited for building images for Raspberry Pi and beyond.

By the end of this chapter, you'll have a solid foundation in the tools and platforms that this book revolves around, and you'll be ready to start building your own embedded Linux images with clarity and confidence.

# 2 Why ELBE?

**Abstract:** This foundational chapter critiques the traditional "golden image" method for Raspberry Pi projects, which is easy to start but plagued by non-reproducibility, lack of version control, configuration drift, and scalability issues. It introduces the superior alternative of treating the OS as declarative code via build systems. It positions ELBE as a Debian-centric tool that leverages mature package management and security updates while offering XML-based configuration for automated, transparent image creation. Comparisons to other build tools highlight ELBE's accessible middle ground, ideal for Raspberry Pi prototypes and production.

## 2.1 The Traditional Approach: Golden Images

When most people start working with Raspberry Pi–based projects, the usual workflow is simple and familiar. You download an operating system image, flash it to an SD card, boot the board, and then begin configuring the system manually. Over time, you install packages, tweak configuration files, enable services, and adjust settings until everything works exactly the way you want.

*Figure 2 Golden Image ecosystem*

Once the system looks "right," the SD card is often cloned or backed up. This cloned image commonly referred to as a golden image is then reused for other boards or stored as a fallback.

While this approach works well for experiments and one-off projects, it starts to break down surprisingly fast.

Small changes become difficult to track. You may not remember which packages were installed manually or which configuration file was edited and why. Reproducing the same system months later becomes challenging. Sharing the setup with others often turns into a game of trial and error. If something goes wrong, debugging is difficult because the image itself does not explain how it was created.

For hobby projects, this may be inconvenient. For larger or long-term projects, it quickly becomes a serious problem.

## 2.2 The Limits of Golden Images

Golden images are fundamentally binary snapshots. They capture a system at one moment in time, but they do not capture the process that created it.

This leads to several common issues:

- Lack of reproducibility: Rebuilding the same image from scratch is nearly impossible.
- No version control: Binary images cannot be meaningfully diffed or reviewed.
- Configuration drift: Two "identical" images often behave differently over time.
- Poor scalability: Managing many devices becomes manual and error-prone.
- Difficult maintenance: Applying security updates or system changes is risky.

As projects grow, even hobby projects, these problems compound. What started as a quick experiment slowly turns into an unmaintainable system.

## 2.3 Build Systems: Treating the OS as Code

A build system approaches the problem from a completely different angle.

Instead of manually configuring a running system and capturing the result, a build system describes the system declaratively. In other words, you write down what the system should contain, not how you manually installed it.

This description includes:

- Which base operating system to use
- Which packages should be installed
- How the system should be configured
- How the final image should be generated

From this description, the build system automatically creates the complete operating system image.

This approach brings powerful advantages:

- The system can be rebuilt at any time
- Changes are tracked in text files
- Builds can be automated
- The process is transparent and repeatable

For beginners, this might sound complex at first—but in practice, it often simplifies development rather than complicating it.

## 2.4 Introducing ELBE

ELBE (Embedded Linux Build Environment) is a build-system specifically designed for creating Debian-based embedded Linux systems.

Instead of reinventing Linux from scratch, ELBE builds directly on top of Debian's existing strengths:

- A mature package ecosystem
- Proven dependency management
- Long-term security updates
- Excellent documentation and tooling

With ELBE, you describe your target system using an XML file. This file defines the Debian release, packages, users, services, filesystem layout, and more. ELBE then uses this description to automatically build a complete bootable image for your Raspberry Pi or other supported targets.

The result is a system that feels like a normal Debian installation—but is created in a controlled, reproducible, and automated way.

## 2.5 ELBE Compared to Other Approaches

It is helpful to briefly understand how ELBE differs from other popular solutions.

Some build-systems compile the entire operating system from source. While this offers maximum control, it also increases complexity and build-time. Others rely on custom scripts that grow organically and become difficult to maintain.

ELBE occupies a middle ground. It offers structure, reproducibility, and automation while staying close to a standard Debian system. This balance makes it particularly suitable for Raspberry Pi–based projects, prototypes, and educational use.

ELBE is not intended to replace all build systems. Instead, it excels when Debian is the right foundation—and for many Raspberry Pi projects, it is.

**Summary**

Golden images are easy to start with, but difficult to maintain. Build systems solve this problem by treating the operating system as code.

ELBE brings this approach to the Debian ecosystem in a way that is accessible, powerful, and beginner friendly. By using ELBE, you gain reproducibility, transparency, and long-term maintainability without sacrificing the convenience of Debian.

The rest of this book builds on this foundation, gradually introducing the tools, concepts, and recipes needed to create reliable embedded Linux systems using ELBE and Raspberry Pi.

# 3 Linux Kernel Basics

**Abstract:** This chapter demystifies the Linux kernel's role in embedded systems, explaining the boot process from hardware initialization to user space handoff, kernel command-line parameters, the strict kernel/user-space divide, and fundamental mechanisms like system calls and libc. Readers build essential understanding of how the kernel interacts with hardware and applications, preparing them to customize and debug boot behavior in later ELBE recipes.

In the world of embedded systems, especially when working with platforms such as Raspberry Pi, understanding of how Linux boots is essential. Unlike general-purpose desktop systems, embedded Linux requires fine-grained control over the boot process, the root file system, and the kernel configuration. Before diving into building images using ELBE, it is important to understand the lifecycle of a Linux system from the moment the device is powered on to the point where your application is up and running.

This section provides an overview of how Linux boots, how the kernel interacts with user space, what role the root file system and kernel modules play, and how hardware is described using the device tree. These fundamentals will help you make better decisions when crafting your own embedded images.

## 3.1 The Linux Boot Process: From Hardware to Kernel

The journey of a Linux system begins with the boot ROM, a tiny, immutable piece of firmware embedded in the system-on-chip (SoC) by the hardware vendor. Its role is simple but crucial: initialize basic hardware (such as memory and clocks) and load the first stage bootloader from a known location such as an SD card, eMMC, or SPI flash.

Typically, the boot ROM loads a bootloader such as U-Boot, Barebox, or any other vendor-specific code and transfers control to it (see Figure 3 for an overview of the boot process). The bootloader reads configuration data from a file or environment variables and is responsible for loading the Linux kernel, initramfs (initial RAM filesystem), and the device tree. Once loaded, it hands over control to the kernel.

The kernel then performs further hardware initialization and searches for the init process to start the user space. If an initramfs is present, the kernel launches the init process from it; otherwise, it loads it from the root file system. The initramfs may also include drivers and utilities (e.g., network drivers, storage utilities) required for specific hardware or boot scenarios.

Once the kernel completes its initialization, it locates the root file system and starts the main init system such as systemd, SysVinit, or another init system.

This structured boot sequence ensures flexibility and modularity, allowing Linux to adapt to a wide variety of hardware platforms. Each stage builds on the previous, with clearly defined responsibilities, from initializing hardware to launching user applications. By separating concerns, system integrators can customize or debug specific layers without impacting the entire process. This modularity is especially valuable in embedded systems, where reliability and tailored configurations are critical.

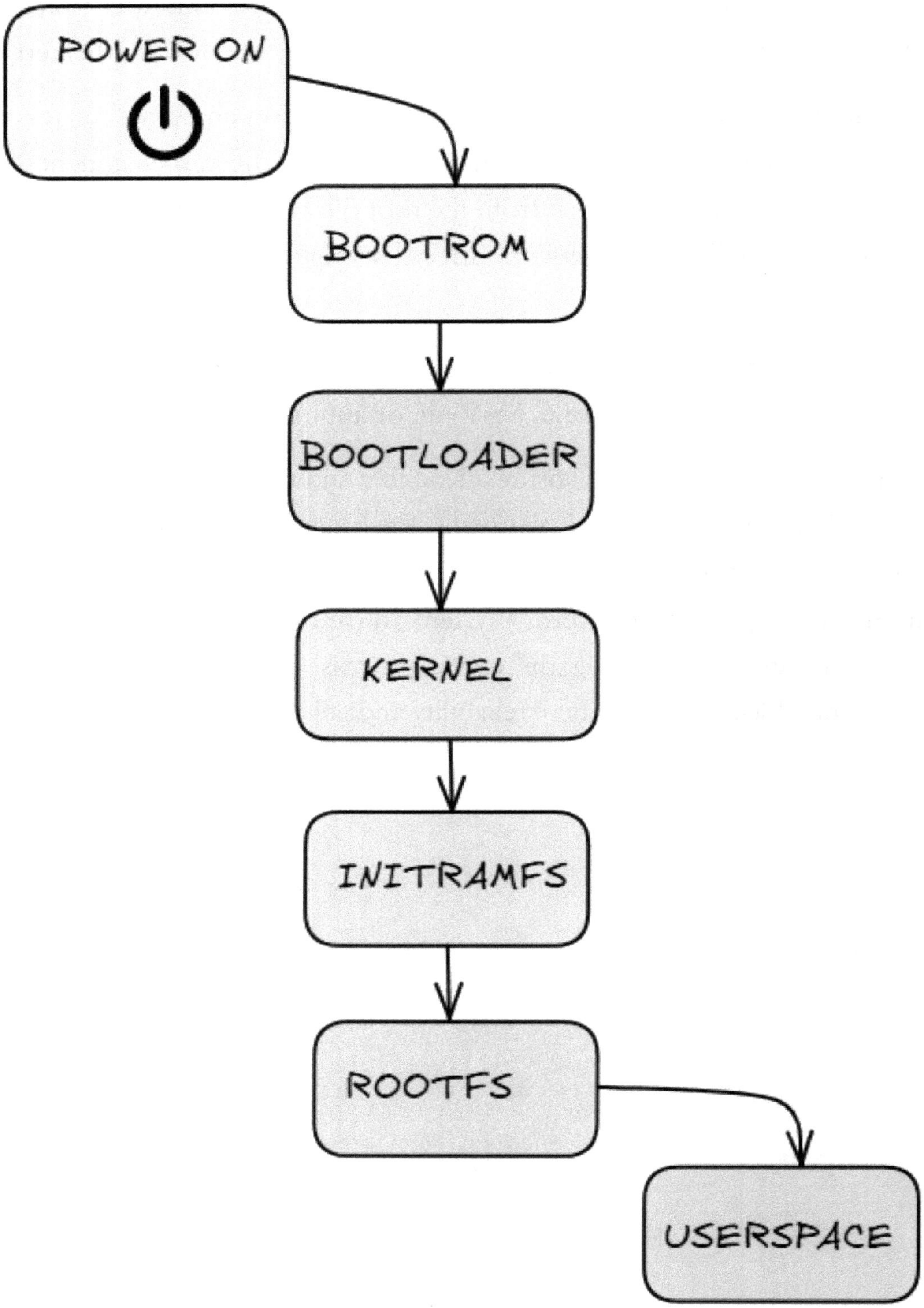


*Figure 3:Linux boot process flow*

On a Raspberry Pi, the BootROM loads the first-stage boot code from the FAT32-formatted boot partition. On older models, this is typically bootcode.bin, On newer Raspberry Pi models, the BootROM uses the EEPROM bootloader to directly load the GPU firmware file start.elf, which initializes the GPU and system memory, then continues the chain of loading additional firmware, configuration files, and the kernel. Alongside the kernel, some important files are used:

- **config.txt** – Configures hardware settings such as video, overlays, etc.
- **cmdline.txt** – Contains kernel boot parameters.
- **Device Tree Blob (.dtb)** – Describes the board's hardware configuration.

These components are loaded into memory and handed over to the kernel to begin the initialization process of the operating system.

## 3.2 Kernel Parameters and Command-Line Interface

The cmdline.txt file holds kernel parameters that modify how the kernel behaves during boot. These parameters are read by the bootloader and passed to the kernel via memory during the boot process.

Common kernel parameters include:

- **root=/dev/mmcblk0p2** – Specifies the root filesystem.
- **init=/sbin/init** – Defines the first user-space process.
- **console=ttyAMA0,115200** – Sets up serial output for debugging.
- **ro or rw** – Mounts the root filesystem as read-only or read-write.

A misconfigured parameter can prevent the system from booting, so precise definition is critical, especially in embedded environments where interactive debugging may not be possible.

## 3.3 Kernel and User Space: A Structured Divide

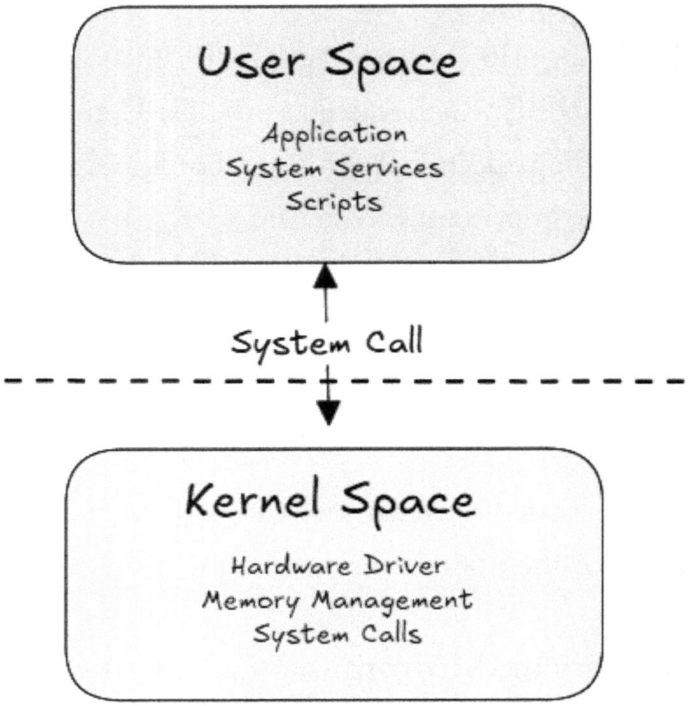


*Figure 4:Kernel space vs user space*

The kernel operates in privileged mode known as kernel space, where it manages low-level operations such as memory management, process scheduling, device drivers, and interrupt handling. In this mode, the kernel has unrestricted access to all hardware resources and is responsible for enforcing protection boundaries between processes

Meanwhile, user space hosts applications, system services, and scripts. Programs in user space run with limited privileges and must request access to hardware or kernel-managed resources through well-defined interfaces such as system calls. This separation ensures stability and security: even if a user-space program crashes, it does not compromise the integrity of the kernel or other running processes.

This clear division between kernel space and user space is fundamental to Linux's design, providing both isolation and controlled interaction. The mechanism that enables this controlled interaction is the system call interface, which serves as the formal gateway from user space into the kernel.

## 3.4 Understanding System Calls and the C Library

A key mechanism that enables controlled interaction between user-space programs and the kernel is the system call interface. Understanding this interface is especially important in embedded systems, such as when targeting a Raspberry Pi using a Debian base, for building stable, portable, and efficient software.

### System Calls: The Kernel's API

At the heart of this interaction are **system calls**. These predefined functions, exposed by the kernel, allow applications to perform privileged operations safely. Common examples include:

- ***read()*** and ***write()*** for file and device I/O
- ***fork()*** and ***execve()*** for process control
- ***mmap()*** for memory mapping
- ***socket()*** for network communication

Unlike ordinary library functions, system calls transition the processor from user mode to kernel mode, giving applications a controlled access to hardware and low-level resources. Direct interaction with system calls is generally cumbersome and architecture-specific. To simplify development, Linux provides a standard C library.

The **GNU C Library (Glibc)** acts as a high-level wrapper around system calls. It provides a standardized interface enabling developers to write portable, maintainable code without dealing directly with low-level kernel details.

For example, calling fopen() invokes a Glibc wrapper around the open() system call. In addition to wrapping system calls, Glibc handles:

- Buffering
- Error reporting (errno)

- Signal management
- Memory allocation
- Localization

As shown in Figure 5, when a program calls fwrite(), the request passes through multiple layers starting from the C library, which provides a high-level interface, down to the kernel interface before ultimately reaching and executing the sys_write system call. This flow illustrates how user space functions interact with the kernel in a controlled and secure manner, allowing applications to perform I/O operations without directly accessing hardware resources.

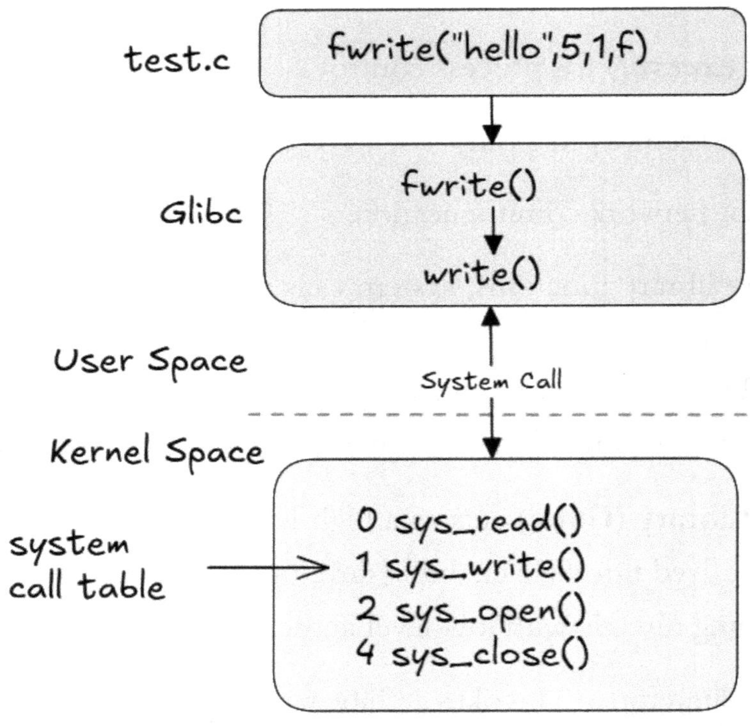


*Figure 5: System call flow*

In the context of Raspberry Pi systems running Debian, Glibc is a core component of the user-space environment. It ensures compatibility with the broader Debian ecosystem and allows applications to run across a wide range of hardware with minimal modification.

## Glibc and Debian in Embedded Development

Debian provides robust support for Glibc through core packages such as:

- **libc6** – the runtime library
- **libc6-dev** – the headers and development files
- **libc-bin** – essential tools such as **ldd, getent**, etc.

These are maintained in sync with Debian's stable release cycles, ensuring long-term support, reliability, and security, which are qualities crucial for embedded systems.

Debian also includes related libraries that work alongside Glibc:

- **libpthread** – POSIX threading support
- **libm** – mathematical operations
- **librt** – real-time extensions
- **libnss** – name service switch support for user and host lookup

When building custom embedded Linux images using ELBE, these libraries are often automatically included or selectively added depending on the image profile. Developers targeting constrained devices can also replace Glibc with lighter alternatives such as musl or uClibc if needed, though this generally means moving away from Debian's standard tooling.

## Importance of Version Compatibility

It's important to note that Glibc is not ABI (Application Binary Interface)-stable across major versions. Binaries compiled against one version may not work correctly or at all on systems with a different Glibc version. When using Debian in embedded environments, it's best to build and test your software using the same Glibc version provided by the target Debian suite (e.g., Bullseye, Bookworm, Trixie).

Using ELBE to define your base image ensures consistency, as you can lock the target suite and architecture, guaranteeing your software is tested against the exact version of Glibc and system headers that will run in production.

**Root Filesystem and Initramfs:**

Before user space can operate, the kernel must mount a root filesystem which is the top-level directory structure of the operating system. But how does the kernel access this root filesystem before all drivers or filesystems are loaded?

That's where initramfs comes in. The Initial RAM Filesystem is a small, compressed, temporary filesystem loaded directly into memory during boot. It contains just enough tools and scripts to prepare the system to mount the real root filesystem. For example, initramfs might:

- Load storage device drivers.
- Decrypt root partition (if encryption is used.).
- Mount remote or read-only filesystems.

Once the real root filesystem is mounted (commonly as ext4, btrfs, or squashfs filesystems), the initramfs is no longer needed and is released from memory, and the kernel pivots to the root filesystem, where the main init system takes over.

**Kernel Modules vs Built-In Features**

Linux provides flexibility through **kernel modules** (. ko files), which allow features to be loaded at runtime rather than compiled directly into the kernel. This modularity helps keep the kernel image minimal, especially in embedded systems, by loading only the required components.

However, certain drivers or features needed before the root filesystem is mounted, such as the ext4 filesystem driver or drivers for the primary storage device, must be built into the kernel. This requires selecting **y (yes)** rather than **m (module)** in the kernel configuration.

Kernel modules are typically stored in **/lib/modules/<kernel-version>/** and managed using commands such as **modprobe, insmod,** or **rmmod**. Using initramfs and modular kernel features together allows embedded systems to remain flexible while ensuring the kernel has the drivers it needs during early boot.

## The Role of the Device Tree

Embedded platforms such as the Raspberry Pi differ from PCs in that they lack standardized BIOS or UEFI to describe hardware configurations. Each board has a unique arrangement of processors, memory, peripherals, and buses. Initially, this hardware information was hardcoded into the Linux kernel for each board, but this approach was inflexible and difficult to maintain.

To address this, Linux uses the **device tree**, a separate data structure passed to the kernel at boot time that describes the hardware layout. The device tree includes information such as:

- CPU architecture and clock speeds
- Memory regions
- Peripheral addresses and interrupts
- GPIO, I2C, SPI and other hardware interfaces

This system allows a single kernel image to support multiple board variants, with the device tree defining the differences. The human-readable device tree source (.dts) file is compiled using the device tree compiler (dtc) into a binary device tree blob (.dtb), which the bootloader loads into memory alongside the kernel. Developers can also apply Device Tree Overlays (dtbo) to add or modify hardware descriptions at runtime, enabling features such as additional GPIO pins, I2C sensors, or HATs without modifying the base.dtb.

## Evolving Standards: usr-merge and the Unified Filesystem

As Linux and Debian evolved, the way system binaries and libraries are organized has also changed. Traditionally, executables and system tools were split across /bin,

/usr/bin, /sbin, and /usr/sbin due to early Unix design constraints. Modern systems, however, rarely need this separation. To simplify the filesystem layout and reduce redundancy, Debian has adopted the **usr-merge** strategy, consolidating:

- **/bin → /usr/bin**
- **/lib → /usr/lib**
- **/sbin → /usr/sbin**

This consolidation makes the filesystem simpler to manage and compatible with modern boot mechanisms, while still supporting setups where /usr may be on a separate partition.

### Summary

Understanding the internals of Linux from the boot sequence to the root filesystem, and from kernel modules to device trees equips you to build custom, efficient, and stable embedded Linux images. These foundational concepts are especially relevant when using a build system such as ELBE, which automates and structures the creation of complete Debian-based images.

In the upcoming sections, we will explore how Raspberry Pi fits into this architecture, why Debian is an ideal base for embedded Linux, and how ELBE orchestrates the entire build process with clarity and reproducibility.

# 4 Raspberry Pi Basics

**Abstract:** Focusing on the Raspberry Pi platform, this chapter traces its history and model evolution, details the unique multi-stage boot process (firmware, bootloader, kernel loading), and explains the critical role of config.txt in configuring hardware parameters, overlays, and boot options. It equips readers with hardware-specific knowledge needed to tailor ELBE-generated images for reliable Raspberry Pi deployment.

In the previous chapters, we explored how applications interact with the Linux kernel using system calls and the role the C standard library in providing a portable and convenient interface to these low-level operations. While these abstractions enable high-level development, an embedded system must ultimately connect bare hardware to a working user space.

This chapter shifts focus to the very beginning of that journey: the boot process on Raspberry Pi platform. To understand how Linux reaches the point where user applications and libraries come into play, we first need to examine what happens immediately after power is applied to the board, following Raspberry Pi's unique boot sequence.

## 4.1 Raspberry Pi Platform: History and Models

The Raspberry Pi is a series of low-cost, credit-card-sized single-board computers developed by Raspberry Pi Foundation, powered by Broadcom system-on-chip (SoC) processors. Originally created to promote computer science education in schools, and has since expanded into widespread use among hobbyists, developers, and the maker community.

Below is a chronological list of the major Raspberry Pi models, each bringing incremental performance, connectivity, and form factor improvements:

### Key Milestones and Models in Raspberry Pi History

- **Raspberry Pi 1 Model B** (2012) - BCM2835 (ARM11, 700 MHz)
- **Raspberry Pi 1 Model A** (2013) - BCM2835 (ARM11, 700 MHz)
- **Raspberry Pi 1 Model B+** (2014) - BCM2835 (ARM11, 700 MHz)
- **Raspberry Pi 1 Model A+** (2014) - BCM2835 (ARM11, 700 MHz)
- **Raspberry Pi 2 Model B** (2015) - BCM2836 (later revised to BCM2837)
- **Raspberry Pi Zero** (2015) - BCM2835 (ARM11, 1 GHz)
- **Raspberry Pi 3 Model B** (2016) - BCM2837 (Quad-core Cortex-A53, 1.2 GHz)
- **Raspberry Pi Zero W** (2017) - BCM2835 variant with wireless
- **Raspberry Pi 3 Model B+** (2018) - BCM2837B0 (Quad-core Cortex-A53, 1.4 GHz)
- **Raspberry Pi 3 Model A+** (2018) - BCM2837B0 (Quad-core Cortex-A53, 1.4 GHz)
- **Raspberry Pi 4 Model B** (2019) - BCM2711 (Quad-core Cortex-A72, 1.5 GHz)
- **Raspberry Pi 400** (2020) - BCM2711 (Quad-core Cortex-A72, 1.8 GHz)
- **Raspberry Pi Zero 2 W** (2021) - RP3A0 (Quad-core Cortex-A53, 1 GHz)
- **Raspberry Pi 5** (2023) - BCM2712 (Quad-core Cortex-A76, 2.4 GHz)

Each new Raspberry Pi generation introduced improved performance, expanded peripheral support, and architectural changes that affected the way the board boots and loads an operating system. These differences are important to understand when building custom Linux images, as they influence everything from firmware expectations to kernel compatibility across different Raspberry Pi targets.

## 4.2 Boot Process of Raspberry Pi

Before the Linux kernel can begin executing and interacting with hardware, several low-level components must be initialized. This sequence, known as the boot process, has evolved across Raspberry Pi models but retains a common structure. All boards start with the SoC's BootROM, which relies on the GPU to initialize memory and load the first-stage firmware. On earlier models, this GPU-driven chain handled the entire process, while newer boards such as the Raspberry Pi 4 and 5 extend it with a dedicated bootloader in EEPROM, adding flexibility and greater configuration options.

In this section, we will break down the shared boot architecture used across the Pi Zero 2, 3, 4, and 5, while also highlighting enhancements unique to each model.

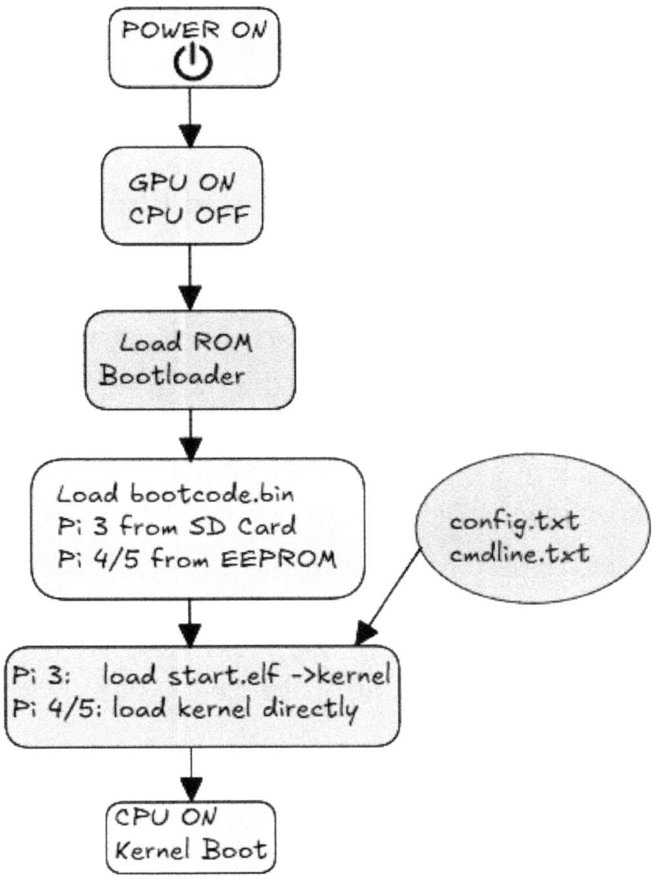


*Figure 6: Raspberry Pi Boot flow*

## Common Boot Process Across Raspberry Pi 3, 4, and 5

Despite hardware differences, the fundamental boot process of Raspberry Pi 3, 4, and 5 follows a similar staged sequence, shown in Figure 6:

1. **Power-On Initialization**
   - When power is applied, the ARM CPU cores remain off, while the GPU inside the SoC becomes active and begins the boot sequence.
2. **Executing the First Stage Bootloader**
   - The GPU executes the first-stage bootloader, which is stored in the SoC ROM. This initial bootloader is extremely minimal and is designed to give GPU access to the SD card or other boot media.
   - The first-stage bootloader's primary task is to load the second-stage bootloader or, in the case of Raspberry Pi 4 and 5, check for recovery files which may trigger an EEPROM update.
3. **Loading the Second Stage Bootloader and Firmware**
   - Once the SD card is accessible, the GPU loads the second-stage bootloader, typically bootcode.bin, into memory. This stage involves enabling the SDRAM, which is critical for proceeding with the boot process.
   - The GPU then loads the firmware files (start.elf and related files such as fixup.dat) from the boot partition of the SD card. These firmware files configure essential system and prepare the system to hand control over to the Linux kernel.
4. **Loading Kernel and Configuration Files**
   - After the firmware is loaded, the GPU loads the kernel.img, config.txt, and cmdline.txt files from the SD card. These files are crucial for setting up the hardware parameters, passing kernel arguments, and eventually booting the operating system.

- The config.txt file allows users to customize hardware settings, such as display resolution, overclocking, and enabling or disabling specific interfaces.
- The cmdline.txt file provides the kernel with command-line parameters necessary for system startup, such as defining the root filesystem location.

5. **Starting Up the ARM CPU and Booting the Kernel**
   - With everything in place, the GPU wakes up the ARM CPU cores, which then begin executing the Linux kernel. The kernel takes over the boot process, initializes hardware, mounts filesystems, and starts system services.
6. **Kernel Boot-Up and Operating System Initialization**
   - The Linux kernel completes its boot process, and the operating system becomes fully operational. At this point, Raspberry Pi is ready for use, whether for desktop applications, embedded systems, or other projects.

**Raspberry Pi Zero 2, 3:**

Use a first-stage bootloader in ROM and a second-stage bootloader (bootcode.bin) on the SD card. Firmware files (start.elf, fixup.dat) handle GPU initialization.

**Raspberry Pi 4 and 5:**

Use an EEPROM-based second-stage bootloader. This EEPROM bootloader, stored within the EEPROM chip, enables advanced boot options and firmware updates.

## 4.3 How config.txt works in the Boot Process

### Reading config.txt During Boot

During Raspberry Pi boot process, after the GPU executes the initial BootROM code and second-stage bootloader, the bootloader accesses the SD card to read the config.txt file located in the boot partition. This file contains a series of key-value pairs that define hardware configuration settings and system instructions, which the bootloader applies before handing control to the Linux kernel.

### Applying Hardware Settings

The bootloader uses the parameters in config.txt to configure essential hardware components:

- **Memory Split:** Allocates a defined portion of RAM to the GPU, with the remainder reserved for the CPU.
- **Display Settings:** Configures HDMI resolution, video modes, and other graphical parameters.
- **Hardware Interfaces:** Enables or disables interfaces such as I2C, SPI, or UART according to the directives in the file.
- **Clock Speeds and Overclocking:** Sets CPU and GPU frequencies when specified in the configuration.

### Interaction with the Kernel

While config.txt is essential for setting up the hardware environment, it does not directly pass parameters to the kernel. Instead, it prepares the system by configuring the hardware and the environment in which the kernel will operate.

- **Indirect Influence:** Some settings in config.txt indirectly affect kernel behavior by ensuring the necessary hardware configuration is in place before the kernel starts.
- **Separate File for Kernel Parameters:** Direct kernel parameters are managed through a different file, cmdline.txt. This file contains a single line of text with parameters which the bootloader passes directly to the kernel.

### Key Points:

- **config.txt:** Configures hardware settings applied by the bootloader before the kernel is loaded. It sets up the environment and hardware configuration but does not pass parameters directly to the kernel.

- **cmdline.txt:** Used to pass command-line parameters directly to the kernel. This file provides specific instructions to the kernel for its operation.

**Precedence of Parameters:**

If both config.txt and cmdline.txt specify parameters such as initramfs, the parameters in cmdline.txt take precedence. The bootloader uses the settings in cmdline.txt to pass parameters directly to the kernel, overriding any related settings specified in config.txt.

For more information refer:
https://www.raspberrypi.com/documentation/computers/config_txt.html

**kernel.img:**

The Linux kernel image. By default, when not specified in the config.txt these filenames are searched by the bootloader depending on the model of Raspberry Pi

- kernel.img: For older ARMv6 devices (Raspberry Pi 1, Zero).
- kernel7.img: For ARMv7 32-bit devices (Raspberry Pi 2, 3, Zero 2 W).
- kernel8.img: For ARMv8 64-bit devices (Raspberry Pi 4 and newer).

An **initramfs** is an optional file that can be used during the boot process. It helps load kernel modules, drivers, and other essential components before the root filesystem is mounted. If used, the initramfs file must be placed in the boot partition (see Figure 7), and its filename must be referenced in the config.txt file.

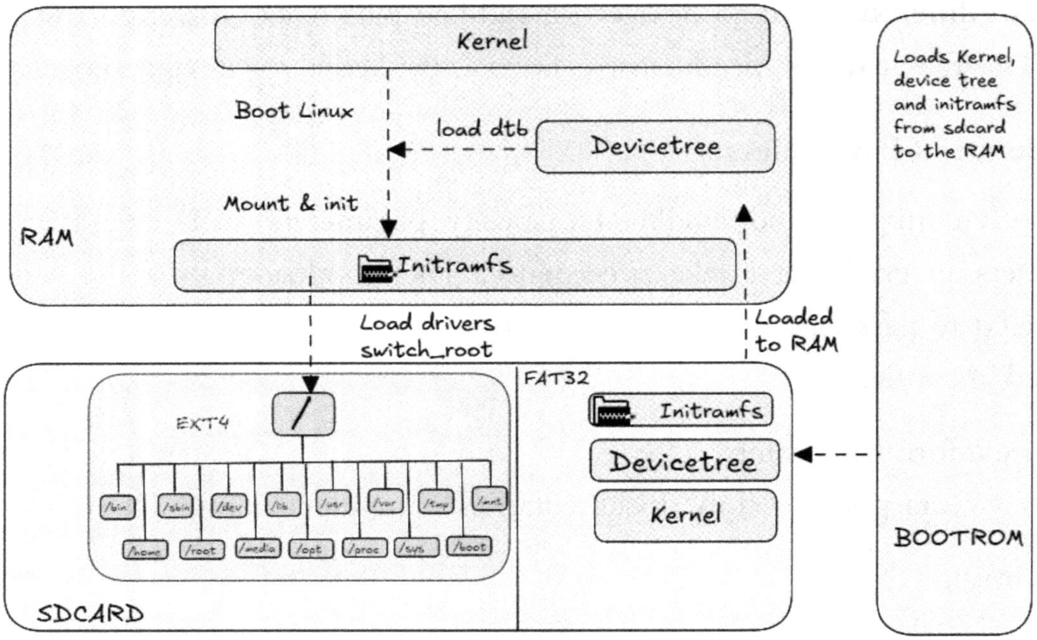


*Figure 7: Kernel, Initramfs, device tree loading and boot flow*

## Common initramfs filenames

Like kernel.img, the initramfs is also searched for in the FAT partition using a default filename, unless a specific one is defined in config.txt. Below are the possible filenames.

1. **initramfs.img**
   - A generic name for the initramfs file.
2. **initramfs-<kernel version>.img**
   - Includes the kernel version in the filename (e.g., initramfs-6.1.0.img).
   - This format is useful when using multiple kernels to ensure the initramfs matches the kernel version.
3. **Custom names**
   - You can name the initramfs file anything you prefer, but the filename must be referenced explicitly in config.txt.

**To use an initramfs on a Raspberry Pi, follow these steps:**

- Place the **initramfs file** in the boot partition. modify the following line in config.txt.
- Replace initramfs.img with your actual filename. The followkernel option ensures the initramfs matches the kernel version.

```
initramfs initramfs.img followkernel
```

**Device tree:**

The device tree in Raspberry Pi serves as a structured way to describe the hardware components and their configurations to the Linux kernel. Instead of hardcoding hardware details into the kernel, the device tree provides a flexible and modular approach, enabling the same kernel to work across different Raspberry Pi models without modification.

**Based on the device model the corresponding device tree file is loaded by the bootloader:**

- **bcm2712-rpi-5-b.dtb**: Pi 5 Model B.
- **bcm2711-rpi-4-b.dtb**: Pi 4 Model B.
- **bcm2711-rpi-400.dtb**: Pi 400 (keyboard computer).
- **bcm2711-rpi-cm4.dtb**: Pi Compute Module 4.
- **bcm2837-rpi-3-b.dtb**: Pi 3 Model B.
- **bcm2837-rpi-3-b-plus.dtb**: Pi 3 Model B+.
- **bcm2837-rpi-cm3.dtb**: Pi Compute Module 3.
- **bcm2837-rpi-2-b.dtb**: Pi 2 Model B (Revision 1.2.
- **bcm2710-rpi-zero-2-w.dtb**: Pi Zero 2 W.

- **bcm2835-rpi-b.dtb**: Pi Model B (1st Generation).
- **bcm2835-rpi-a.dtb**: Pi Model A.
- **bcm2835-rpi-b-plus.dtb**: Pi Model B+.
- **bcm2835-rpi-a-plus.dtb**: Pi Model A+.
- **bcm2835-rpi-zero.dtb**: Pi Zero.
- **bcm2835-rpi-zero-w.dtb**: Pi Zero W.
- **bcm2835-rpi-cm1.dtb**: Compute Module 1 (uses BCM2835).
- **bcm2711-rpi-cm4.dtb**: Compute Module 4 (uses BCM2711).
- **bcm2837-rpi-cm3.dtb**: Compute Module 3 (uses BCM2837).

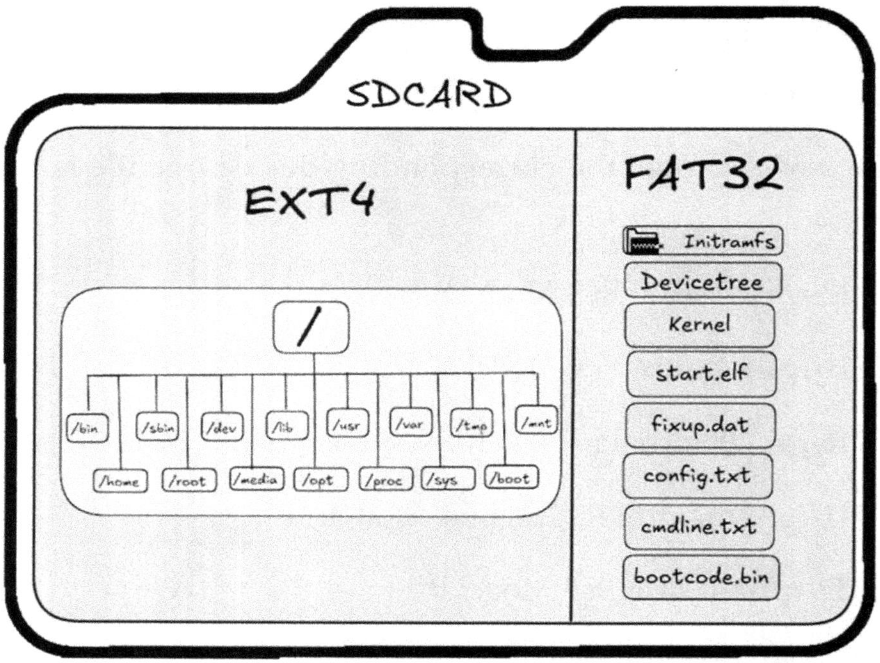


*Figure 8: Example Files in the Boot Partition*

To boot any Raspberry Pi, the boot partition must be formatted using the FAT file system, typically FAT32. The root filesystem is usually formatted as ext4 and contains the operating system along with user data (see Figure 8). During the boot process, the kernel searches the /lib/modules directory for the appropriate modules, based on the version encoded within the kernel itself. Although the kernel file may be named something like kernel8.img, its internal version (e.g., 6.1.0-v7+) determines the path used for loading modules—such as /lib/modules/6.1.0-v7+/.

**Summary:**

In this chapter, we explored Raspberry Pi platform from both a historical and technical perspective, covering its model evolution, unique GPU-driven boot architecture, and the critical role of configuration files, firmware, and device trees in system initialization. Understanding these components is essential for gaining control over the boot process and tailoring systems for specific applications. These insights form a crucial foundation for embedded Linux development on Raspberry Pi.

# 5 Debian Basics

**Abstract:** This comprehensive chapter explores Debian as the robust foundation for ELBE-built systems. It covers Debian's history, architecture (including the OS structure, package management tools like apt/dpkg, and repository organization), and advanced features beyond packages, such as debconf for configuration prompts, preseeding for automated installs, debootstrap for bootstrapping root filesystems (including foreign architecture support via QEMU), and keyring management for secure package verification. Readers learn why Debian's ecosystem excels for embedded reproducibility and long-term maintenance.

## 5.1 History and Milestones

Debian is one of the oldest and most influential Linux distributions, renowned for its stability and unwavering commitment to open-source principles. It was founded in 1993 by Ian Murdock, who envisioned a community-driven operating system prioritizing quality, reliability, and transparency. The name Debian is a blend of Debra (Murdock's then-girlfriend) and Ian.

The first release, Debian 0.91, introduced a novel approach to Linux distribution: Debian introduced centralized package management, with packages rigorously tested for quality, and distributed under free software licenses. Over the decades, Debian has evolved into a base for many popular distributions, including Ubuntu, Kali Linux, and Raspberry Pi OS.

Today, the Debian Project is managed by a worldwide community of developers who coordinate through mailing lists, forums, and annual conferences. Since its first stable release in 1996, Debian has progressed through numerous major versions, each introducing new features and enhancements while maintaining a focus on stability and security. The release cycle is meticulously planned, with each stable version undergoing extensive testing before being deemed production ready.

Debian releases are named after characters from Pixar's Toy Story, a tradition that adds a playful touch to its serious technical mission. Each release delivers improvements in functionality, security, and hardware compatibility. Below is a timeline of key releases:

1. Debian 1.1 - "*Buzz*" (1996)
2. Debian 1.2 - "*Rex*" (1996)
3. Debian 1.3 - "*Bo*" (1997)
4. Debian 2.0 - "*Hamm*" (1998)
5. Debian 2.1 - "*Slink*" (1999)
6. Debian 2.2 - "*Potato*" (2000)
7. Debian 3.0 - "*Woody*" (2002)
8. Debian 3.1 - "*Sarge*" (2005)
9. Debian 4.0 - "*Etch*" (2007)
10. Debian 5.0 - "*Lenny*" (2009)
11. Debian 6.0 - "*Squeeze*" (2011)
12. Debian 7.0 - "*Wheezy*" (2013)
13. Debian 8.0 - "*Jessie*" (2015)
14. Debian 9.0 - "*Stretch*" (2017)
15. Debian 10.0 - "*Buster*" (2019)
16. Debian 11.0 - "*Bullseye*" (2021)
17. Debian 12.0 - "*Bookworm*" (2023)
18. Debian 13.0 - "*Trixie*" (2025)

### Debian's Philosophy and Community

At the heart of Debian lies its *Social Contract*, a set of principles that guide its development and community:

1. **Free Software**: All software in Debian's main repository is free to use, modify, and redistribute.
2. **Transparency**: Contributors ensure openness in development processes and bug reporting.
3. **User-Centric Development**: Debian prioritizes its users, offering tools for customization and control.

The *Debian Free Software Guidelines (DFSG)* define the standards for software inclusion, ensuring that only software adhering to strict freedom principles is part of the main repository.

Debian's governance is democratic and managed by its developer community. Major decisions are made through votes, and annual events such as DebConf foster collaboration among contributors and users.

## 5.2 Debian Architecture Overview

The architecture of the Debian system is organized to balance stability, modularity, and maintainability. Figure 9 illustrates the key components that make up Debian and how they interact to form a complete operating system.

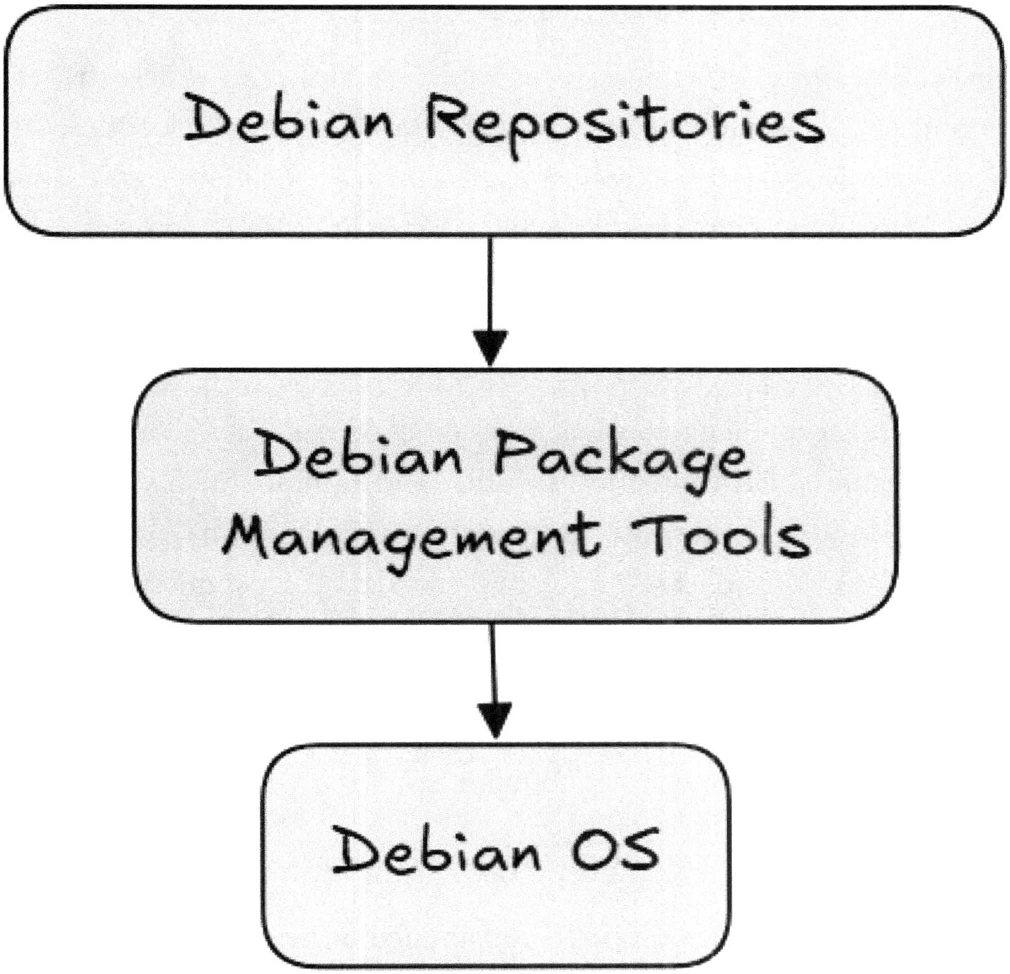


*Figure 9: Debian Architecture Overview*

## Essential Elements of the Debian System

The Debian system is founded on three primary components. These elements work in harmony to deliver a streamlined and effective environment for software deployment and system administration.

- **Debian Operating System**
- **Package Management Tools**
- **Debian Repositories**

### 5.2.1 Debian Operating System

The Debian Operating System is a versatile, stable, and widely trusted Linux distribution used across industries, ranging from consumer electronics to space exploration. Renowned for its robust performance, flexibility, and open-source foundation, Debian powers systems where reliability and long-term support are essential.

#### Stability and Reliability

Debian is known for its meticulously tested stable releases. These undergo extensive validation to ensure system integrity, security, and uptime. Such characteristics are essential in embedded, enterprise, and research applications, where stability is important. Debian's long release cycles make it ideal for production environments requiring years of dependable operation.

#### Flexibility and Customization

Debian's modular design allows users to tailor installations to meet specific needs:

- Deploy minimal systems with only essential packages.
- Customize setups for resource-constrained or headless devices.
- Support for cross-compilation enables building various platforms.

Tools such as debootstrap simplify building lightweight Debian-based systems tailored for specific use cases particularly in embedded development.

#### Comprehensive Hardware Architecture Support

Debian supports a wide range of processor architecture, making it a strong choice for both modern and legacy hardware:

- x86 (32-bit and 64-bit) - Common in desktops, servers, and industrial PCs.
- ARM - Popular in embedded systems, mobile devices, and single-board computers such as the Raspberry Pi.

- RISC-V - An emerging, open-source instruction set architecture (ISA) gaining traction in research and IoT.
- Debian also supports PowerPC, MIPS, s390x, ia64, and other architectures, ensuring backward compatibility and broader hardware reach.

**Extensive Software Repository**

Debian's package repository includes over 50,000 software packages, covering:

- Core libraries, utilities, and development tools.
- Network and security tools.
- Support for graphical user interfaces and headless systems.
- Pre-compiled binaries and source packages.
- Optional access to non-free software when licensing permits.

This rich ecosystem makes Debian adaptable to diverse use cases, including scientific research, education, IoT, and enterprise infrastructure.

**Filesystem Hierarchy Standard (FHS) Compliance**

Debian adheres strictly to the FHS, which standardizes the directory structure across Linux systems. This improves system maintainability and cross-platform compatibility:

- /bin, /sbin, /usr/bin - Essential binaries.
- /etc - Configuration files.
- /var - Logs and transient data.

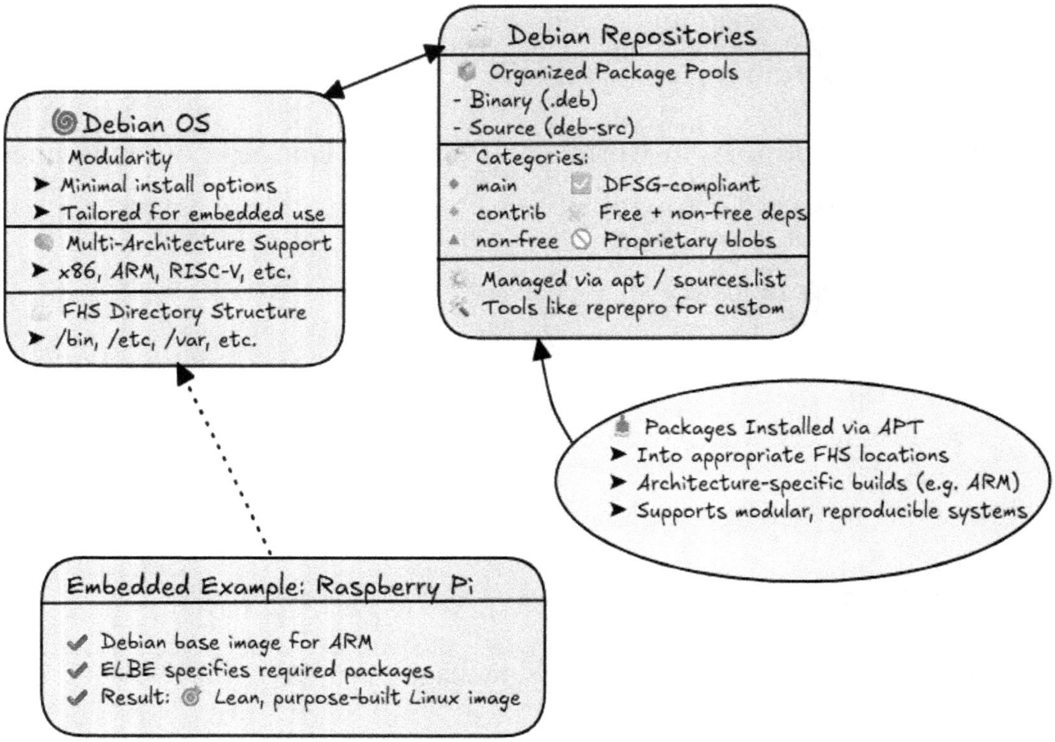


*Figure 10: Debian Repository and OS relationship*

### 5.2.2 Debian Package Management Tools

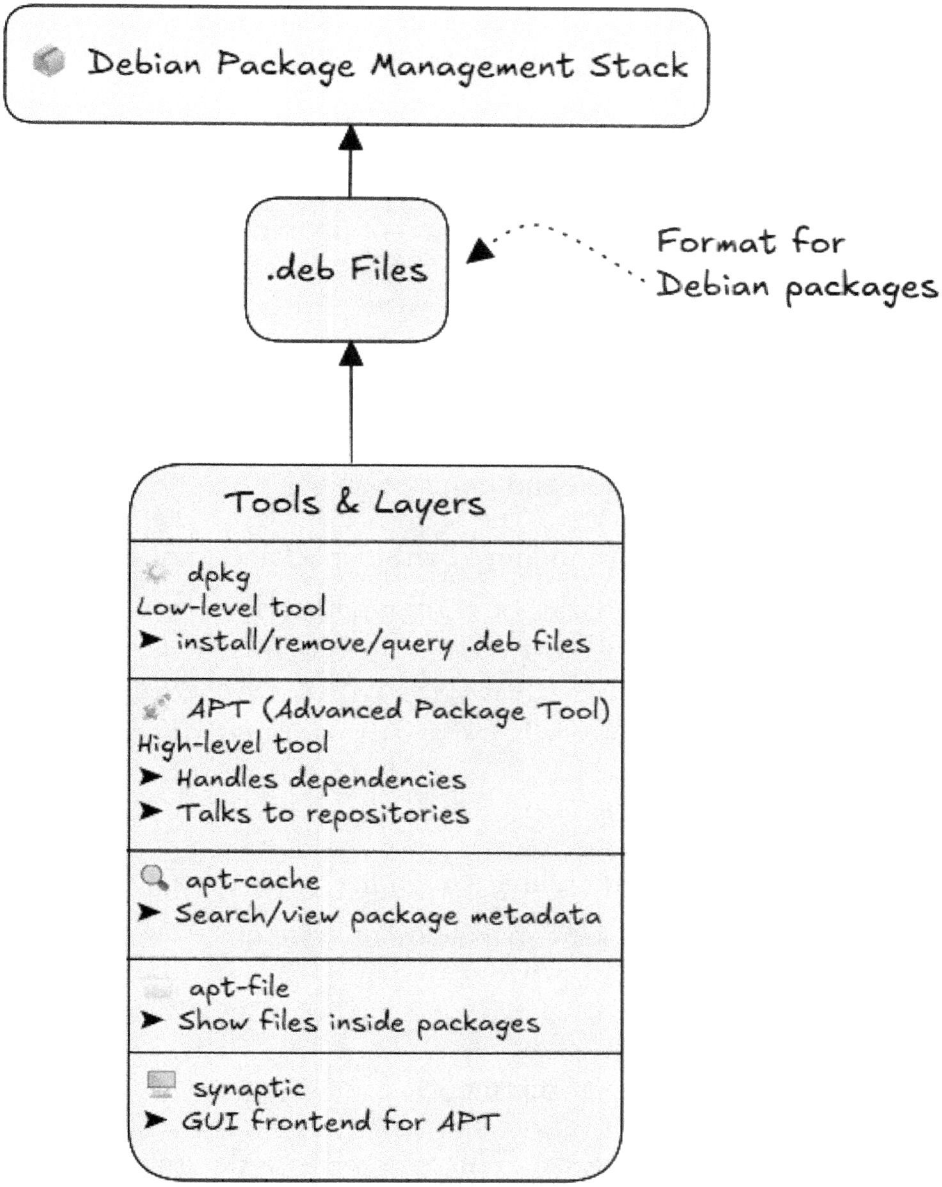


*Figure 11: Debian Package Management Stack*

Debian employs a sophisticated and mature package management system based on the .deb package format. This system relies on a combination of low-level and high-level tools to ensure reliable software installation, removal, and maintenance. Understanding these tools and how they interact with each other is essential.

1. **dpkg**: This is the foundational, low-level utility used for installing, removing, and querying .deb packages directly. It does not handle dependencies automatically and is typically used when working with local package files.

2. **apt (Advanced Package Tool)**: APT is a higher-level package management tool that builds on dpkg, providing features such as dependency resolution, remote repository access, and automation of upgrades. It interacts with package lists defined in /etc/apt/sources.list.

3. **Additional Tools**:

    - **apt-cache**: Allows users to search and query package metadata such as version, dependencies, and descriptions.

    - **apt-file**: Lists files contained within packages, useful for locating the origin of specific binaries or configuration files.

    - **synaptic**: A graphical front-end to APT, ideal for users who prefer a GUI-based experience when installing or removing packages.

### Understanding DEB Packages

A .deb package is a specialized archive, much like a .tar or .zip file (see Figure 12), designed for use by Debian's package management system.

### Structure of a .deb Package

It typically contains the following components:

1. **Control Files (control.tar.xz)**: This archive includes the control file, which defines metadata such as package name, version, maintainer, dependencies, and other important fields.

2. **Data Files (data.tar.xz)**: Contains the actual files that will be installed on the system (e.g., binaries, man pages, config files).

3. **Scripts**: Pre- and post-installation scripts that are executed to configure the software during installation or removal (e.g., postinst, prerm).

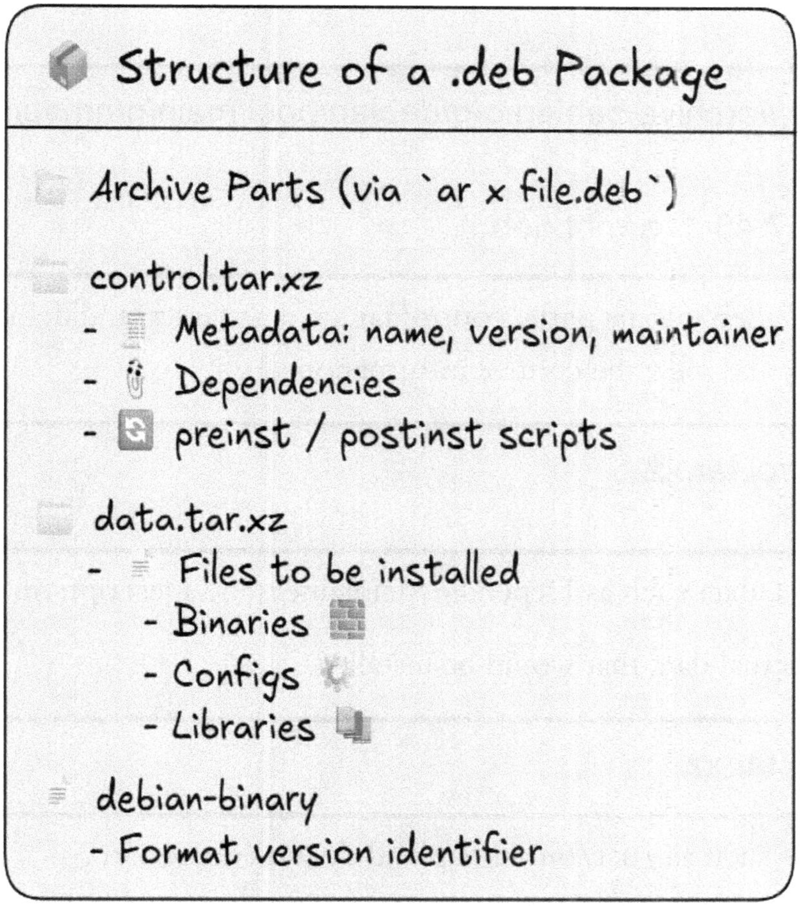


*Figure 12: Structure of a Debian package*

### Binary vs. Source Packages

- **Binary Packages**: These are ready-to-install .deb files that contain compiled code and resources.

  Example: nmap_7.70_armhf.deb

- **Source Packages**: Include source code, patch sets, and a rules file for building the software from scratch. Useful for developers or when a user needs to apply custom modifications.

### Inspecting Debian Packages (e.g., nmap)

To better understand a package's structure, you can manually download and inspect it:

```
$ wget https://archive.debian.org/debian/pool/main/n/nmap/nmap_7.40-
1_armhf.deb
$ ar x nmap_7.40-1_armhf.deb
```

This extracts the .deb into its parts: control.tar.xz, data.tar.xz, and debian-binary. You can then unpack and view the control information:

```
$ tar xvf control.tar.xz
$ cat control
```

This outputs metadata such as Depends, Maintainer, and Description.

To inspect the actual data that would be installed:

```
$ tar xvf data.tar.xz
```

This reveals files such as /usr/bin/nmap and documentation in /usr/share/doc/nmap.

### Package Management Fundamentals

1. **dpkg (Low-Level Tool)**

    - dpkg -i package.deb: Install a .deb file.
    - dpkg -r package: Remove a package (but leave config files).
    - dpkg -P package: Purge package and its configuration.
    - dpkg -L package: List files installed by the package.
    - dpkg -s package: Show detailed package information.

2. **APT (High-Level Tool)**

   - apt install package: Installs a package and resolves dependencies.
   - apt remove package: Uninstalls a package.
   - apt update: Updates local metadata about repositories.
   - apt upgrade: Upgrades all installed packages.

3. **APT and dpkg: How They Work Together**

APT serves as a front-end, downloading .deb files and resolving dependencies, while dpkg handles the actual installation/removal process. For example:

   - apt install nmap will download the nmap package and its dependencies, then pass them to dpkg for installation.
   - The system's state is tracked in /var/lib/dpkg/status.

4. **Usage Example**

```
$ apt install nmap
```

This will also install any required libraries such as libc6 or libpcap etc

To list dependencies:

```
$ apt-cache depends nmap
```

**Handling Dependencies: Types and Resolution**

1. **Types of Dependencies**

      - Depends: Must be present for the package to function.
      - Recommends: Not essential but enhances functionality.
      - Suggests: Additional tools or enhancements.

- Pre-Depends: Required before package installation begins.
- Conflicts: Incompatible packages that cannot coexist.

2. **APT's Dependency Resolver**

   APT automatically manages dependencies to:

   - Ensure necessary packages are installed.
   - Prevent incompatible packages from being installed together.

**Example**: Installing nmap automatically pulls in required packages such as libpcap.

### Building a Simple Debian Package from Scratch

Creating your own .deb package can be an enlightening exercise in understanding how Debian packaging works.

```
$ sudo apt install build-essential devscripts dh-make
```

### Set Up a Sample Project

```
$ mkdir -p hello-deb/usr/local/bin
$ cd hello-deb
$ echo -e '#!/bin/bash\necho "Hello, Debian!"' > usr/local/bin/hello-deb
$ chmod +x usr/local/bin/hello-deb
```

### Generate Debian Packaging Files

```
$ dh_make --indep --createorig -p hello-deb_0.1
```

Modify debian/control with details:

```
Source: hello-deb
Section: utils
```

```
Priority: optional
Maintainer: Your Name <you@example.com>
Standards-Version: 4.6.0
Package: hello-deb
Architecture: all
Depends: ${misc:Depends}
Description: A simple Hello World script packaged as a .deb
```

Specify what to install in debian/install:

```
usr/local/bin/hello-deb usr/local/bin/
```

Build the Package

```
$ dpkg-buildpackage -us -uc
```

-us -uc skips signing (acceptable for local/testing use).

**Install and Test**

```
$ sudo dpkg -i ../hello-deb_0.1_all.deb
$ hello-deb
```

If everything was successful, you'll see:
Hello, Debian!

**Summary:**

This section laid the groundwork for understanding Debian's package management system, from the core tools and package formats to inspecting and even building your own .deb files. In the next subsection, we'll explore Debian repositories, including their structure, categorization, configuration, and how they serve as the upstream sources these tools rely on for software installation and updates.

### 5.2.3 Debian Repositories:

Debian repositories, often referred to as "repos" are centralized storage locations where software packages both binary (.deb) and source (deb-src) are organized in a special directory tree. These repositories form the backbone of Debian's software distribution system, enabling client computers to securely download, install, and update software in an organized and efficient manner. They are categorized based on licensing and software freedom, configured via the /etc/apt/sources.list file, and can be managed using tools such as reprepro for custom setups.

#### Repository Categories

Repositories are divided into three logical components:

- **Main**:
    - Contains software fully compliant with the *Debian Free Software Guidelines (DFSG)*.
    - Default and primary repository for most installations.
    - Examples: bash, gcc, vim.
- **Contrib**:
    - Includes free software that depends on non-free components (e.g., proprietary firmware or libraries).
    - Example: Software requiring non-free drivers.
- **Non-Free**:
    - Contains proprietary or restricted software not compliant with the DFSG, provided for user convenience.
    - Examples: nvidia-driver.

- **Non-free-firmware**:
  - Introduced in Debian 12 (Bookworm), this section specifically provides firmware packages that are not DFSG-free but are required for many modern devices.
  - Examples: firmware-iwlwifi, firmware-amd-graphics.

This separation ensures users can choose software aligning with their preferences, such as avoiding non-free components if desired.

## Repository Structure and Configuration

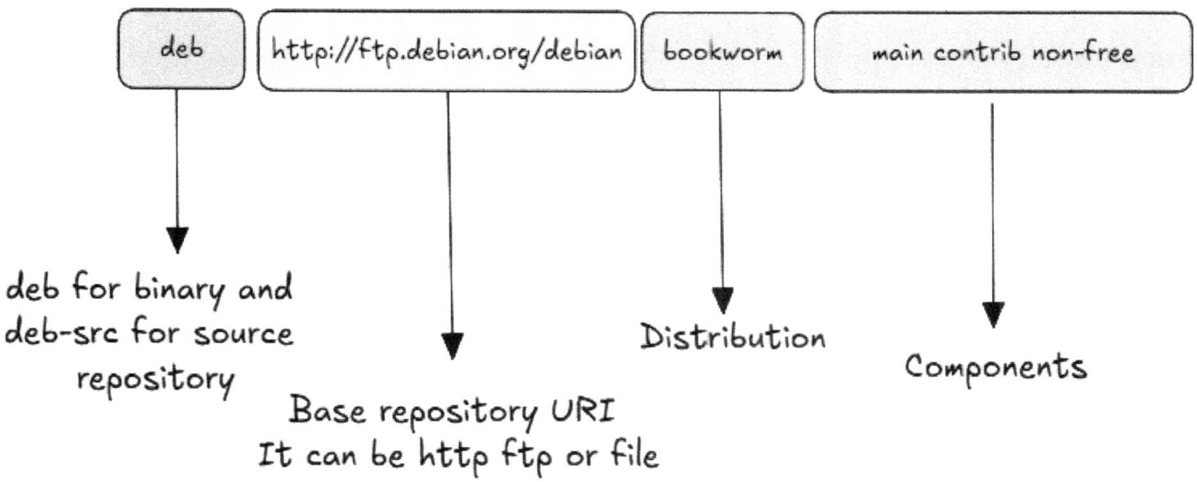


*Figure 13: Repository URL Structure*

Repositories are accessed via URLs specified in /etc/apt/sources.list. Each line defines:

1. **Repository Type**: deb (binary packages) or deb-src (source packages).
2. **Base URI**: Server address (e.g., https://deb.debian.org/debian).
3. **Distribution**: Codename or suite (e.g., stable, bullseye).
4. **Components**: Sections such as main, contrib, non-free.

**Example configuration of /etc/apt/sources.list:**

```
deb https://deb.debian.org/debian stable main contrib non-free
deb-src https://deb.debian.org/debian stable main contrib non-free
deb https://security.debian.org/debian-security stable-security main
contrib non-free
```

**Binary Packages (deb)**: Precompiled software for direct installation.

**Source Packages (deb-src)**: Source code for debugging, custom builds, or modifications.

### The Deb822 Format

While the classic /etc/apt/sources.list format remains widely used, Debian now provides a modern alternative for defining repositories in a more structured and flexible way: the **Deb822 format**. This format allows repository definitions to be written as multi-line key–value blocks in. sources files, improving readability, modularity, and security, while also enabling advanced features such as multi-URI definitions and per-source GPG signing.

### Deb822 File Location and Structure

Deb822-style repository definitions are stored as individual files inside the /etc/apt/sources.list.d/ directory, each using the. sources extension. Instead of single-line entries, these files use a structured, multi-line block format made up of key–value pairs. A typical. sources file includes core fields such as:

**Types**: Specifies the package types (e.g., deb for binary packages, deb-src for source packages).

**URIs**: One or more repository base URLs.

**Suites**: Distribution names or suites (e.g., stable, bookworm, trixie).

**Components**: Repository sections such as main, contrib, non-free, and non-free-firmware.

Additional optional fields allow for fine-grained control:

- **Architectures**: Limits downloads to specific architectures.
- **Signed-By**: Assigns a per-source GPG key for enhanced security.
- **Enabled**: Enables or disables the repository entry without removing it.

**Example: Equivalent Deb822 Entry**

Classic sources.list line:

```
deb https://deb.debian.org/debian stable main contrib non-free
```

Deb822 version (/etc/apt/sources.list.d/debian.sources):

```
Types: deb
URIs: https://deb.debian.org/debian
Suites: stable
Components: main contrib non-free
```

**Example With Signed-By and Architecture Filtering**

This example shows how Deb822 allows per-repository GPG keys and architecture-specific filtering:

```
Types: deb
URIs: https://deb.example.org/repo
Suites: bookworm
Components: main
Architectures: amd64
Signed-By: /usr/share/keyrings/example.gpg
```

With the repository structure now explained, we will next cover creating a custom repository, managing packages within it, and configuring clients to use it.

### Creating Custom Repositories with reprepro:

Reprepro is a lightweight and efficient tool for managing Debian repositories. It supports both binary and source packages, automates metadata generation (such as Release files), and includes GPG signing for package integrity and security.

### Setting Up a Repository

Before you begin, ensure you have root or sudo privileges on your Debian machine.

### Install Reprepro:

Reprepro is available directly from Debian's official repositories

```
$ sudo apt  install reprepro
```

### Create Repository Structure

Choose a base directory where your repository will live. A common convention is /var/www/debian-repo, especially for serving it over HTTP.

```
$ sudo mkdir -p /var/www/debian-repo/{conf,incoming}
```

Here's what each directory is for:

**conf:** Stores configuration files (e.g., distributions).

**incoming:** Optional directory for holding uploaded packages.

### Configure the Repository

The key configuration file is distributions, located in the /var/www/debian-repo/conf/ directory. This file defines the distributions (or "suites") your repository will support, the architectures you build for, and the cryptographic keys used for signing. Add the following content as an example:

```
Codename: stable
Suite: stable
Components: main
Architectures: amd64 i386
SignWith: YOUR_GPG_KEY_ID
```

**Codename and Suite** define the release name.

**Components** typically include main but can include others such as contrib or non-free if applicable.

**Architectures** should match the package types you intend to serve.

**SignWith** refers to your GPG key ID (discussed below), ensuring packages and metadata are signed for security.

### Make the Repository Available for HTTP

To serve the repository over the network, install and configure a web server such as Apache

```
$ sudo apt  install apache2
$ sudo ln -s /var/www/debian-repo /var/www/html/debian
```

By creating a symbolic link in the web root, your repository becomes accessible via: https://your-server/debian.

### Managing Packages in Your Repository

Once your repository is configured, you can start adding, removing, and listing packages with reprepro commands.

### Add a Package

```
$ reprepro -b /var/www/debian-repo includedeb stable package.deb
```

This command places the package in the appropriate location, updates metadata, and signs the repository.

**Remove a Package**

```
$ reprepro -b /var/www/debian-repo remove stable package-name
```

**List all the Packages**

```
$ reprepro -b /var/www/debian-repo list stable
```

### Integrating GPG for Repository Security

A crucial aspect of managing a Debian repository is ensuring package integrity. GPG signing protects users from tampered or malicious packages

**Generate a GPG Key:**

If you don't already have a GPG key, generate one with:

```
$ gpg --gen-key
```

Follow the interactive prompts to choose the key type (RSA 4096 etc.), expiration date, and your identity details (name and email). Protect the key with a strong passphrase.

**Retrieving Your GPG Key ID**

List and identify the relevant key's ID from the output.

```
$ gpg --list-keys
pub   rsa3072 2025-06-08 [SC] [expires: 2027-06-08]
B6083C0F236A7EBFD9515F61AA9EBCD81D0838F8
uid [ultimate] Rootfx <rootfx@local>
sub   rsa3072 2025-06-08 [E] [expires: 2027-06-08]
```

In the output the GPG_KEY_ID is

```
B6083C0F236A7EBFD9515F61AA9EBCD81D0838F8
```

or a shorter version with last 8 bytes

```
1D0838F8
```

Use that string in the SignWith field of the /var/www/debian-repo/conf/distributions file.

```
SignWith: 1D0838F8
```

For better compatibility and clarity, it's recommended to use the **long key ID**

**Behind the Scenes: What reprepro Does:**

When you run reprepro includedeb or update the repository, reprepro automatically updates the repository metadata files, most importantly the Release file and internally invokes GPG to sign it using the key specified in the SignWith directive. This process produces three important files: Release (the unsigned metadata), Release.gpg (a detached GPG signature), and InRelease (a clear signed version of Release). These signatures are essential for APT clients, which verify them during apt update to ensure the repository's integrity and authenticity.

**Exporting and Distributing the Public GPG Key**

Once you've generated your GPG key and used it to sign your repository, you need to make the public part of the key available to your users. This allows their APT package managers to verify that the repository and its contents are trusted.

```
$ gpg --armor --output public-key.gpg --export 1D0838F8
```

Place this public-key.gpg file in a location that is accessible via your web server, for example in /var/www/html

## Client Setup: Trusting and Using the Repository

On client systems that need to use your custom Debian repository, follow these steps:

### Add the GPG Key

First, the client must import your public GPG key so that APT can verify package signatures.

Instead of using the deprecated apt-key add, save the key directly into /etc/apt/trusted.gpg.d/:

```
$ wget -O - https://your-server/public-key.gpg | sudo tee
/etc/apt/trusted.gpg.d/your-repo.gpg > /dev/null
```

This ensures that APT will trust the metadata and packages signed by your repository.

Add the Repository to /etc/apt/sources.list

```
deb https://your-server/debian-repo stable main
```

This tells APT to pull packages from your repository's stable distribution and the main component.

### Update the Package Index:

```
$ sudo apt  update
```

APT will now fetch metadata from your repository, verify it using your GPG key, and make the packages available for installation.

### Summary:

We explored the structure and role of Debian repositories in the software distribution ecosystem, focusing on the use of *reprepro* for creating and managing custom repositories. We covered how repositories are categorized (main, contrib, non-free, non-free-firmware), configured via the sources.list file, and served over HTTP using a web server such as Apache. We also detailed how to set up the repository structure, define distributions and architectures, manage packages using *reprepro*, and secure the repository using GPG key signing. Clients were then configured to trust the repository by importing the public GPG key and updating their package index. With a solid understanding of how repositories are structured and maintained, the next subsection will move on to the following topic in the chapter, building upon this foundation.

## 5.3 Beyond Package Management

### 5.3.1 Debconf

Debconf is Debian's configuration management system that facilitates package configuration during installation and upgrades. It standardizes how packages collect input from users, enabling smoother automated and manual setups.

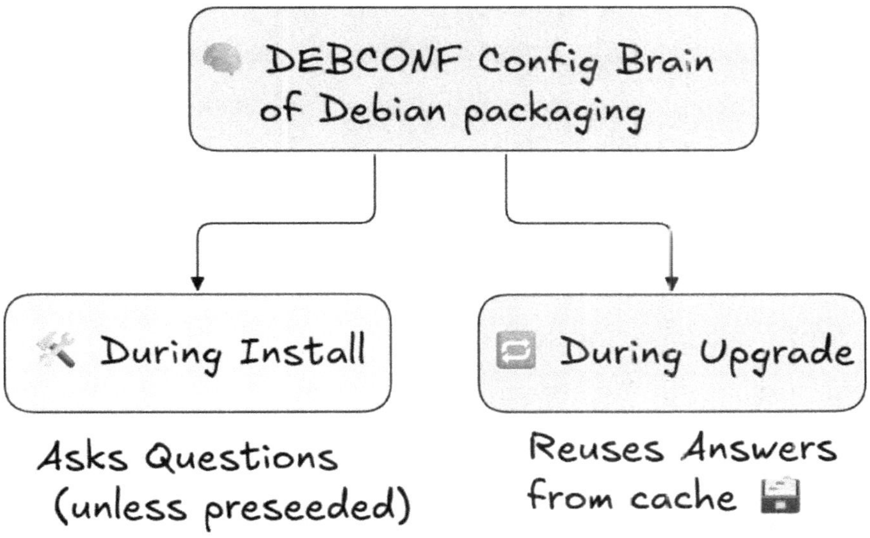


*Figure 14: Debconf configuration management*

#### How Does Debconf Work?

Debconf operates in four stages:

1. **Pre-Configuration Check**: Before prompting the user, Debconf checks whether answers for a package's configuration questions are already stored in

its database. If values are found, it uses them automatically, enabling seamless reinstallation or scripting without user intervention. This is particularly useful during unattended installations or system imaging.

2. **Interactive Prompts**: If no existing answers are found, Debconf prompts the user for necessary information. It supports several front-end interfaces depending on the system configuration:
    - **dialog**: Text-based (default for terminal environments).
    - **readline**: Command-line prompt interface.
    - **gtk**: Graphical interface used in GUI environments.
    - **noninteractive**: Skips prompts entirely used in automated scripts and headless servers.

    **Example:** When installing lightdm (or any display manager package), Debconf may detect that multiple display managers are present (e.g., gdm3, sddm, lightdm) and prompt the user to choose a default display manager. The user's choice determines which manager will be started automatically during system startup.

3. **Configuration Storage**: All responses provided during configuration are saved in Debconf's database, located in /var/cache/debconf/. This ensures that the same answers can be reused in future package reinstalls or upgrades without requiring additional user input

4. **Applying Changes**: Once the configuration is complete, the package uses these stored answers to modify system files or execute post-install scripts. For example, setting the root password for MySQL during mysql-server installation updates the database's internal user credentials accordingly

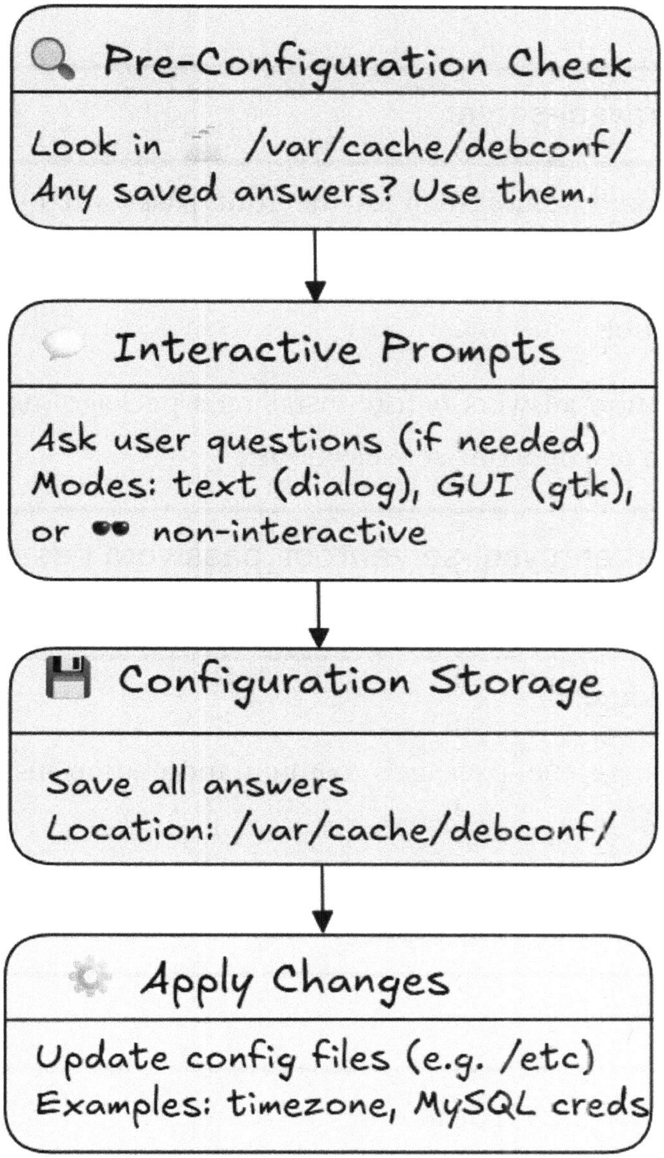


*Figure 15: Debconf stages*

## Checking and Modifying Debconf Settings

### View Stored Values:

You can inspect the answers saved for any package with the following command:

```
$ debconf-show package_name
```

**Example**

```
$ debconf-show mysql-server
```

This will display stored values such as the root password question and selected options.

**Manually Set a Value:**

To pre-set configuration answers before installing a package (useful for scripting or automation), you can use debconf-set-selections:

```
$ echo "mysql-server mysql-server/root_password password
MySecurePass" | sudo debconf-set-selections
```

**Reconfigure a Package:**

If you need to change the package's configuration after installation, use dpkg-reconfigure:

```
$ sudo dpkg-reconfigure package_name
```

**Example**

```
$ sudo dpkg-reconfigure tzdata
```

This allows you to interactively select a new timezone and update the system configuration accordingly.

With Debconf, Debian offers a flexible mechanism to manage package configurations, balancing automation with user control. Whether you're building automated deployment scripts or tweaking settings post-install, understanding Debconf is key to efficient Debian administration.

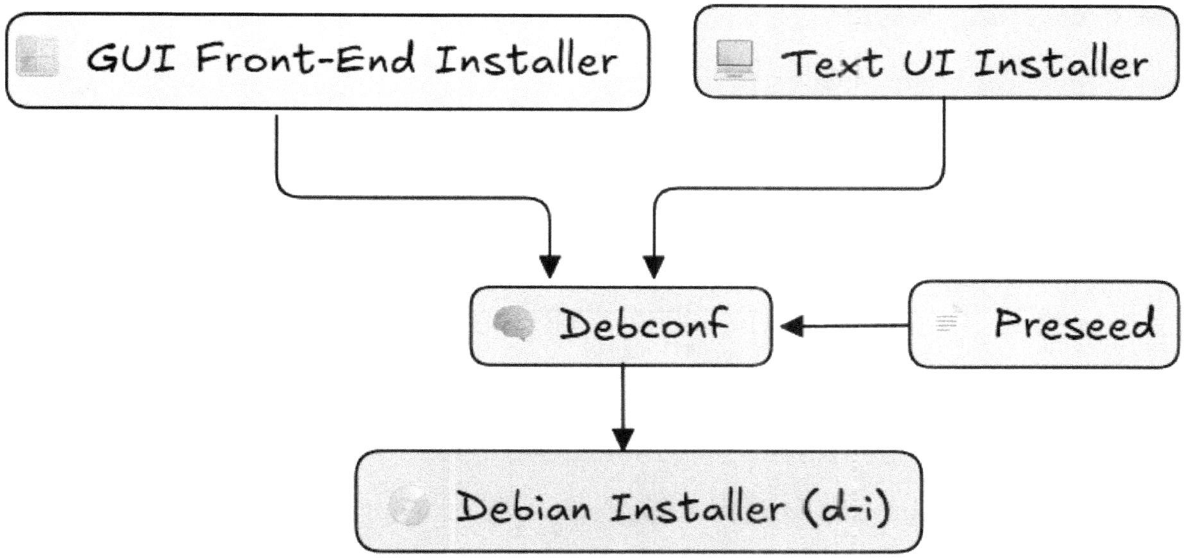


Figure 16: Debconf Preseed Installation

Figure 16 illustrates how *debconf* serves as the central configuration management system during a Debian installation. It interfaces with both graphical and text-based installer frontends and communicates directly with the Debian Installer—laying the groundwork for automation through tools such as Preseed, which will be discussed in the following section.

### 5.3.2 Preseed

**Preseeding** enables fully automated Debian installations by supplying predefined answers to Debconf prompts. This approach is ideal for unattended setups, mass deployments, and ensuring consistency across multiple systems

## How Preseeding Works

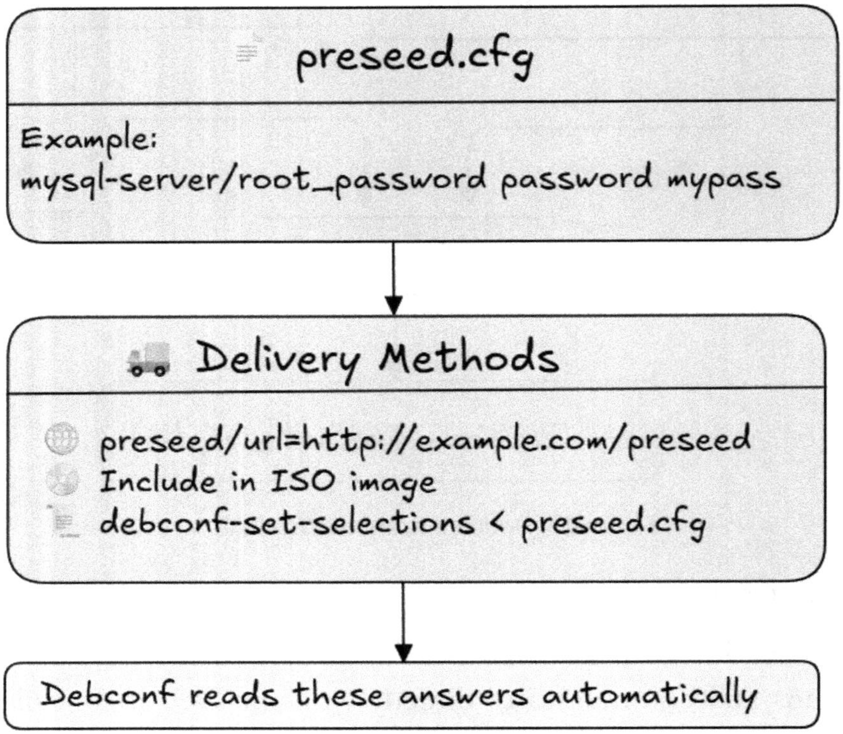


*Figure 17: Preseeding methods*

## Create a Preseed File

The file contains configuration directives in the following format:

```
package-name/setting question-type value
```

Each line defines a Debconf question, the expected input type (such as string, select, or boolean), and the desired answer. These settings map directly to Debconf questions that would otherwise be presented during installation.

Provide the Preseed File:

You can deliver the file in various ways:

- Embedded in a custom ISO: Ideal for distributing installation media with built-in configuration.

- Hosted remotely and fetched during installation: The installer downloads and processes it on-the-fly.
- Applied directly using Debconf before installation: Suitable for setting values in advance on a running system.

Automatic Configuration:
During installation, Debconf reads the preseeded answers instead of prompting the user, enabling a fully automated flow. The installer processes each directive sequentially, using values from the preseed file to configure the system. This includes disk partitioning, package selection, user creation, and network setup.

**Example: Preseed Configuration Snippets**

Setting a Default Display Manager:

```
lightdm lightdm/daemon_name string lightdm
```

This ensures LightDM is selected automatically without asking the user to choose a display manager.

Configure Timezone:

```
tzdata tzdata/Areas select Europe
tzdata tzdata/Zones/Europe/Paris select Paris
```

This configures the system's timezone non-interactively.

Setting MySQL Root Password:

```
mysql-server mysql-server/root_password password yourpassword
mysql-server mysql-server/root_password_again password
yourpassword
```

Prevents interactive password prompts during installation of MySQL.

### How to Use a Preseed File

#### Method 1: Apply Before Installing Packages

This method is useful for configuring specific packages on an already installed system:

```
$ sudo debconf-set-selections < preseed.cfg
$ sudo apt  install -y package-name
```

Debconf will apply the preset values from preseed.cfg before installing the package, avoiding prompts.

#### Method 2: Automate Full System Installations:

Preseed files can be passed at boot time when launching an installer. This is commonly used in PXE boot environments or cloud-init configurations:

```
preseed/url=https://example.com/preseed.cfg
```

This boot parameter tells the Debian installer to fetch the configuration file from the given URL and use it to drive the entire installation process automatically.

By leveraging preseeding, administrators can eliminate repetitive setup tasks, enforce policy-compliant configurations, and accelerate provisioning at scale.

### 5.3.3 Debootstrap

debootstrap is a command-line utility used for creating a minimal Debian environment by downloading and installing only essential base system packages into a specified directory. It does not require an existing Debian installation and can run from other Linux distributions. This makes it highly effective for bootstrapping new systems, building chroot environments, container bases, or crafting custom images for embedded systems.

debootstrap supports installation for any Debian or Debian-based release, including stable, testing, and unstable branches, as well as derivatives such as Ubuntu. It allows precise control over which packages are installed and provides a clean foundation without superfluous software.

**Common Use Cases Include:**

- Creating isolated development or testing environments (chroot, LXC, Docker)
- Custom image creation for embedded devices
- Recovery or rescue systems
- Building root filesystems for virtualization

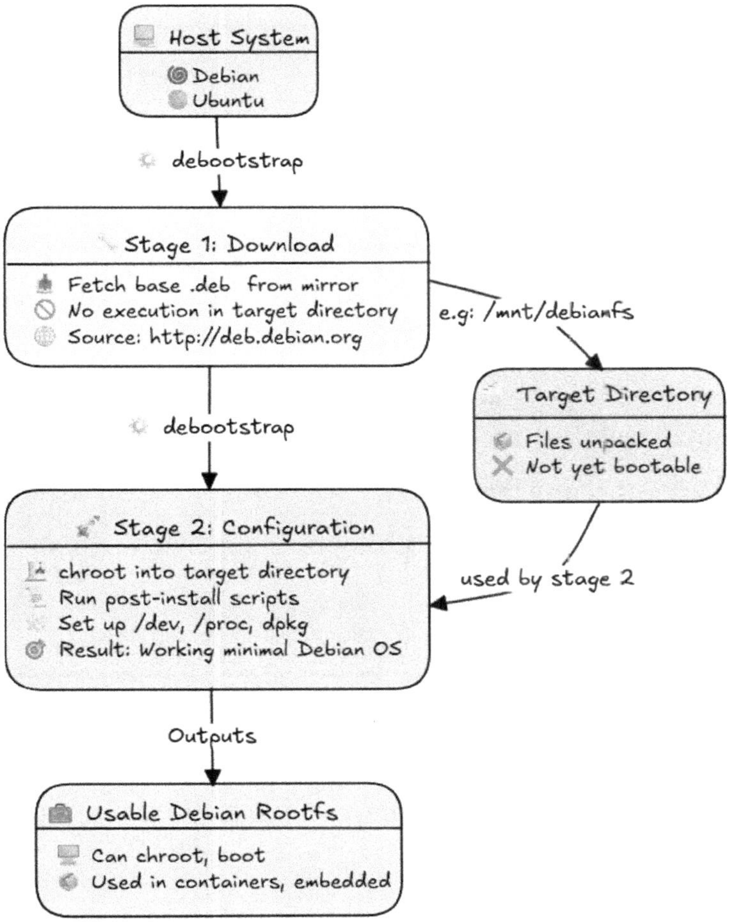


*Figure 18: Debootstrap Basic Flow*

## Cross-Architecture Bootstrapping with QEMU

For cross-architecture environments such as building an ARM Debian system on an x86 host debootstrap works in tandem with QEMU, which provides user space CPU emulation.

This technique enables system administrators and developers to build and test software for different architectures without dedicated hardware.

### Step-by-Step Process

### Install QEMU and Support Tools

```
$ sudo apt  install qemu qemu-user-static
```

This installs the necessary emulators to handle foreign architecture such as ARM, MIPS, or RISC-V.

### Run Debootstrap (Stage 1)

```
$ sudo debootstrap --foreign --arch=armhf stable /mnt/debian
https://deb.debian.org/debian
```

This command initializes the target directory /mnt/debian with an ARM (armhf) minimal system. The --foreign flag tells debootstrap to stop after downloading and unpacking, skipping the execution of architecture-specific scripts.

### Copy QEMU Binary

```
$ sudo cp /usr/bin/qemu-arm-static /mnt/debian/usr/bin/
```

This places the ARM emulator inside the new root so it can execute ARM binaries during the second stage.

### Complete Installation (Stage 2)

```
$ sudo chroot /mnt/debian /debootstrap/debootstrap --second-stage
```

Inside the chroot, debootstrap completes the remaining setup steps, such as configuring base system packages and preparing the environment for first boot.

After this process, /mnt/debian contains a fully functional ARM Debian root filesystem that can be used for further configuration, packaging, or testing.

**Note**: ELBE internally uses debootstrap to generate reproducible Debian-based root filesystems.

## 5.3.4 Keyring

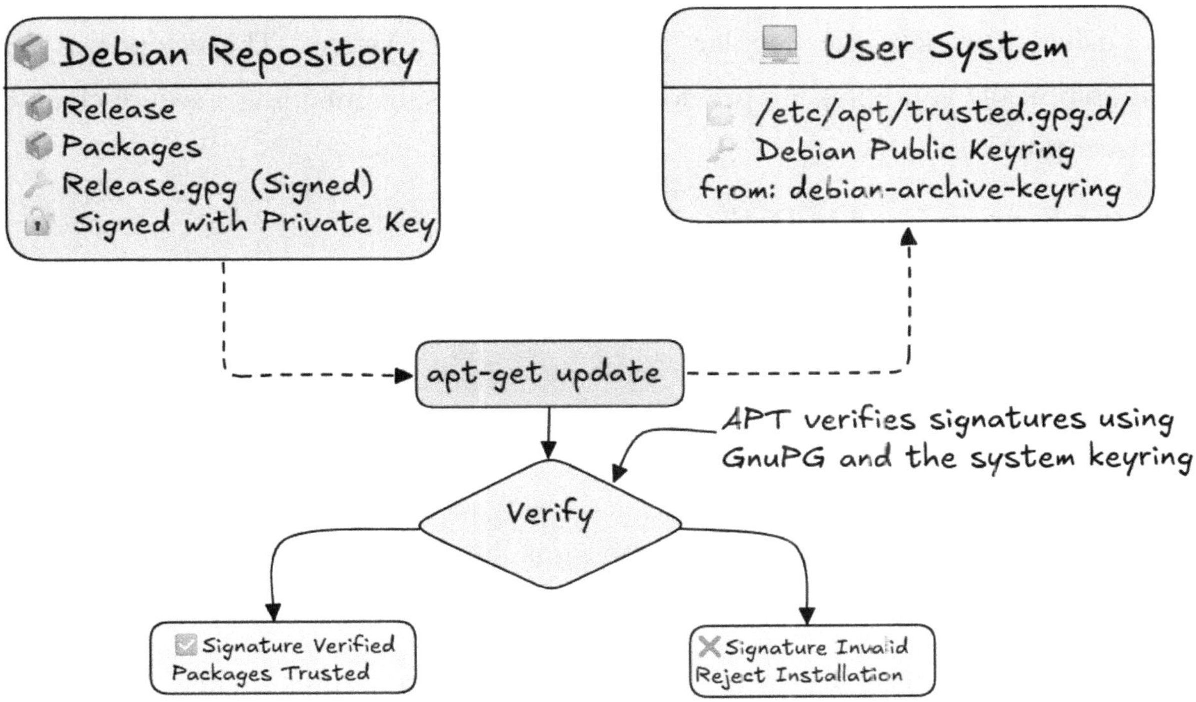


*Figure 19: Keyring basics*

In Debian, a keyring is a collection of GPG (GNU Privacy Guard) keys used to verify the authenticity of software packages and ensure secure installations. These keys are essential for validating the signatures of Release files and individual packages, protecting users from tampered or unauthorized software. The keyring is typically managed by a daemon that handles key verification during package operations such as apt update or apt install.

One of the most important keyring packages in Debian is **debian-archive-keyring**. This package contains the trusted GPG public keys used to verify the signatures of official Debian archive releases. Similarly, Ubuntu maintains a separate but related package called ubuntu-archive-keyring for the same purpose in Ubuntu systems.

These keyring packages are carefully maintained by the respective distribution's security and archive teams. The process involves securely generating and managing GPG key pairs, where the private key is used to sign archive metadata (e.g., Release files), and the public key is distributed via the keyring package. When new release keys are introduced or old ones are retired, the keyring packages are updated accordingly and pushed through the regular package update system. These updates are cryptographically verified using previously trusted keys, maintaining a secure chain of trust over time.

### How is a Keyring Used in Debian?

1. **Package Verification**: Keys in debian-archive-keyring verify repository signatures.
2. **Trusted Installation**: Ensures packages are untampered, with keys stored in /etc/apt/trusted.gpg.d/.
3. **Public Key Cryptography**: Debian signs Release files with a private key; users verify with the public key.
4. **APT and Secure Archives**: apt update checks signatures against the keyring.

### How Release Files Are Created

A Release file provides repository metadata and checksums, signed with a GPG signature (Release.gpg).

**Step 1: Generate the Release File:**

```
$ apt-ftparchive release /path/to/repository > /path/to/repository/Release
```

apt-ftparchive scans the repository directory and generates a Release file that serves as a metadata summary for the repository. This file includes references to package indexes such as Packages.gz, lists the repository components such as main, contrib, and non-free, and specifies supported architecture such as amd64 and i386. Additionally, it contains cryptographic hash checksums (MD5, SHA1, SHA256) for the index files, which are used by APT to verify the integrity and authenticity of these files, ensuring they have not been altered or tampered with.

**Step 2: Sign the Release File with GPG**

```
$ gpg --default-key GPG_KEY_ID -abs -o /path/to/repo/Release.gpg
/path/to/repo/Release
```

This command uses GPG to create a detached ASCII-armored signature of the Release file, producing a file named Release.gpg. The -abs option passed to GPG instructs it to perform three actions: a generates an ASCII-armored output suitable for easy distribution as a plain text file; b creates a detached signature that is stored separately from the original file; and s indicates that the file should be signed. To perform this operation, the private key associated with the specified GPG_KEY_ID must be available on the system executing the command, as it is required to generate the digital signature.

**Step 3: (Optional) Create an InRelease File (Signed Inline)**

```
$ gpg --default-key GPG_KEY_ID -clearsign -o /path/to/repo/InRelease
/path/to/repo/Release
```

This command creates a clear-signed version of the Release file, resulting in a file called InRelease. Unlike Release.gpg, which is a separate detached signature, the InRelease file combines both the repository metadata and the GPG signature into a single file. This format is preferred by newer versions of APT because it simplifies the verification process and reduces the number of network requests required during package updates.

```
$ gpg --verify Release.gpg Release
```

This step confirms the authenticity of the Release file using the public GPG key installed on the system. If the signature is valid and the corresponding public key is trusted, then it is typically because it is included in the debian-archive-keyring package which the system can verify that the repository contents have not been tampered with and can be safely trusted for package installation or updates.

**Summary:**

This chapter introduces Debian as a stable, versatile, and community-driven Linux distribution, emphasizing its historical significance, open-source philosophy, and role in embedded systems. It explores Debian's architecture, including its operating system, extensive hardware support, and adherence to the Filesystem Hierarchy Standard (FHS). The chapter details Debian's structured repository system organized into main, contrib, non-free, and non-free-firmware components and explains how software is distributed via binary and source packages. It covers essential package management tools such as apt, dpkg, and debootstrap, and provides a practical guide to creating and managing custom repositories using reprepro, including GPG signing for security and client configuration for trusted access. Together, these elements form a reliable and customizable foundation for embedded Linux development.

# 6 Basics of ELBE

**Abstract:** The core of the book's tooling section, this chapter provides an end-to-end overview of ELBE: its workflow, installation on a host system, creation and purpose of the InitVM (a controlled build container), and the structure of ELBE XML files for defining targets, packages, users, services, and filesystems. Readers gain hands-on familiarity with ELBE's architecture, enabling them to start authoring and executing their own build recipes.

The Embedded Linux Build Environment, abbreviated as ELBE, is a build-system used for creating Debian-based root filesystems or boot images. ELBE simplifies the development of customized embedded Linux systems by allowing users to define system configurations through XML recipe files (see Figure 20). These recipe files act as blueprints, specifying how the system should be set up. ELBE processes these files to generate root filesystems in the required formats, making it an efficient and flexible solution for creating customized embedded Linux systems.

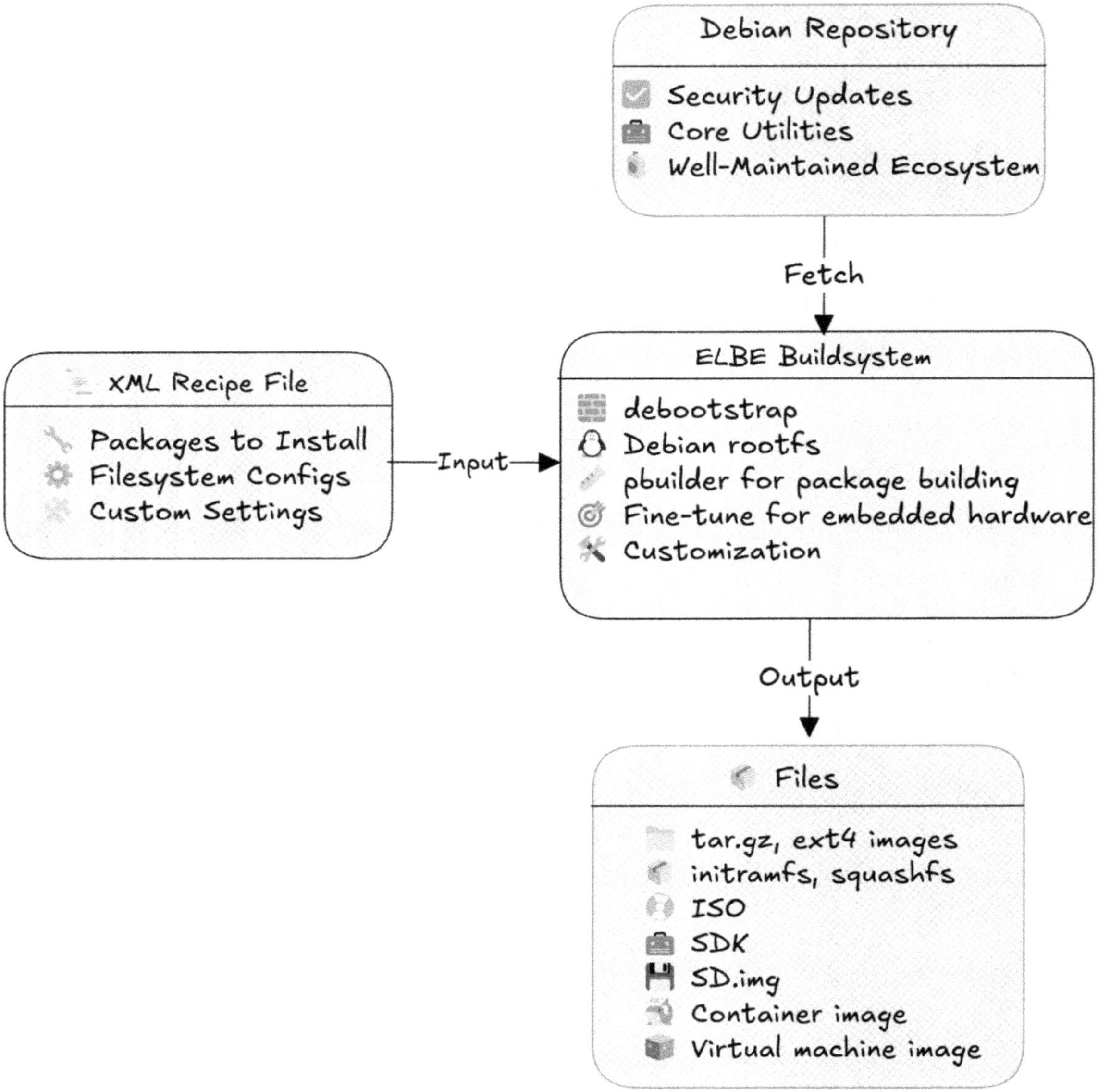


*Figure 20: ELBE Basics*

Written in Python, ELBE relies on debootstrap, (a tool to create a minimal Debian installation) as its underlying mechanism to construct root filesystems. This ensures a clean and consistent foundation for the system generated, adhering to Debian standards. Debian provides several advantages, such as access to a vast ecosystem of precompiled, well-maintained packages, and robust security updates. By leveraging Debian's stability and rich software repository, ELBE enables developers to focus on customization without having to worry about low-level dependency management or package compatibility.

Though ELBE works on top of debootstrap, its functionality, however, extends well beyond basic image creation. ELBE supports system updates, enabling seamless modification of existing configurations. It integrates with pbuilder (Personal Builder a Debian Package Building system) for streamlined package building and testing, allowing developers to maintain consistency across builds. It also offers fine-tuning capabilities, providing granular control over system customization.

Additionally, ELBE simplifies cross-compilation and development workflows by facilitating SDK and sysroot generation, which are essential for building and testing software on target architectures. It supports the creation of source and binary CDROMs for easy distribution and includes mechanisms for generating license files, ensuring compliance with software licensing requirements. ELBE also accommodates multiple filesystem formats, such as ext4, btrfs, and squashfs, catering to the diverse needs of embedded projects.

With its robust feature set and the inherent advantages of the Debian ecosystem, ELBE has become an indispensable tool for embedded Linux development. It offers unparalleled flexibility, efficiency, and comprehensive customization options, making it a top choice for developers building reliable, scalable, and tailored Debian embedded Linux systems

## 6.1 ELBE Workflow at a Glance:

Now let us assume that we are planning to build an image for a Raspberry Pi board. Figure 21 shows a very basic workflow.

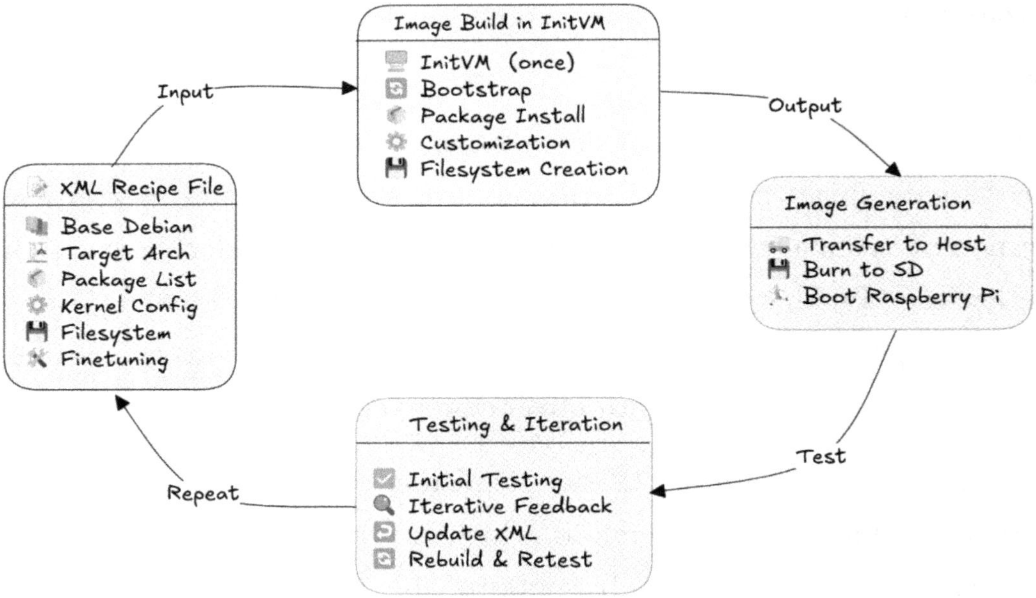


*Figure 21: ELBE Workflow*

## Define the Project Configuration (XML Recipe)

The first step in the ELBE workflow is to define the project configuration using an XML recipe file. This recipe serves as the blueprint for the embedded system image you want to create. Within the recipe, you define several key aspects of the system:

- **Base Debian Version**: Specify the base Debian release (e.g., bookworm or trixie) that the system will be built from.
- **Target Architecture**: Define the target system architecture, such as ARM, ARM64, or x86.
- **Package Selection**: List the Debian packages that should be included in the root filesystem. These can range from standard libraries to specific applications required by your embedded system.
- **Kernel Configuration**: Define the kernel package available as part of the distribution, or you can compile a custom kernel. The custom kernel can be copied to the target using the overlay feature, or you can build a Debian package for it and integrate it with the XML recipe.

- **Filesystem Format**: Specify the format of the root file system, such as ext4, btrfs, or squashfs, depending on your project requirements.
- **Custom Software or Features:** ELBE allows you to add custom software, such as third-party applications, tools, or drivers that are required for your specific embedded hardware.

The XML recipe ensures consistency across builds and provides a centralized configuration that can be modified or reused as needed. It simplifies managing the complexity of embedded system configuration by organizing all these parameters in a single, easily editable file.

### Image Build Process in InitVM

Once the project configuration is defined, the next step is to initiate the image build process, which ELBE automates using a virtual machine (VM), referred to as **InitVM**. The build process includes several key tasks:

- **VM Initialization**: ELBE creates and configures a virtual environment (a minimal Debian installation) to build the recipe image. This ensures a clean and isolated build environment, reducing the risk of errors. This is a one-time task.
- **Bootstrap Process**: ELBE uses **debootstrap** to set up a minimal Debian installation in a directory. This serves as the basis for the root filesystem.
- **Package Installation and Configuration**: ELBE installs the selected packages from Debian repositories and configures them as per the recipe, ensuring all dependencies are correctly handled for the target system.
- **Customization and Fine-Tuning**: If the recipe specifies custom configurations or additional software, ELBE handles fine-tuning, ensuring custom modules and settings are applied seamlessly during the build.
- **Filesystem Creation**: Based on the specified format (e.g., ext4, squashfs), ELBE generates the root filesystem, resulting in a deployable image that meets the system requirements.

By using a virtual machine (InitVM) to perform the build, ELBE ensures that the process remains consistent and isolated, reducing errors and ensuring reproducibility across different environments.

### Image Generation and Booting on Raspberry Pi

After successfully building the image, the next step is to transfer it from the InitVM to the host machine and burn it to an SD card.

Once the image is deployed to the SD card, you can boot the Raspberry Pi. The system will load the custom embedded Linux environment defined in the XML recipe, including the specified packages, kernel options, and configurations.

ELBE automates the boot configuration process, making it easier to deploy customized systems on hardware such as the Raspberry Pi without manual setup of the bootloader or partitions.

### Testing and Iteration (Going Back to XML Recipe)

After booting Raspberry Pi or another target device, you test the system to ensure it meets the desired specifications.

- **Initial Testing**: After booting the image, verify that essential services, drivers, and applications are working. Test network connectivity, hardware support (e.g., GPIO, USB), and performance.
- **Iterative Feedback**: Based on the outcome, you may identify areas for improvement, such as adding packages, tweaking the kernel, or adjusting system configurations.
- **Returning to the XML Recipe**: If changes are needed, go back to the XML recipe to adjust. This could involve adding software, updating the kernel, or modifying configurations.
- **Rebuilding and Retesting**: Once the XML recipe is updated, rebuild the image and retest it on Raspberry Pi or target hardware. This process is repeated until the image meets the required specifications.

This iterative process allows rapid adjustments to the embedded system, ensuring the final image is optimized. ELBE's automation streamlines testing and iteration, making it easier to develop customized embedded Linux images.

## 6.2 Installation

With a basic understanding of ELBE, we can now proceed with its installation. ELBE officially supports Debian as the host operating system, though it is also compatible with Ubuntu. At the time of writing, Debian 12 (codename Bookworm) was used as the host system, and the ELBE version was v15.2.

### Method 1: Install from ELBE repository

Let us install the Debian way using prebuilt .deb packages. For this, you either need root access or a user with sudo privilege.

**Install the Repository Key:**

First, you need to add the repository key. You can do this in one of two ways:

Using apt to install the key:

This command installs the ELBE repository key from the standard Debian repository if the above fails, then directly download the key from the Linutronix website, where the ELBE packages are hosted

```
$ apt install elbe-archive-keyring || wget -O /usr/share/keyrings/elbe-archive-keyring.gpg https://debian.linutronix.de/elbe/elbe-repo.pub.gpg
```

Now, add the ELBE repository to your APT sources list:

```
$ echo "deb [signed-by=/usr/share/keyrings/elbe-archive-keyring.gpg] https://debian.linutronix.de/elbe buster main" >> /etc/apt/sources.list
```

The binaries hosted on the Linutronix website support Debian *Buster* and work well with Bookworm as well

**Update the APT Package Database:**

After adding the repository, update your APT package database to fetch the latest package information:

```
$ apt update
```

**Install ELBE:**

Once the package information is updated, you can install ELBE from the Linutronix Debian repository:

```
$ apt install elbe
```

If all goes well, you have installed elbe successfully

**Method 2: Installation using Git Version:**

If you prefer to install ELBE directly from the source repository instead of installing it from a Debian package, you can fetch the ELBE repository using Git. If Git is not yet installed on your system, you can install it with the following command:

```
$ apt install git
```

After successfully installing Git, clone the ELBE repository into a directory of your choice using the following command

```
$ git clone https://github.com/Linutronix/elbe.git
```

**Add ELBE to Your Default Path:**

Navigate into the ELBE directory and add it to your default path:

```
$ cd elbe
$ export PATH=$PWD:$PATH
```

### Install Core ELBE, Python Dependencies, and Virtualization Tools

Begin by installing the essential Python packages needed to run ELBE, as well as the required virtualization tools and supporting utilities.

```
$ sudo apt  install python3 python3-debian python3-mako \
                    python3-lxml python3-apt python3-gpg \
                    python3-suds python3-libvirt p7zip-full  \
                    qemu-kvm make qemu-utils python3-passlib\
                    libvirt-clients libvirt-daemon-system \
                    debian-archive-keyring
```

This command installs:

- **Python dependencies**: Required for running ELBE scripts and handling various tasks such as package installation, virtualization management, and more.
- **Virtualization tools**: Includes libvirt, qemu-utils, qemu-kvm, and associated packages, allowing interaction with KVM and virtualization management.
- **Additional utilities**: Includes p7zip-full, make, and debian-archive-keyring, which are useful for system configuration, package management, and secure repository access.

After successfully installing ELBE, let us continue configuring user permission etc.

### Configure User Permissions for Virtualization

Next, add the user (e.g., u1) to the necessary groups for working with libvirt and KVM:

```
$ sudo adduser u1 libvirt
$ sudo adduser u1 libvirt-qemu
$ sudo adduser u1 kvm
```

This ensures that the u1 user has the necessary permissions to interact with virtualization services and tools. For virtualization, appropriate settings need to be enabled in the BIOS/UEFI configuration of your PC.

## 6.3 Creating the InitVM

The InitVM is a virtual machine that serves as the environment where ELBE builds the root filesystem (rootfs) for your embedded Linux image. It helps to isolate the build process, ensuring consistency and preventing potential conflicts with the host system. Below is a detailed breakdown of how to create and manage the InitVM.

```
$ elbe initvm create
```

This command creates a directory named "initvm" and sets up a virtual machine using ELBE's default configuration. It downloads the kernel and initrd from the Debian repository, then initializes the InitVM. The virtual machine runs with KVM if supported or falls back to QEMU if not.

The process produces a single image file, typically over 10GB, in the current directory. This setup prepares a minimal Debian environment equipped with all the necessary tools to build embedded Linux images with ELBE. The installation usually takes just a few minutes and only needs to be done once, the resulting InitVM image can be reused to build multiple Debian recipes.

For machines without KVM support, the output looks like shown below.

```
$ elbe initvm create
~~~
Build initvm
KVM accelerated emulation is not available for the initvm, builds will be
slow
*****
```

### Create InitVM with Development (Git) Source

If you are using ELBE directly from the source code downloaded from https://github.com/Linutronix/elbe , you can use the –devel option:

```
$ elbe initvm create --devel
```

This ensures that the InitVM is created using the latest development version of ELBE, which may include changes or features not present in the stable release. This option is useful if you are developing a feature, fixing a bug, or need the InitVM to be built in sync with that version.

### Create InitVM with Custom XML

In some cases, you may want to customize the InitVM. For instance, to enable SSH access or adjust other specific settings, you can provide a custom XML file when creating the InitVM

```
$ elbe initvm create initvm-ssh-access.xml
```

Here, initvm-ssh-access.xml is a custom XML file that defines specific configurations for the VM, such as enabling SSH access or configuring network settings. You can specify any custom settings required for your embedded image build in this XML file. If no XML file is provided, ELBE uses the default one located at elbe/elbepack/init/default-init.xml. An example XML recipe is available at the following path

```
https://github.com/Linutronix/elbe/blob/master/examples/elbe-init-big-
machine.xml
```

### Deleting and Recreating InitVM Using ELBE

If you need to delete an old InitVM and recreate a new one, follow these steps:

```
$ elbe initvm destroy
```

This command will:

- Clean up the existing InitVM.
- Remove the associated virtual machine configuration files.
- Allow you to create a new InitVM with a fresh configuration.

By using this command, you avoid having to manually remove directories or undefine the virtual machine from the virtualization management system (libvirt). ELBE handles everything for you, making the process easier and more streamlined.

Now, after using elbe initvm destroy, you can proceed to recreate the InitVM using the elbe initvm create command, as previously described, to set up a new environment for building your embedded Linux images.

In case if you are using an older version of elbe, then use the below commands to delete the InitVM.

```
$ rm -rf initvm
$ virsh --connect qemu:///system undefine initvm
```

**Starting and Stopping InitVM Using ELBE**

ELBE provides commands to start and stop the InitVM, making it easy to manage the virtual environment during development. Here's how to use these commands:

**Starting the InitVM**

To start the InitVM, use the following command:

```
$ elbe initvm start
```

**Stopping the InitVM**

To stop the InitVM, use the following command:

```
$ elbe initvm stop
```

### Attaching to the InitVM Shell

Once the InitVM is started, you can connect to it using the **attach** command. This connects you to the virtual console (a login shell) of the InitVM and provides direct access to its environment.

```
$ elbe initvm attach
```

**What this command does:**

- Connects to the InitVM's console through the virtualization platform, such as KVM/QEMU.
- Displays a login prompt where you can authenticate and access the InitVM directly.
- **Login Information:**
- If you are using the default InitVM XML configuration, the username is root and the password is root.
- For custom InitVM XML configurations, use the credentials specified in the custom XML file.

**InitVM SSH Access:**

In the latest elbe version starting from 15.7, it is possible to access the InitVM shell via ssh command like shown below.

```
$ elbe initvm ssh
```

### Direct SSH Access to InitVM

- If the XML used to create the InitVM includes an **SSH service with port redirection**, it is possible to directly SSH into the InitVM without using elbe initvm attach. This can be done with the following command:

```
$ ssh -p 5022 root@localhost
```

**Important Notes:**

- **Root Login:** By default, SSH root login is restricted for security reasons. However, if the recipe explicitly enables root login, this command will work.
- **Custom Configurations:** Ensure that your XML configuration contains the necessary directives to enable SSH and set up port forwarding.

**Steps to Follow After Running the command elbe initvm attach:**

1. **Wait for the Login Prompt:**

Sometimes, you might need to press the **Enter** key twice to bring up the login prompt.

2. **Login:**
   - Use the username: root.
   - Enter the password: default is root, or the password specified in your custom XML configuration.
3. **Perform Your Tasks:**

   Once logged in, you can interact with the InitVM as needed, such as inspecting logs, troubleshooting, or manually managing build dependencies.
4. **Detaching from the InitVM**

- To exit the InitVM console and return to your host system, follow these steps:
- Use one of the following key combinations:
  - **Ctrl +]**
  - **Ctrl + 5** (depending on your keyboard layout).

This will safely detach from the virtual console and return you to the host machine's command prompt.

**Key Notes:**

- Ensure you have started the InitVM with elbe initvm start before attempting to attach or SSH.
- If you encounter issues with login or connection, verify that the InitVM is running using the command elbe initvm ensure.
- **SSH Access:** If configured, SSH access is a more convenient way to connect to the InitVM compared to elbe initvm attach, especially for automated workflows.
- Detaching does not stop the InitVM, it continues running in the background.

**Developer Note: Synchronizing Changes to InitVM**

The elbe initvm sync command is a valuable tool for developers working with ELBE. It ensures that updates made to the ELBE source code on the host system are mirrored in InitVM without requiring manual file transfers. Since the ELBE source code is split into client (host-side) and server (InitVM-side) components, synchronization is necessary to keep both parts aligned. The sync command uses rsync to efficiently transfer only modified files based on their timestamps, automating what would otherwise be a tedious process.

To use the sync command, certain configurations must be in place. Root login via SSH must be enabled on the InitVM, and the client system's SSH key should be added to the root/.ssh/authorized_keys file in the InitVM to allow passwordless access. The InitVM exposes internal services such as SSH (port 22) and rsync (port 873) to the host through ports 5022 and 8730, respectively. However, enabling root SSH login can pose a security risk, so it should be configured with care.

To run the sync, execute:

```
$ elbe initvm sync
```

from the host system. By default, the command prompts for the InitVM's root password unless password less SSH is configured. Developers can verify synchronization by modifying or creating a file in the host's ELBE project directory and checking its presence in the InitVM after running the command. This streamlined process is essential for efficient development and testing in ELBE environments.

## 6.4 Understanding the InitVM

Now that we know how to create and manage the InitVM, let's explore its internal architecture and role in the ELBE build process.

The ELBE source code is divided into two main components: the **client** and the **server**, which communicate through a **SOAP interface**. The server performs the operations required to build the root filesystem, based on the inputs provided by the client. The client gathers input from the user, typically as an XML file along with command-line parameters.

ELBE provides a wide range of commands that support both service provider (server-side) and requester (client-side) roles. On the server side, commands are handled by the elbe-daemon process (see Figure 22), which runs as a SOAP server and forwards incoming requests to the appropriate ELBE commands for execution.

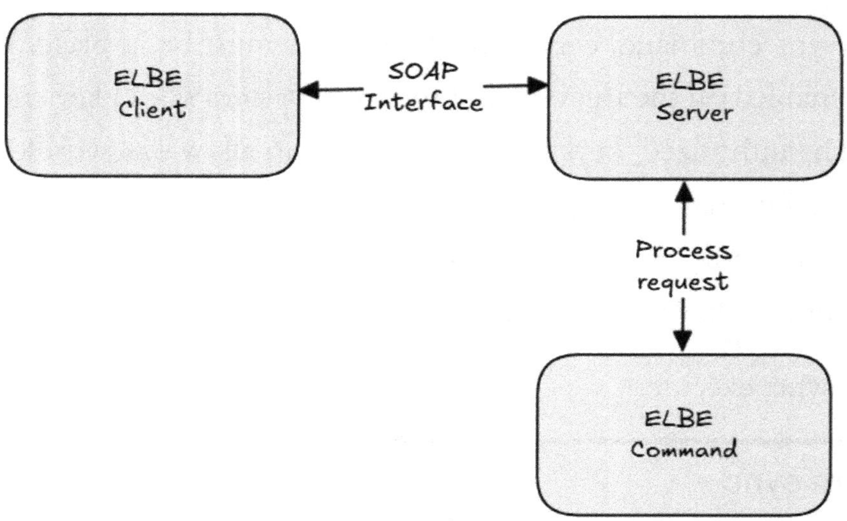


*Figure 22: ELBE Building Blocks*

The operations carried out by the ELBE service provider require root access. To support this, both the elbe-daemon and the ELBE service provider are bundled together and installed within the **InitVM**. This environment includes not only the ELBE components but also essential tools such as debootstrap, mkfs utilities, chroot, and others required to create a root file system in the desired format.

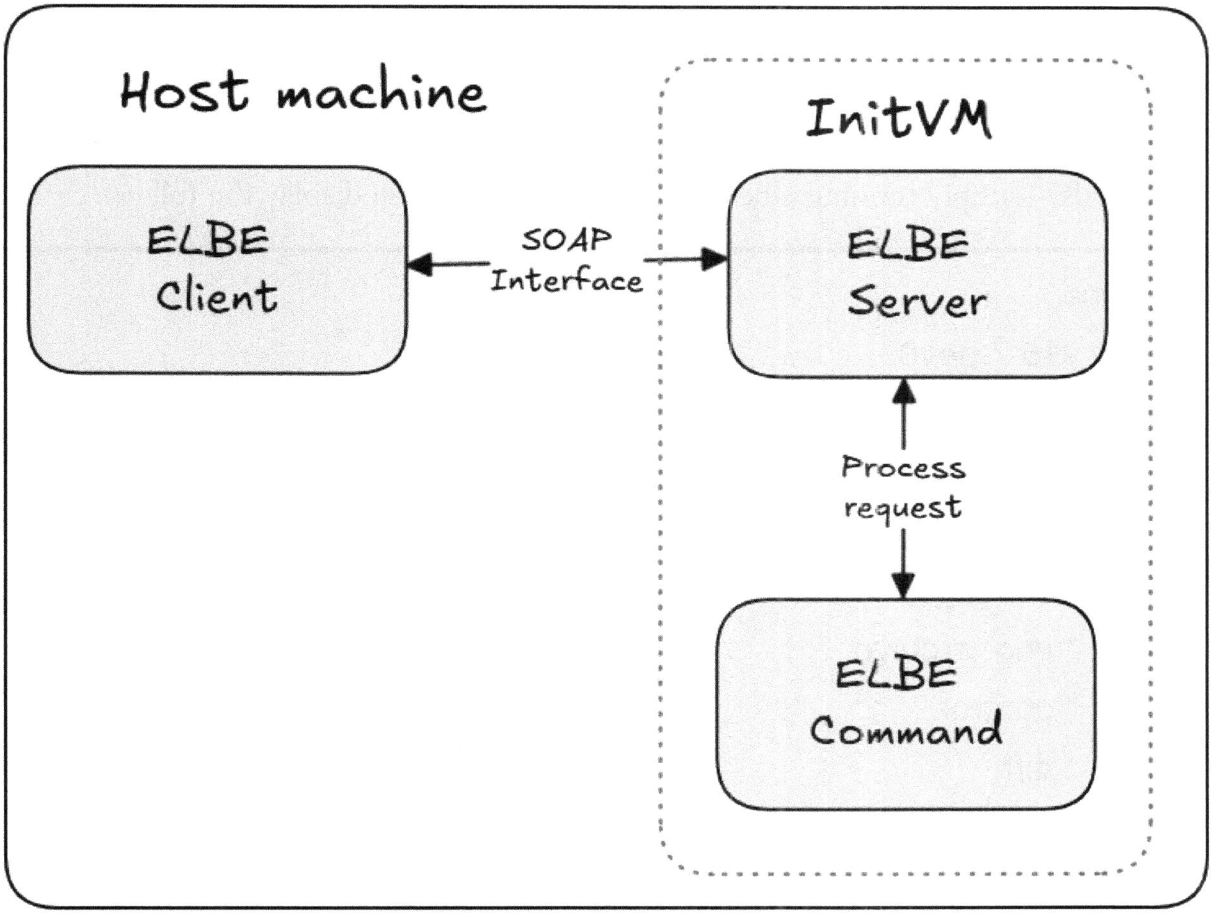


*Figure 23: ELBE InitVM Host Communication*

InitVM is essentially a Debian machine equipped with ELBE and all the required tools. For flexibility, it can also be deployed in Docker, LXC, or other container environments. In such cases, the SOAP interface requires port **5788** to be open, so the container must map its local port to the host port for proper communication.

Alternatively, the components that normally run inside the InitVM can be installed and executed directly on the host system with root privileges. While this removes the isolation provided by a virtual machine, it generally works as expected. This book, however, focuses on the KVM-based setup, as it is the most used and best supported by the ELBE community.

**ELBE Build Process, Internals by example:**

Now that we understand ELBE's capabilities, let's explore how an example build works and examine its internal workflow. The ELBE client offers a variety of commands—simply running elbe in the command line will display the full list.

```
$ elbe
elbe v15.7.dev0
need a subcommand: e.g. 'elbe initvm'.
  Available subcommands are:
    * add
    * check_updates
    * chg_archive
    * control
    * diff
    * get_archive
    * init
    * initvm
    * parselicence
    * pbuilder
    * pin_versions
    * pkgdiff
```

```
        * preprocess
        * prjrepo
        * remove_sign
        * repodir
        * setsel
        * show
        * sign
        * validate
    * xsdtoasciidoc
```

Among all the available commands, this book primarily focuses on the elbe control subcommand.

```
$ elbe control
available subcommands are:
  rm_log
  list_projects
  list_users
  add_user
  create_project
  reset_project
  del_project
  set_xml
  build
  build_sysroot
  build_sdk
```

```
    build_cdroms
    get_file
    build_chroot_tarball
    dump_file
    get_files
    wait_busy
    set_cdrom
    set_orig
    shutdown_initvm
    set_pdebuild
    status
    build_pbuilder
    update_pbuilder
  install_elbe_version
```

Let's start with a recipe named recipe.xml. The recommended and simplest way to build an image with ELBE is using a single high-level command that handles the entire workflow automatically:

```
$ elbe initvm submit recipe.xml
```

This one command:

- Starts or connects to the ELBE InitVM (the build virtual machine).
- Creates a new project (if none exists for this XML).
- Uploads/submits the XML recipe.
- Triggers the build process.

- Monitors progress and waits for completion.
- Provides error handling, validation, logging, and cleanup.

Once finished successfully, the generated image and artifacts (e.g., root filesystem tarball, logs, reports) are available in the project directory or via retrieval commands.

For reference and deeper understanding especially when debugging, customizing scripts, or learning how ELBE works internally the following sections describe the underlying low-level steps that elbe initvm submit orchestrates behind the scenes using elbe control. These are not intended for everyday use.

The steps are straightforward: create a project, submit the XML recipe to it, start the build process, and monitor the logs. Once the build finishes successfully, the generated image can be downloaded.

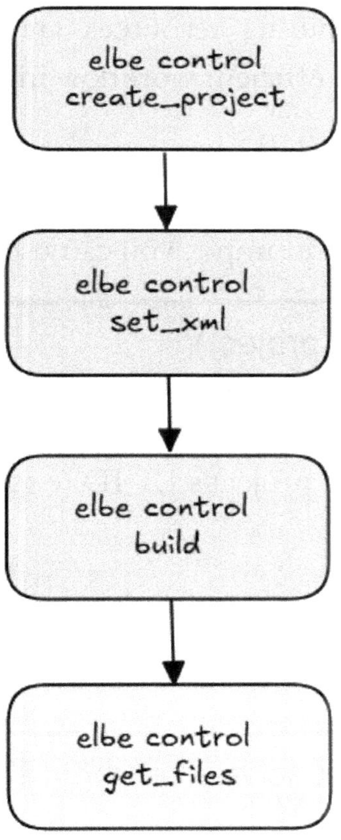


*Figure 24: ELBE Workflow*

### Create a project

```
$ elbe control create project
/var/cache/elbe/0bf64350-12fc-4761-a80d-acb82290e4cf
```

The create_project command, when executed successfully, returns a UUID representing a newly created directory under /var/cache/elbe/. Each project created by ELBE gets its own unique UUID-based folder at this location.

For example, running **elbe control create_project** might output something like **/var/cache/elbe/0bf64350-12fc-4761-a80d-acb82290e4cf**, this indicates that a directory with the specified UUID has been created. UUID serves as the project identifier, and all subsequent operations such as submitting recipes or managing the build reference it.

The **create_project** command simplifies project initialization by ensuring each project is uniquely tracked and its resources are cleanly organized, laying the foundation for a structured and efficient workflow in ELBE.

To streamline handling the UUID in scripts or automation workflows, you can capture it directly into a variable. This eliminates manual copying and ensures seamless integration into automation. For example, you can use the following command:

```
$ ID=$(elbe control create_project)
```

In this example, the **ID** variable stores the output of the **create_project** command, which is the path containing the project's UUID (e.g., **/var/cache/elbe/0bf64350-12fc-4761-a80d-acb82290e4cf**).

### Submit XML Recipe:

The next step is submitting an XML recipe file to the InitVM using **set_xml** command

```
$ elbe control set_xml /var/cache/elbe/0bf64350-12fc-4761-a80d-
acb82290e4cf  recipe.xml
```

Or

```
$ elbe control set_xml $ID recipe.xml
```

This command pushes the XML file recipe.xml into the InitVM, to the specified UUID path. The next step is to build the project.

**Build the Project:**

This command is used to initiate the build process for a project. This command processes the project, creating the target root filesystem or other outputs as specified in the XML recipe file.

```
$ elbe control build $ID
```

The build process produces logs and outputs that can be reviewed for troubleshooting or verification purposes. Once the build is complete, the generated root filesystem and related artifacts are stored within the project directory for deployment or further customization.

```
$ elbe control wait_busy $ID
```

The **elbe control wait_busy** command is used to monitor a project build and wait until it completes. It continuously checks the build status, ensuring that you know when the build process finishes or encounters any issues.

```
$ elbe control wait_busy /var/cache/elbe/0bf64350-12fc-4761-a80d-acb82290e4cf
...
[INFO] Build finished successfully
```

The message indicates that the build process for the ELBE project completed without errors or issues. If there were any errors during the build, you would see a different log message indicating failure or issues to investigate.

**Download files:**

This command is used to retrieve the output files from the ELBE project.

```
$ elbe control get_files --output downloads  $ID
```

**--output downloads**: Specifies where the retrieved files should be saved. In this case, the files will be saved in the **download's** directory.

An example downloads

```
$ elbe control get_files --output downloads  $ID
source.xml      (Current source.xml of the project)
nfsroot.tar.gz  (Image)
licence-chroot.txt      (License file)
licence-chroot.xml      (xml License file)
licence-target.txt      (License file)
licence-target.xml      (xml License file)
validation.txt  (Package list validation result)
elbe-report.txt         (Report)
log.txt  (Log file)
```

**How it works:**

When the elbe control build command is issued, the ELBE daemon, start a deboostrap stage1 base image installation, which happens inside InitVM in x86 environment.. Under the /var/cache/elbe/UUID/ it creates bunch of folder as listed below.

- chroot - contains the chroot environment used by ELBE
- target - contains the target-specific files or directories that will be included in the final image.

- filesystems hold the filesystems used in the build process such as FAT, Ext4 etc.
- imagemnt is used as a mount point for the image during the build process in project-finetuning
- repo contains the minimal repository for the local packages submitted before build

Here, the target directory is denoted as **t** (or *target*), and its parent directory—the build environment—is referred to as **b** (or *build environment*).

**Note**: This distinction is important when using XML tags such as b2t_cp and t2b_cp within the <finetuning> section.

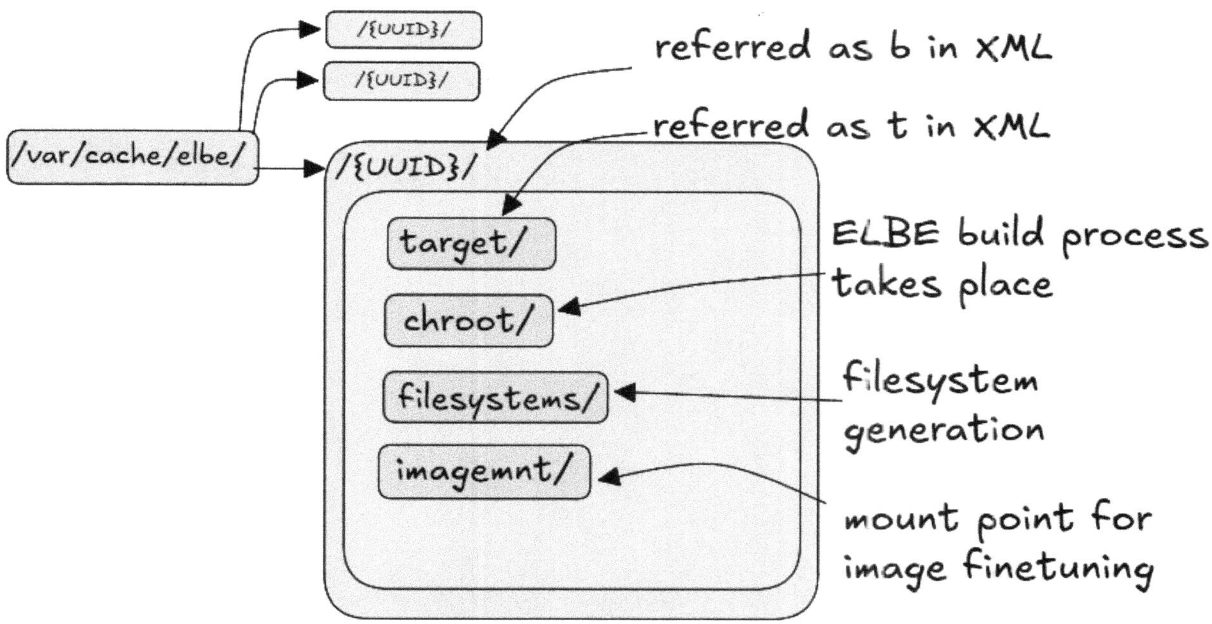


*Figure 25: ELBE Build Internals*

After the first stage of the debootstrap process, the initial root filesystem prepared in the chroot/ directory is copied into the target/ directory. The second stage of debootstrap is then executed inside the target/ directory, but within an **emulated ARM environment provided by QEMU**, allowing the configuration of ARM-specific packages and settings.

Following this, the **<finetuning> section** is processed, where customizations such as file operations, script execution, or cleanup tasks are performed within the ARM-emulated target environment.

Next, for each filesystem defined in the XML recipe using <fstab> and <mountpoint> tags, a corresponding directory is created inside the filesystems/ folder. These directories represent individual mount points or partitions and are eventually assembled into a complete disk image, typically output as something like sdcard.img.

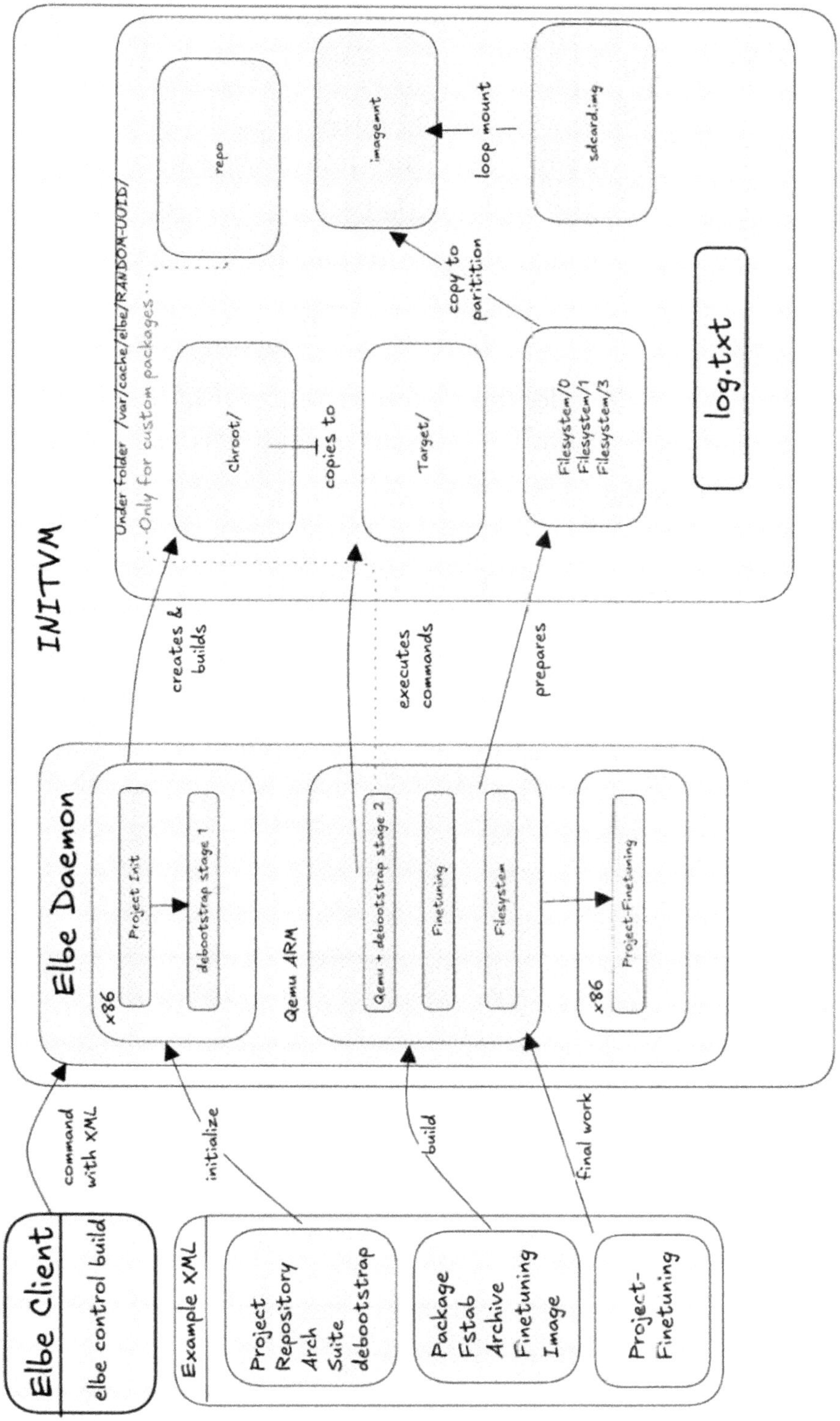


*Figure 26: ELBE Project workflow*

After the image has been successfully built, **ARM emulation is no longer used**. At this stage, ELBE switches to native execution on the host x86 system. The image is mounted as a loopback device under the imagemnt/ directory, and the **<project-finetuning> section** is then executed. This final step allows additional host-side modifications, such as applying final configurations or removing temporary build artifacts, before the image is finalized and ready for deployment.

**InitVM Maintenance:**

As we create project and download and repeat this process, the InitVM will keep growing in size. Eventually it may fail to build if there is no space left in the device. To maintain and clean up the InitVM following commands are necessary

**Lists all the project**

```
$ elbe control list_projects
```

This command displays all currently active or previously created ELBE projects inside the InitVM, showing their UUIDs and basic metadata. Use this as a reference for identifying which projects to manage.

**Delete the project**

```
$ elbe control del_project UUID
```

This removes a project identified by its UUID from the InitVM, including associated build artifacts and data. It's useful for freeing up disk space once the project is no longer needed.

**Delete all the project**

```
$ elbe control del_all_projects UUID
```

This removes all the projects from the InitVM, this command was introduced in version 15.7.

### Check the status

```
$ elbe control status
{
  "version": "15.7.dev0",
  "is_devel": true,
  "storage_free_bytes": 62395224064,
  "memory_total_bytes": 1005576192,
  "memory_available_bytes": 584740864
}
```

This command shows the free storage and free memory; this command was introduced in version 15.7.

### Reset the project

```
$ elbe control reset_project UUID
```

If you want to reuse the same project for different purposes, you can simply reset it instead of creating a new one. Additionally, in cases where a project has exited in an undefined or incomplete state and the del_project command fails to remove it, performing a reset first can allow the project to be deleted successfully afterward.

**Important Note:** elbe control is an internal command for low-level daemon interaction and should not be used by end-users. It bypasses critical steps (project setup, validation, error handling, cleanup) performed automatically by elbe initvm submit. Always use the latter for all builds.

### Summary:

We've covered the fundamentals of ELBE, including its installation, architecture, internal structure, example recipes, and overall workflow. From here, you're encouraged to explore ELBE further and discover additional command sets on your own. This book intentionally limits the number of commands introduced, focusing instead on helping you understand and experiment with various recipe.

## 6.5 ELBE XML Overview

**Key Elements:**

1. **project:**
    - **Description**: This section provides general information about the project.
    - **name**: The name of the project, which identifies the specific root filesystem image being built.
    - **version**: The version of the image, which helps track different builds and releases.
    - **description**: A short description of what the project is for, providing context about the purpose of the image.
2. **buildtype:**
    - **Description**: Specifies the architecture for which the root filesystem image is built (e.g., x86_64, arm64).
    - **Importance**: It ensures the appropriate architecture-specific packages are installed.
3. **mirror:**
    - **Description**: Defines the mirror settings used to fetch packages during the build process.
    - **primary_host**: URI of the primary Debian mirror.
    - **primary_path**: Path to the directory on the mirror containing package files.
    - **primary_proto**: Protocol used to access the mirror (e.g., http, https, ftp).

- **primary_proxy**: Optional proxy configuration for accessing the mirror.
- **options:** Additional mirror settings such as trusted=yes|no to skip or enforce signature checks and check-valid-until=yes|no to respect or ignore repository expiration.
    - trusted=yes|no
    - check-valid-until= yes|no

**4. noauth:**

- **Description**: A boolean that indicates whether authentication is required to access the package repositories.
- **True/False**: If set to true, no authentication credentials are required.
- Note: This feature is deprecated, use the options

**5. preference:**

- **Description**: Configures APT (Advanced Package Tool) preferences for managing package versions.
- **Purpose**: Helps control which versions of packages are preferred or excluded, ensuring package version consistency.

**6. raw-preference:**

- **Description**: Provides raw preference settings, typically used for more advanced or custom APT configurations.

**7. suite:**

- **Description**: Specifies the Debian suite from which packages are fetched (e.g., stable, buster, bullseye).
- **Importance**: Ensures the correct set of packages is used based on the Debian release being targeted.

**Target Section:**

**1. hostname:**

- **Description**: Defines the hostname for the target system.
- **Example**: webserver01 or myserver.

**2. domain:**

- **Description**: Specifies the domain name for the target system.
- **Example**: example.com.

**3. passwd_hashed:**

- **Description**: Configuration for hashed passwords of system users, typically used for secure user authentication.
- **Example**: You may provide a hashed password such as SHA256 or bcrypt.

**4. console:**

- **Description**: Configures console settings (such as terminal settings and output configurations).
- **Example**: ttyS0 or tty1.

**5. debootstrapvariant:**

- **Description**: Specifies how the root filesystem is created (e.g., minbase, buildd).
- **Purpose**: Controls the packages included during the bootstrap process.

**6. package:**

- **Description**: Defines configurations for package installation.
- **tar, cpio, squashfs**: Compression methods used for packages during installation.

**7. images:**

- **Description**: Defines the structure of different image formats such as MTD, MSDOSHD, GPTHD.
- **Purpose**: Specifies how disk images are partitioned and formatted.

**8. pkg-list:**

- **Description**: A list of packages to be installed on the target system.
- **Usage**: Ensures the required packages are included in the final image.

**9. fstab:**

- **Description**: Configures the file system table (fstab) with mount points and file system types.
- **Purpose**: Ensures proper partitioning and mounting of filesystems during boot.

**10. diet:**

- **Description**: Includes packages, settings, or optimizations that reduce the size of the root filesystem.
- **Usage**: Helps keep the image lightweight.

**11. tighten:**

- **Description**: Removes unnecessary packages to tighten up the installed environment.
- **Example**: Removing debug packages or unused libraries.

**12. install-recommends:**

- **Description**: Configures whether recommended packages should be installed during the build.
- **Usage**: Helps reduce the size of the root filesystem by avoiding installing recommended packages.

**13. finetuning:**

- **Description**: Includes custom operations such as file manipulations, copying, and executing commands to fine-tune the image.
- **Example**: Copying configuration files, removing files, or creating directories.

**14. pbuilder:**

- **Description**: Configures settings for pbuilder, which provides a clean environment for package building.
- **Usage**: Ensures packages are built in a clean, isolated environment.

**15. pkg-blacklist:**

- **Description**: Specifies packages to exclude from being installed.
- **Purpose**: Helps filter out unwanted or incompatible packages.

**16. project-finetuning:**

- **Description**: Additional customizations specific to the project.
- **Example**: Removing artifacts after the build or setting up device mappings.

**17. img_convert:**

- **Description**: Converts image formats between different types, such as MTD, MSDOSHD, or GPTHD.

**18. unit-tests:**

- **Description**: Defines unit tests for image validation, ensuring the image meets specific criteria.

**19. src-cdrom:**

- **Description**: Specifies the source for additional packages from a CD-ROM.

**20. archive:**

- **Description**: **<archive>** section in ELBE XML recipes is designed to include additional files or directories as overlays on the target root filesystem.
- **Example**: Copying configuration files, removing files, or creating directories.

**Conclusion**:

The **Target** section provides extensive configuration options for customizing the root filesystem image, focusing on user authentication, package selection, filesystem structure, and environment setup. The **passwd_hashed** field ensures secure user authentication by allowing hashed password configurations.

# RECIPES

# 7 Docker Build Environment

**Abstract:** This chapter demonstrates building a Docker-capable Debian Trixie image using ELBE. It details customer requirements, implementation steps, the docker-trixie.xml recipe, and explanations of key configurations for container runtime support. Readers learn to create lightweight, container-ready embedded bases suitable for modern DevOps-inspired workflows.

## 7.1 Company Introduction

**Skybridge Embedded Systems** specializes in developing robust, custom embedded solutions for a wide range of industries, including automotive and aerospace. The team is renowned for its deep expertise in embedded Linux and frequently works on projects involving ARM architecture. Recently, their focus has shifted toward creating tailored Linux environments for ARM-based systems, optimized for both performance and security.

## 7.2 Customer Requirements

Skybridge is approached by **Orryx Dronetics**, a startup developing drones for deployment in remote locations, such as scientific research in the Arctic and search-

and-rescue operations in harsh terrains. Orryx Dronetics has selected 64-bit ARM architecture processors for their drones due to their low power consumption and efficient performance. They require a custom Linux environment to power the onboard control systems, and they want the entire system built from the ground up.

Orryx Dronetics presents a unique challenge: They need a Docker image that will serve as a portable development environment for their engineers, but they want everything in the image to be built from scratch. The image must include an ARM 64-bit cross-compiler, kernel compilation tools, and support for mounting host directories inside the container, but no pre-built or off-the-shelf Docker images are allowed. The entire environment must be custom built to ensure maximum control over every aspect of the build process.

### Company Response

Skybridge's engineering lead, *Leila*, takes on the challenge. She knows that ELBE can be used to build highly customized Debian-based root file system for embedded devices, and she sees an opportunity to extend this capability to a Docker tailored for Orryx Dronetics' ARM-based drone development.

Leila begins by setting up an ELBE project. She outlines the requirements for the Docker image:

- **ARM 64-bit Cross-Compiler**: To compile code for the drone's ARM processors.
- **Kernel Compilation Tools**: To build custom kernels tailored to the drone's hardware.
- **Host Directory Mounting**: To allow developers to work on code outside the container and compile it within the containerized environment.

## 7.3 Implementation

Leila starts by configuring ELBE to create a minimal Debian-based root file system that will serve as the base for the Docker image. Rather than focusing solely on an embedded device image, she adapts the ELBE configuration to build a versatile environment suitable for running inside a Docker container.

She defines the necessary packages in ELBE's XML configuration files:

- The gcc-aarch64-linux-gnu package is included to provide the ARM 64-bit cross-compiler.
- Kernel development tools such as make, git, bc, and libncurses-dev are added to the package list to ensure that everything needed for kernel compilation is present.
- ELBE is configured to set up the appropriate user and environment variables to ensure the tools run efficiently within Docker.

**Finalization and Results:**

ELBE then handles the entire build process: creating the root file system, installing the specified packages, and configuring the environment. Leila's ELBE project generates a fully customized Debian image, which she then packages into a format that can be used as a Docker image.

One of the key challenges Leila faces is ensuring that the Docker container can work seamlessly with host-mounted directories. While Docker typically handles volume mounting, Leila configures the ELBE-built environment to recognize the mounted directories and ensure that permissions and access controls work correctly when moving between the container and the host system.

After several iterations, Leila successfully builds the complete environment using ELBE, resulting in a Docker image that includes:

- A custom-built Debian environment.
- ARM 64-bit cross-compilation tools.
- Kernel development tools.
- Configurations to support host directory mounting.

**Outcome**:

Leila presents the finished Docker image to Orryx Dronetics. The image provides a portable, consistent development environment that all their engineers can use, regardless of their host machine setup. With this solution, the engineers can now focus on developing and compiling code for the drones' ARM 64-bit processors, confident that the entire environment has been built from the ground up using ELBE.

As Orryx Dronetics progresses with their development, they see other potential applications for the ELBE-built Docker image. For instance, they consider automating the image build process and integrating it into their CI/CD pipeline—ensuring that every time a developer pushes new code, it is compiled and tested in a fresh, custom-built environment.

Leila starts exploring how this ELBE-based approach to support other architectures and use cases, ensuring that Skybridge remains at the cutting edge of embedded systems development.

The following steps outline the process used to build the custom Docker image using ELBE:

```
$ elbe initvm submit docker-trixie.xml --output downloads
```

The above command connects to (or starts) the ELBE InitVM, creates a project, submits and validates the XML file, downloads the required packages, sets up the root filesystem, builds the Docker cross-build environment, then waits for the process to complete and reports the final status.

**Output:**

```
Build started, waiting till it finishes
[INFO] Build started
~
```

```
~
[INFO] Build finished successfully

Build finished !

ELBE Package validation
========================

Package List validation
----------------------

No Errors found
Binary CD
Source CD

Getting generated Files

Saving generated Files to /home/u1/elbe-cookbook-recipes/01-
docker/downloads
source.xml      Current source.xml of the project
crossbuildenv.tgz       Image
licence-chroot.txt      License file
licence-chroot.xml      xml License file
licence-target.txt      License file
licence-target.xml      xml License file
validation.txt  Package list validation result
```

```
elbe-report.txt Report
log.txt Log file
bin-cdrom.iso   Repository IsoImage
src-cdrom-target.iso    Repository IsoImage
src-cdrom-main.iso      Repository IsoImage
src-cdrom-added.iso     Repository IsoImage
```

- The key output is crossbuildenv.tgz, which contains the Docker environment for ARM 64-bit cross-compilation.

### Docker Integration

After retrieving the crossbuildenv.tgz file from the ELBE build process, the following steps are used to import and run the Docker image:

### Import the Docker Image

```
$ sudo docker import crossbuildenv.tgz crossbuildenv
```

This command imports the crossbuildenv.tgz file as a Docker image.

- **docker import**: Imports a tarball as a Docker image
- **crossbuildenv.tgz**: The tarball generated by ELBE, containing the cross-compilation environment
- **crossbuildenv**: The name assigned to the resulting Docker image

### Run the Docker Container

```
$ sudo docker run -it --user $(id -u):$(id -g) -w /workspace -v
"$PWD:/workspace" --hostname crossbuilder  crossbuildenv bash
```

This command runs a Docker container using the crossbuildenv image with specific options to configure the development environment.

- **docker run -it**: Starts an interactive terminal session.
- **--user $(id -u):$(id -g)**: Runs the container with the same user and group IDs as the host user, preventing permission issues when accessing mounted volumes.
- **-w /workspace**: Sets the working directory inside the container to /workspace.
- **-v "$PWD:/workspace"**: Mounts the current host directory into the container's /workspace directory, allowing access to host files.
- **--hostname crossbuilder**: Assigns the hostname crossbuilder to the container
- **crossbuildenv**: Specifies the Docker image to use.
- **bash**: Launches a Bash shell inside the container for interactive use

## 7.4 Recipe: docker-trixie.xml

```
<?xml version="1.0"?>
<ns0:RootFileSystem
xmlns:ns0="https://www.linutronix.de/projects/Elbe"
xmlns:xsi="http://www.w3.org/2001/XMLSchema-instance"
created="2009-05-20T08:50:56" revision="6"
xsi:schemaLocation="https://www.linutronix.de/projects/Elbe
dbsfed.xsd">
<project>
<name>Cross Compiler Container Environment</name>
<version>1.0</version>
<description>
  The Docker Container image for cross compilation
</description>
```

```
<buildtype>amd64</buildtype>
<mirror>
  <primary_host>deb.debian.org</primary_host>
  <primary_path>/debian</primary_path>
  <primary_proto>http</primary_proto>
  <url-list>
        <url>
          <binary>https://deb.debian.org/debian-security trixie-security
main</binary>
          <source>https://deb.debian.org/debian-security trixie-security
main</source>
        </url>
  </url-list>
</mirror>
<suite>trixie</suite>
</project>
<target>
<hostname>crossbuildenv</hostname>
<domain>arm64</domain>
<passwd_hashed>$6$bOQ4Sf4rSdI1IfRd$3Hai04jz2OYEW108SZWew
eGO/rGvO65ITthDDtDuaC/8Gpwek/xT4rUvKBkBHFIjTDd6.kIFdNJ685k
xgabHh/</passwd_hashed>
<debootstrap>
  <variant>minbase</variant>
</debootstrap>
<package>
```

```
  <tar>
        <name>crossbuildenv.tgz</name>
  </tar>
</package>
<finetuning>
  <mkdir>/workspace</mkdir>
  <adduser
passwd_hashed="$6$bOQ4Sf4rSdI1IfRd$3Hai04jz2OYEW108SZWew
eGO/rGvO65ITthDDtDuaC/8Gpwek/xT4rUvKBkBHFIjTDd6.klFdNJ685k
xgabHh/" shell="/bin/bash" uid="1000"
create_group="true">u1</adduser>
</finetuning>
<pkg-list>
  <pkg>bash</pkg>
  <pkg>bc</pkg>
  <pkg>bison</pkg>
  <pkg>flex</pkg>
  <pkg>libssl-dev</pkg>
  <pkg>libc6-dev</pkg>
  <pkg>crossbuild-essential-arm64</pkg>
  <pkg>gcc</pkg>
</pkg-list>
</target>
</ns0:RootFileSystem>
```

## 7.5 Recipe Explanation

### Root Element: <ns0: RootFileSystem>

This is the root element of the XML, specifying the namespace https://www.linutronix.de/projects/Elbe and providing metadata such as the creation date (created="2009-05-20T08:50:56") and schema version (revision="6"). It also links to an external schema (dbsfed.xsd) to validate the document structure.

### <project>: Project Metadata

Defines basic information about the ELBE project:

- **<name>**: Cross compiler Container Environment
  Identifier for the project.
- **<version>**: 1.0
  The version number for this project.
- **<description>**:
  Describes the purpose—building a Docker container image for cross-compilation.
- **<buildtype>**: amd64
  Specifies the architecture of the build target

### <mirror>: Debian Package Source Configuration

Specifies where ELBE fetches packages.

- **<primary_host>**: deb.debian.org
- **<primary_path>**: /debian
  The path on the Debian server that contains the base Debian package repositories.
- **<primary_proto>**: http
  This specifies that the protocol used to fetch the packages is HTTP, it can also be FTP.

- **<url-list>**: Includes URLs for binary and source packages for **Debian security updates** (Trixie suite).

**<suite>: Debian Distribution**

- **trixie**: Specifies Debian 13 as the base system

**<target>: Target Configuration**

This section defines details about the environment that will be built.

**<hostname>:** crossbuildenv

Hostname for the container.

**<domain>:** arm64

Domain name of the container

**<passwd_hashed>: User Password Hash**

This line defines a pre-hashed password for the root user. The hash is generated using SHA-512 (indicated by $6$) and is a secure way of setting a password within the image.

This is the hashed version of the password, which ensures that the raw password is not exposed in the configuration file.

**Password Hash Creation**

Example command:

```
$ openssl passwd -6 -salt ANkqTWpA RockPaperScissors

$6$ANkqTWpA$.qy1Wf5S.g5lYioOvZVx.XKawLVAziaZox0j1n6tQnTPYj
oUem0jhcHVBQDt/SnA2fUbsklNiZ80IEpqncEq50
```

1. **-6**: SHA-512 algorithm
2. **-salt ANkqTWpA**: ANkqTWpA: Custom salt

3. **RockPaperScissors**: Plaintext password

## <debootstrap>: Base System Creation

- **<variant>:** minbase
  Creates a minimal Debian system with essential packages only

## <package>: Output Package Definition

- **<tar>**:**<name>**: crossbuildenv.tgz
  Specifies the output tarball to be imported into Docker.

## <finetuning>: File System and User Setup

This section is used for additional file system setup and user configuration within the target environment.

### <mkdir>: /workspace

Creates a shared working directory inside the container.

### <adduser>: Adding a User

- **passwd_hashed=**Hashed password.
- **shell="/bin/bash"**: The default shell for the user.
- **uid="1000"**: The user ID for u1will be 1000, which is typical for a non-root user on most systems. The uid and the username matches the host username and id.
- **create_group="true"**: A new group will be created for the user u1, matching the user ID.

## <pkg-list>: Package List

Essential packages for cross-compilation and development:

- **bash**: Shell

- **bc**: Caclulator tool.
- **bison**: Parser generator.
- **flex**: Lexical analyzer.
- **libssl-dev**: SSL development libraries.
- **libc6-dev**: The GNU C library development package.
- **libncurses5-dev**: Terminal interface libraries.
- **crossbuild-essential-arm64**: ARM64 cross-compilation toolchain.
- **gcc**: The GNU Compiler.

## Summary

This XML recipe defines a complete ELBE project for building a **cross-compilation Docker image** tailored for ARM64 development. The resulting image (crossbuildenv.tgz) can be used with Docker, Podman, or systemd-nspawn, and is suitable for kernel and application development as well as integration into CI/CD pipelines.

## Further Reading and Resources

Readers interested in extending this approach can consult the official ELBE documentation for advanced root filesystem customization, multi-architecture builds, and CI/CD integration workflows. The Docker Engine documentation provides deeper insight into image import mechanisms, user namespace mapping, and volume mounting strategies relevant to embedded cross-build environments. For ARM-specific toolchains and kernel development, the Debian Cross Toolchains and Linux Kernel documentation offer valuable background and best practices.

# 8 Desktop Environment

**Abstract:** This chapter walks through creating a full x86_64 desktop image with LXDE on Debian Trixie using ELBE. It includes company context, requirements, implementation details, the x86_64-lxde-trixie.xml recipe, and in-depth explanations. It shows how ELBE extends beyond minimal embedded targets to graphical environments, useful for development stations or hybrid systems.

## 8.1 Company Introduction

**Oxenyx Research Group** specializes in providing advanced computing solutions for scientific research institutions. Their focus is on creating high-performance computing environments tailored to the specific needs of scientists and researchers working on complex simulations and data analysis.

## 8.2 Customer Requirements

**Neurekos Labs** a leading scientific research institution, requires a specialized desktop environment to support its researchers, who work on large-scale simulations and data analysis in fields such as quantum physics and computational biology. Their requirements include:

- A Debian-based desktop environment with the LXDE graphical user interface (GUI) for a lightweight and responsive experience.
- Pre-installed scientific computing tools such as Octave, R, and Python with relevant scientific libraries.
- The ability to run the desktop environment on QEMU for testing and virtual deployment.

### Company Response

Victor, a systems engineer at Oxenyx Research Group, is tasked with creating the solution for Neurekos Labs. He recognizes that ELBE can be used to build a highly customized Debian environment optimized for scientific research. Using ELBE, he plans to build an LXDE-based desktop image that includes essential scientific tools.

## 8.3 Implementation

The following steps document the implementation process used to build and run the LXDE-based desktop environment for Neurekos Labs.

### ELBE Build Process

```
$ elbe initvm submit x86_64-lxde-trixie.xml --output downloads
```

The command starts build process and automatically downloads the artifacts to downloads directory. The main output is debian-amd64-lxde.img, a bootable Debian desktop image for QEMU (amd64 architecture).

### Run the QEMU Machine

```
$ qemu-system-x86_64 -hda debian-amd64-lxde.img -m 2G -enable-
kvm -cpu host -net nic,model=virtio -net user,hostfwd=tcp::2222-:22 -
virtfs
local,path=$HOME,mount_tag=host0,security_model=mapped,id=host0
```

This command launches the built image in a QEMU virtual machine with the following options:

- **qemu-system-x86_64**: Launches QEMU for x86_64 architecture.
- **-hda debian-amd64-lxde.img**: Uses the built image as the VM's hard disk.
- **-m 2G**: Allocates 2GB of RAM to the virtual machine.
- **-enable-kvm**: Enables Kernel-based Virtual Machine (KVM) acceleration for better performance
- **-cpu host**: Uses the host CPU model for compatibility.
- **-net nic,model=virtio**: Creates a virtual NIC using the virtio model
- **-net user,hostfwd=tcp::2222-:22**: Enables user-mode networking and forwards port 2222 on the host to port 22 (SSH) in the VM.
- **-virtfs local,path=$HOME,mount_tag=host0, security_model=mapped, id=host0**: Shares the host's home directory ($HOME) with the VM using the virtfs (9p filesystem).

**Sharing host directory:**

Using the below commands, it's possible to share the host folder with guest virtual machine.

```
$ sudo mkdir -p /mnt/host0
$ sudo mount -t 9p -o trans=virtio host0 /mnt/host0
```

- Creates a mount point /mnt/host0
- Mounts the shared folder using the host0 tag defined in the QEMU command

## Output:

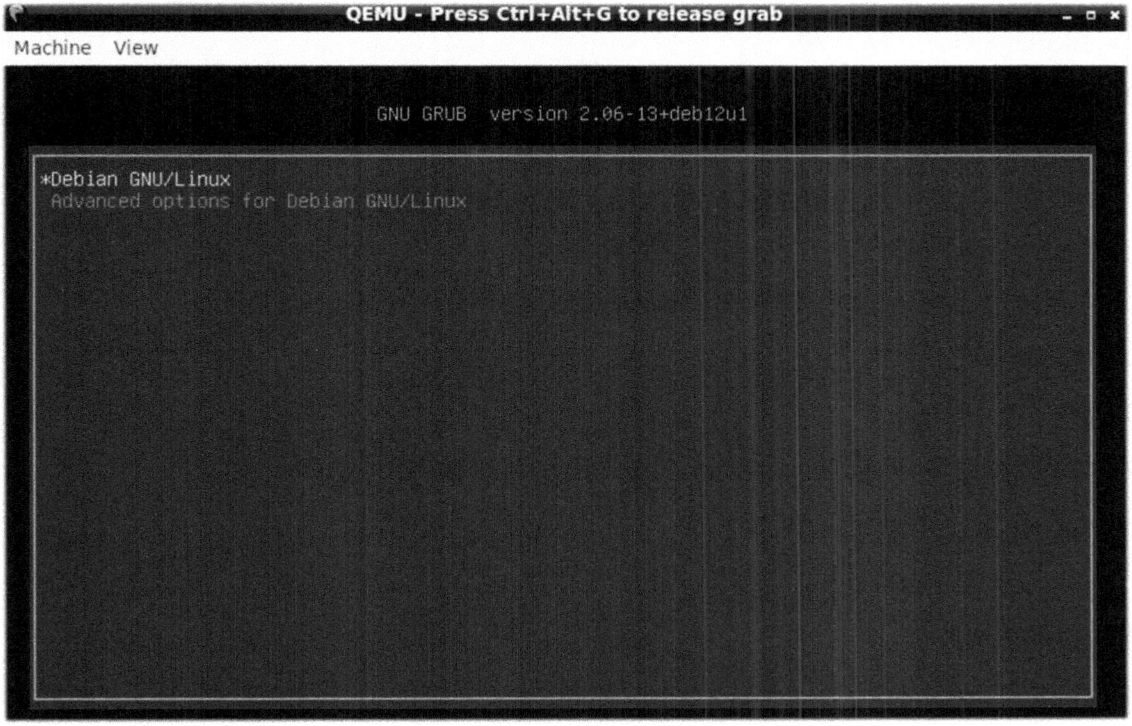
QEMU - Press Ctrl+Alt+G to release grab
Machine View
GNU GRUB version 2.06-13+deb12u1
*Debian GNU/Linux
Advanced options for Debian GNU/Linux

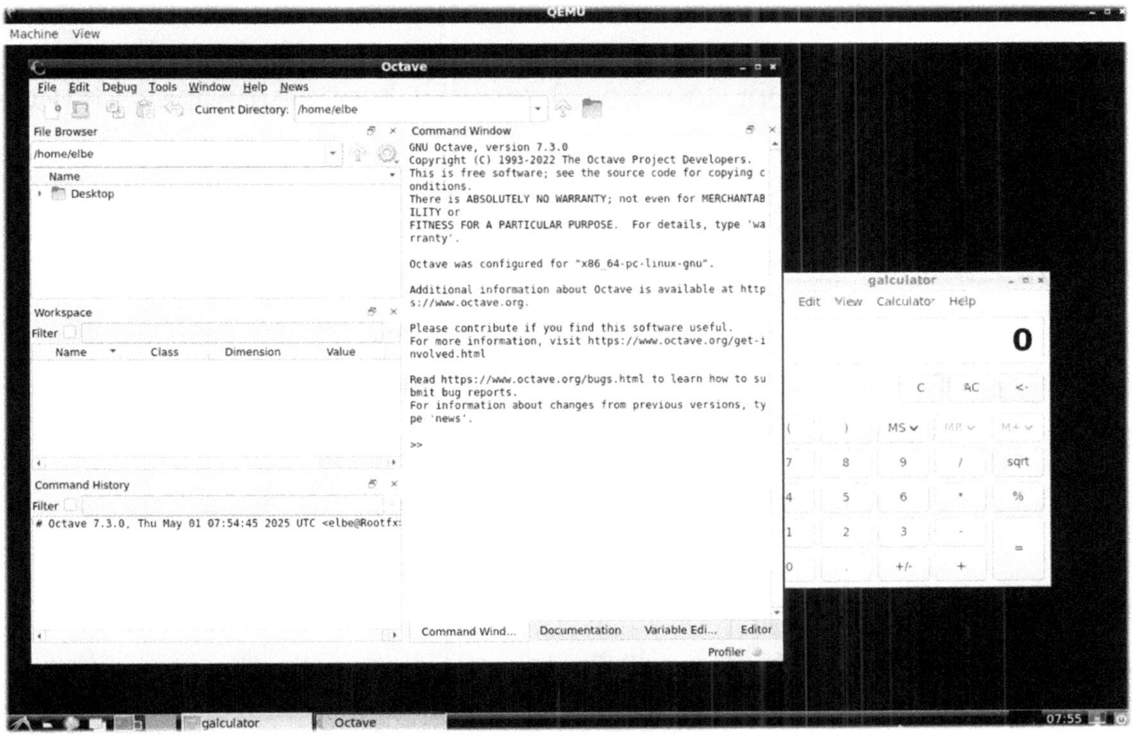
QEMU
Machine View
Octave
File Edit Debug Tools Window Help News
Current Directory: /home/elbe
File Browser
/home/elbe
Name
Desktop
Workspace
Filter
Name Class Dimension Value
Command History
Filter
# Octave 7.3.0, Thu May 01 07:54:45 2025 UTC <elbe@Rootfx:
Command Window
GNU Octave, version 7.3.0
Copyright (C) 1993-2022 The Octave Project Developers.
This is free software; see the source code for copying conditions.
There is ABSOLUTELY NO WARRANTY; not even for MERCHANTABILITY or
FITNESS FOR A PARTICULAR PURPOSE. For details, type 'warranty'.
Octave was configured for "x86_64-pc-linux-gnu".
Additional information about Octave is available at https://www.octave.org.
Please contribute if you find this software useful.
For more information, visit https://www.octave.org/get-involved.html
Read https://www.octave.org/bugs.html to learn how to submit bug reports.
For information about changes from previous versions, type 'news'.
>>
Command Wind... Documentation Variable Edi... Editor
Profiler
galculator
Edit View Calculator Help
0
galculator
Octave
07:55

## 8.4 Recipe: x86_64-lxde-trixie.xml

```
<?xml version="1.0"?>
<ns0:RootFileSystem
xmlns:ns0="https://www.linutronix.de/projects/Elbe"
xmlns:xsi="http://www.w3.org/2001/XMLSchema-instance"
created="2009-05-20T08:50:56" revision="6"
xsi:schemaLocation="https://www.linutronix.de/projects/Elbe
dbsfed.xsd">
<project>
<name>Debian LXDE virtual machine image</name>
<version>1.0</version>

<description>
 qemu-system-x86_64 -hda debian-amd64-gnome3.img -m 2G -enable-
kvm -cpu host -net nic,model=virtio   -net user,hostfwd=tcp::2222-:22  -
virtfs
local,path=$HOME,mount_tag=host0,security_model=mapped,id=host0
</description>

<buildtype>amd64</buildtype>
<mirror>
 <primary_host>deb.debian.org</primary_host>
 <primary_path>/debian</primary_path>
 <primary_proto>http</primary_proto>

 <url-list>
 <url>
```

```
  <binary>https://deb.debian.org/debian-security trixie-security
main</binary>
  <source>https://deb.debian.org/debian-security trixie-security
main</source>
 </url>
 <url>
  <binary>https://deb.debian.org/debian trixie non-free-
firmware</binary>
  <source>https://deb.debian.org/debian trixie non-free-
firmware</source>
 </url>
 <url>
  <binary>https://deb.debian.org/debian-security trixie-security non-free-
firmware</binary>
  <source>https://deb.debian.org/debian-security trixie-security non-
free-firmware</source>
 </url>
 </url-list>

</mirror>
<suite>trixie</suite>
</project>
<target>
<hostname>Rootfx</hostname>
<domain>vm</domain>
```

```
<passwd_hashed>$6$bOQ4Sf4rSdl1lfRd$3Hai04jz2OYEW108SZWew
eGO/rGvO65ITthDDtDuaC/8Gpwek/xT4rUvKBkBHFIjTDd6.klFdNJ685k
xgabHh/</passwd_hashed>

<console>ttyS0,115200</console>
<images>
 <msdoshd>
 <name>debian-amd64-gnome3.img</name>
 <size>8000MiB</size>
 <grub-install/>
 <partition>
   <size>6GiB</size>
   <label>rfs</label>
 </partition>
 <extended>
   <size>remain</size>
   <logical>
     <size>remain</size>
     <label>home</label>
   </logical>
 </extended>
 </msdoshd>
</images>
<fstab>
 <bylabel>
  <label>rfs</label>
  <mountpoint>/</mountpoint>
```

```
  <fs>
   <type>ext4</type>
   <fs-finetuning>
    <device-command>tune2fs -i 0 {device}</device-command>
   </fs-finetuning>
  </fs>
 </bylabel>
 <bylabel>
  <label>home</label>
  <mountpoint>/home</mountpoint>
  <fs>
   <type>ext4</type>
   <fs-finetuning>
    <device-command>tune2fs -i 0 {device}</device-command>
   </fs-finetuning>
  </fs>
 </bylabel>
 <bydev>
  <source>none</source>
  <mountpoint>/sys/kernel/debug</mountpoint>
  <fs>
   <type>debugfs</type>
  </fs>
 </bydev>
</fstab>
<finetuning>
```

```
  <rm>var/cache/apt/archives/*.deb</rm>

  <adduser
passwd_hashed="$6$bOQ4Sf4rSdl1IfRd$3Hai04jz2OYEW108SZWew
eGO/rGvO65ITthDDtDuaC/8Gpwek/xT4rUvKBkBHFIjTDd6.klFdNJ685k
xgabHh/" shell="/bin/bash">elbe</adduser>

  <file dst="/etc/network/interfaces" mode="755">
     auto ens33
     iface ens33 inet dhcp
  </file>
</finetuning>
<pkg-list>

 <pkg>grub-pc</pkg>
 <pkg>linux-image-amd64</pkg>
 <pkg>openssh-client</pkg>
 <pkg>openssh-server</pkg>
 <pkg>less</pkg>
 <pkg>bash</pkg>
 <pkg>zsh</pkg>
 <pkg>vim-nox</pkg>
 <pkg>locales</pkg>

 <pkg>lxde</pkg>
 <pkg>x11-utils</pkg>
```

```
<pkg>x11-xkb-utils</pkg>
<pkg>x11-xserver-utils</pkg>
<pkg>lxde-core</pkg>
<pkg>lxde-icon-theme</pkg>
<pkg>lxterminal</pkg>
<pkg>lightdm</pkg>
<pkg>lightdm-gtk-greeter</pkg>
<pkg>xfce4-settings</pkg>
<pkg>xserver-xorg</pkg>
<pkg>xinit</pkg>
<pkg>xserver-xorg-video-all</pkg>
<pkg>xserver-xorg-input-all</pkg>
<pkg>lxsession-edit</pkg>
<pkg>lxrandr</pkg>
<pkg>lxpolkit</pkg>
<pkg>lxinput</pkg>
<pkg>lxappearance</pkg>

<pkg>octave</pkg>
<pkg>r-base</pkg>
<pkg>python3</pkg>
<pkg>python3-numpy</pkg>
<pkg>python3-scipy</pkg>
<pkg>python3-matplotlib</pkg>
<pkg>python3-pandas</pkg>
```

```
    <pkg>apache2</pkg>
    <pkg>nfs-kernel-server</pkg>

    <pkg>htop</pkg>
    <pkg>iotop</pkg>
    <pkg>sysstat</pkg>
    <pkg>gparted</pkg>
    <pkg>isc-dhcp-client</pkg>

    <pkg>fonts-dejavu</pkg>
    <pkg>firefox-esr</pkg>
    <pkg>vlc</pkg>
    <pkg>gimp</pkg>
    <pkg>evince</pkg>
  </pkg-list>
  </target>
</ns0:RootFileSystem>
```

## 8.5 Recipe Explanation

This XML file is a configuration document for a system build environment, formatted to work with the ELBE build framework. It describes a Debian-based target system featuring a lightweight LXDE desktop environment, pre-installed tools, and specific configurations.

Note: Standard XML elements such as <project>, <mirror> and other common tags are explained in detail in Chapter 5.5: ELBE XML Overview. This section focuses on the unique aspects of the current recipe.

Defines the configuration of the target environment.

- **<hostname>**: Rootfx - Sets the hostname of the target system to Rootfx.
- **<domain>**: vm - Specifies the domain name, indicating this is a virtual machine.
- **<passwd_hashed>** - Contains a SHA-512 hashed password for the default user, securely embedded in the configuration.
- **<console>**: ttyS0,115200 - Configures the console to use serial communication at 115200 baud for debugging or login purposes.

### How the Password Hash is Created

To securely define a user password in the ELBE XML configuration, a **SHA-512 hash** is generated using the openssl utility. This hash is then embedded in the <passwd_hashed> tag.

```
$ openssl passwd -6 -salt ANkqTWpA RockPaperScissors

$6$ANkqTWpA$.qy1Wf5S.g5lYioOvZVx.XKawLVAziaZox0j1n6tQnTPYj
oUem0jhcHVBQDt/SnA2fUbsklNiZ80IEpqncEq50
```

### Components of the Command:

- **openssl passwd**: This invokes the OpenSSL utility to create password hashes.
- **-6**: Specifies the use of the SHA-512 hashing algorithm.
- **-salt ANkqTWpA**: Adds a custom salt to the hash, enhancing security against rainbow table attacks.
- **RockPaperScissors**: The plaintext password being hashed.

### <images>: Disk Image Configuration

This section defines the virtual disk image and its partitioning scheme for the LXDE desktop environment build. It specifies how storage is allocated and structured within the image.

### <msdoshd>: Main Disk Image

Represents the virtual hard disk used as the root file system.

- **<name>:** debian-amd64-lxde.img - The name of the output disk image file. It contains the Debian system with LXDE, built for the AMD64 architecture.
- **<size>:** 8000MiB - Total size of the disk image is 8 GB.
- **<grub-install/>** - Installs the GRUB bootloader, enabling the system to boot properly.

### Partitioning Scheme

- **<partition>**
    - **<size>:** 6GiB - Allocates 6 GB for the root file system (/).
    - **<label>:** rfs - Labels the partition as rfs (root filesystem).
- **<extended> -** Defines an extended partition using the remaining space (2 GB).
- **<logical>**
    - **<size>:** Uses all remaining space within the extended partition.
    - **<label>:** home - Labels the logical partition as home, used for the /home directory where user data is stored.

### <fstab>: Filesystem Mount Points

The <fstab> block is used to create entries in **/etc/fstab**, either by referring to partitions by their labels or by using device names. The labels correspond to the partitions defined in the <images> block. For pseudo filesystems such as sysfs or debugfs, entries are created without reference to a physical device.

### Root Filesystem (<bylabel>)

The root filesystem is defined using the label "**rfs**", mounted at **/**, formatted as ext4, with automatic inode checking disabled via tune2fs -i 0

### Home Filesystem (<bylabel>)

The /home filesystem is defined using the label "**home**", mounted at **/home**, formatted as ext4, with automatic inode checking disabled using the same tune2fs -i 0 command as the root filesystem

### <finetuning>: System Configuration and Optimization

- This section is used for fine-tuning the configuration of the system after the initial setup. It includes commands for cleaning up unnecessary files, adding users, and modifying system configurations.
- **<rm>: Removing Files**
    - <rm>var/cache/apt/archives/*.deb</rm>
      This command removes all .deb package files stored in /var/cache/apt/archives/. These files are downloaded packages used for installation or updates. By removing them after installation, this helps to free up disk space by deleting cached package files that are no longer needed.
- **<adduser>: Adding a New User**
    - **<passwd_hashed>: "$6$bOQ4Sf4rSdI1IfRd$3Hai04jz2OYEW108SZWeweGO/rGvO65ITthDDtDuaC/8Gpwek/xT4rUvKBkBHFIjTDd6.klFdNJ685kxgabHh/"**
      This tag adds a new user named elbe to the system with a pre-hashed password.

  - **<shell>: "/bin/bash"**
    The new user elbe will use /bin/bash as their default shell, which is the most common and widely used shell in Linux-based systems.

- **<file>: Creating or Modifying Files**
  - **<dst>: "/etc/network/interfaces"**
    This specifies that a file should be written at the destination path /etc/network/interfaces, which is the configuration file for network interfaces in Debian-based systems.

```
auto ens33
iface ens33 inet dhcp
```

These lines configure the network interface ens33 to use DHCP for obtaining an IP address automatically. The auto ens33 line tells the system to bring the interface up during boot, while the iface ens33 inet dhcp configures it to use DHCP to acquire network settings.

**<pkg-list>: Package List**
This section specifies the packages that will be installed in the target environment. These packages provide essential system tools, development environments, desktop utilities, scientific software, and server functionality:

- **grub-pc**: The GRUB bootloader for BIOS-based systems, enabling the system to boot various OS kernels.
- **linux-image-amd64**: The Linux kernel image optimized for AMD64 systems.
- **openssh-client**: SSH client for secure remote login from the target system.
- **openssh-server**: SSH server to allow remote login to the target system.
- **less**: A pager program used to view text files interactively in the terminal.
- **bash**: The GNU Bourne Again Shell for command-line interaction.

- **zsh**: An enhanced shell designed for interactive use, with features such as improved autocompletion.
- **vim-nox**: A version of Vim with support for scripting languages such as Python and Lua.
- **locales**: Provides localization support including language and regional settings.
- **lxde**: Lightweight X11 Desktop Environment, suitable for systems with limited resources.
- **x11-utils**: Basic utilities for managing X11 window systems.
- **x11-xkb-utils**: Utilities for managing X keyboard extension components.
- **x11-xserver-utils**: Miscellaneous X server utilities, including configuration tools.
- **lxde-core**: Core components of the LXDE desktop environment.
- **lxde-icon-theme**: Default icon theme for LXDE, providing a consistent look.
- **lxterminal**: Lightweight terminal emulator for LXDE.
- **lightdm**: Display manager that handles graphical logins.
- **lightdm-gtk-greeter**: GTK-based greeter for LightDM, providing the login screen interface.
- **xfce4-settings**: Settings manager from the XFCE desktop, used for configuring display, keyboard, and other options.
- **xserver-xorg**: The X.Org X server, responsible for managing the graphical display.
- **xinit**: Utility for initializing X sessions from the command line.
- **xserver-xorg-video-all**: Metapackage that installs all available X video drivers.
- **xserver-xorg-input-all**: Metapackage for installing all available input drivers.
- **lxsession-edit**: Tool to manage session autostart programs for LXDE.

- **lxrandr**: Lightweight GUI tool to manage screen resolutions and multiple displays.
- **lxpolkit**: Lightweight PolicyKit authentication agent for LXDE.
- **lxinput**: GUI tool to configure mouse and keyboard settings.
- **lxappearance**: GTK theme switcher for adjusting LXDE's appearance.
- **octave**: High-level programming language primarily intended for numerical computations (similar to MATLAB).
- **r-base**: Core R statistical computing and graphics system.
- **python3**: Python 3 interpreter, widely used in modern development.
- **python3-numpy**: Fundamental package for scientific computing with Python, providing array support.
- **python3-scipy**: Scientific computing tools for Python, including optimization, integration, and more.
- **python3-matplotlib**: Plotting library for Python, enabling generation of high-quality graphs.
- **python3-pandas**: Powerful data analysis and manipulation library for Python.
- **apache2**: Widely used web server software.
- **nfs-kernel-server**: NFS server for sharing directories across a network.
- **htop**: Interactive process viewer for monitoring system resource usage.
- **iotop**: Tool for monitoring disk I/O by processes in real time.
- **sysstat**: Performance monitoring tools including iostat, mpstat, and more.
- **gparted**: Graphical tool for partitioning disks.
- **isc-dhcp-client**: DHCP client for automatic IP address assignment.
- **fonts-dejavu**: A collection of high-quality, DejaVu fonts covering a wide range of characters.

- **firefox-esr**: Extended Support Release of the Firefox browser, suitable for stable environments.
- **vlc**: Versatile media player supporting numerous audio and video formats.
- **gimp**: GNU Image Manipulation Program for advanced image editing.
- **evince**: Lightweight document viewer for formats such as PDF and PostScript.

## VMware Image

After successfully building and testing the LXDE-based Debian desktop environment in QEMU, **Neurekos Labs** requested compatibility with **VMware** to support their broader virtual infrastructure.

To meet this need, Victor used the qemu-img utility to convert the QEMU image into VMware's VMDK format:

```
$ qemu-img convert -O vmdk debian-amd64-lxde.img debian-amd64-lxde.vmdk
```

After testing the VMDK image in VMware, Victor confirmed its functionality and delivered it to Neurekos Labs. The final product was a lightweight, high-performance Debian desktop environment tailored for scientific computing and compatible with both QEMU and VMware.

### Summary

This recipe creates a **Debian-based x86 virtual machine image** featuring the **LXDE desktop environment**. It includes:

- Pre-installed tools for system management, development, and scientific computing
- Networking and server capabilities
- A lightweight design optimized for minimal resource consumption

- Compatibility with both **QEMU** and **VMware**

## Further Reading and Resources

For deeper customization of graphical Debian systems, the ELBE documentation covers advanced image layouts, desktop integration, and post-install finetuning techniques. The Debian LXDE and X.Org documentation provide background on lightweight desktop components, display managers, and performance tuning for resource-constrained environments. Readers interested in virtualization can refer to the QEMU and KVM manuals for advanced networking, filesystem sharing (9p), and performance optimization strategies.

# 9 QEMU ARM Environment

**Abstract:** This chapter covers building an emulated ARM64 environment with QEMU virt machine support on Debian Trixie. It presents company scenarios, requirements, implementation, the arm64-qemu-virt-trixie.xml recipe, and detailed breakdowns. Readers gain tools for testing ARM-based images without physical hardware.

## 9.1 Company Introduction

**Thryvion Edge** is an innovative company specializing in the development of edge computing solutions. They focus on creating robust development and testing environments that allow engineers to simulate applications across a variety of edge devices and architectures.

## 9.2 Customer Requirements

**Datarion Pulse**, a key client of Thryvion Edge, is developing a suite of edge computing devices designed for real-time data processing and IoT applications. To ensure broad compatibility and performance across their product line, they require a comprehensive testing environment capable of simulating both ARM64 and ARM32 architectures.

Specifically, **Datarion Pulse** requires:

- **An ARM64 Debian image for QEMU:** This image should emulate a high-performance edge device with full network capabilities and support for file sharing between the host and the virtual machine. This setup is essential for testing applications that demand strong compute resources and reliable connectivity.
- **An ARM32 Debian image for QEMU:** This image should be optimized for lightweight applications and services intended for lower-end edge devices. It must include essential development tools and provide a flexible environment suitable for a variety of testing scenarios.

**Company Response**

Krishna, a senior software architect at Thryvion Edge, is assigned to develop the solution for **Datarion Pulse**. He knows that ELBE can facilitate the creation of tailored Debian images for both ARM64 and ARM32 architectures. Krishna plans to use ELBE to build these images, ensuring they meet Datarion Pulse's requirements for simulation, development, and testing.

## 9.3 Implementation

Krishna begins creating custom Linux images tailored specifically for Datarion Pulse's needs. To ensure precision and reproducibility, he follows a structured process using ELBE.

With the environment prepared, Krishna submits the ELBE project directly to the InitVM using the XML configuration file

```
$ elbe initvm submit arm64-qemu-virt-trixie.xml --output  qemu-arm64
```

After submission, ELBE automatically builds the image inside the InitVM, handling package installation, system configuration, and image generation. Build progress is streamed directly to the console, so no separate monitoring command is needed. Once the build completes, ELBE downloads all generated artifacts to the specified output directory, including **vmlinuz** (kernel image), **sdcard.qcow2.tar.xz** (compressed QEMU disk image), and **initrd** (initial RAM disk).

### Extracting the Disk Image

Krishna navigates to the qemu-arm64 directory and extracts the QEMU disk image for testing:

```
$ cd qemu-arm64
$ tar xvf sdcard.qcow2.tar.xz
```

This provides the sdcard.qcow2 file, ready for use in QEMU to simulate an ARM64 edge computing device.

### QEMU command

```
$ qemu-system-aarch64 \
  -M virt \
  -cpu cortex-a57 \
  -m 1024 \
  -smp 2 \
  -initrd initrd \
  -kernel vmlinuz \
  -append "root=/dev/sda2 console=ttyAMA0" \
  -global virtio-blk-device.scsi=off \
  -device virtio-scsi-device,id=scsi \
```

```
-drive file=sdcard.qcow2,id=rootimg,cache=unsafe,if=none \
-device scsi-hd,drive=rootimg \
-netdev user,id=unet \
-device virtio-net-device,netdev=unet \
-nic user,hostfwd=tcp::2022-:22 \
-nographic \
-virtfs
local,path=$HOME,mount_tag=host0,security_model=mapped,id=host0
```

**Breakdown of the command**

- **qemu-system-aarch64**: Launches the QEMU emulator for the AArch64 (ARM 64-bit) architecture.
- **-M virt**: Specifies a generic virtual ARM machine.
- **-cpu cortex-a57**: Emulates an ARM Cortex-A57 CPU.
- **-m 1024**: Allocates 1024 MB (1 GB) of RAM.
- **-smp 2**: Enables 2 CPU cores for symmetric multiprocessing.
- **-initrd initrd**: Loads the initial RAM disk.
- **-kernel vmlinuz**: Uses vmlinuz as the kernel image.
- **-append "root=/dev/sda2 console=ttyAMA0"**:
    - root=/dev/sda2: Specifies that the root filesystem location.
    - console=ttyAMA0: Directs console output to the first ARM serial port.
- **-global virtio-blk-device.scsi=off**: Disables SCSI support for virtio block devices.
- **-device virtio-scsi-device,id=scsi**: Adds a virtio SCSI controller.

- **-drive file=sdcard.qcow2,id=rootimg,cache=unsafe,if=none**:
  - Attaches the QCOW2 disk image.
  - cache=unsafe: Enables faster but less safe caching.
  - if=none: Prevents automatic interface assignment.
- **-device scsi-hd,drive=rootimg**: Connects the drive as a SCSI hard disk.
- **-netdev user,id=unet**: Sets up user-mode networking.
- **-device virtio-net-device,netdev=unet**: Adds a virtual network interface.
- **-nic user,hostfwd=tcp::2022-:22**: Forwards host TCP port 2022 to guest port 22 (SSH). This allows SSH access with ssh -p 2022 user@localhost.
- **-nographic**: Disables graphical output; uses serial console
- **-virtfs local,path=$HOME,mount_tag=host0,security_model=mapped,id=host0**: Shares the host's home directory ($HOME) with the VM using the 9p filesystem.
  - mount_tag=host0: Used inside the VM to mount the shared folder.
  - security_model=mapped: Maps file ownership between the host and guest.
  - id=host0: Assigns an identifier to the shared folder.

### Output

The **9p filesystem** (Plan 9 Filesystem) is a lightweight and efficient networked filesystem commonly used in virtualized environments to facilitate file sharing between the host and guest. In this setup, the 9p mount point (host0) is attached to /mnt/shared within the VM, enabling access to files from the host system. The filesystem utilizes the virtio transport, which is optimized for QEMU's paravirtualized interface, ensuring low overhead and efficient communication.

```
Debian GNU/Linux 12 arm64 ttyAMA0
arm64 login: root
Password:
root@arm64:~# arch
aarch64
root@arm64:~# mount
~
host0 on /mnt/shared type 9p
(rw,relatime,sync,dirsync,access=client,trans=virtio)
```

This confirms that the system is running on an ARM64 architecture (aarch64) and that the host's home directory has been successfully mounted inside the VM at /mnt/shared using the 9p filesystem.

## 9.4 Recipe arm64-qemu-virt-trixie.xml

```
<?xml version="1.0"?>
<ns0:RootFileSystem
xmlns:ns0="https://www.linutronix.de/projects/Elbe"
xmlns:xsi="http://www.w3.org/2001/XMLSchema-instance"
created="2009-05-20T08:50:56" revision="6"
xsi:schemaLocation="https://www.linutronix.de/projects/Elbe
dbsfed.xsd">
<project>
<name>ARM Virtual machine</name>
<version>2.0</version>


<description>
```

```
 qemu-system-aarch64 -M virt -cpu cortex-a57 -m 1024 -smp 2 -initrd
initrd.img-6.1.0-27-arm64   -kernel vmlinuz  -append "root=/dev/sda2
console=ttyAMA0" -global virtio-blk-device.scsi=off  -device virtio-scsi-
device,id=scsi -drive
file=sdcard.qcow2,id=rootimg,cache=unsafe,if=none  -device scsi-
hd,drive=rootimg  -netdev user,id=unet -device virtio-net-
device,netdev=unet -nic user,hostfwd=tcp::2022-:22  -nographic -virtfs
local,path=$HOME,mount_tag=host0,security_model=mapped,id=host0
</description>

<buildtype>aarch64</buildtype>
<mirror>
 <primary_host>deb.debian.org</primary_host>
 <primary_path>/debian</primary_path>
 <primary_proto>http</primary_proto>
</mirror>
<suite>trixie</suite>
</project>
<target>
<hostname>arm64</hostname>
<domain>Rootfx</domain>
<passwd_hashed>$6$bOQ4Sf4rSdI1IfRd$3Hai04jz2OYEW108SZWew
eGO/rGvO65ITthDDtDuaC/8Gpwek/xT4rUvKBkBHFIjTDd6.klFdNJ685k
xgabHh/</passwd_hashed>
<console>ttyAMA0,115200</console>
<images>
 <msdoshd>
```

```
  <name>sdcard.img</name>
  <size>3500MiB</size>
  <partition>
   <size>200MiB</size>
   <label>boot</label>
   <bootable/>
  </partition>
  <partition>
   <size>remain</size>
   <label>rfs</label>
  </partition>
 </msdoshd>
</images>
<fstab>
 <bylabel>
  <label>boot</label>
  <mountpoint>/boot</mountpoint>
  <fs>
   <type>vfat</type>
  </fs>
 </bylabel>
 <bylabel>
  <label>rfs</label>
  <mountpoint>/</mountpoint>
  <fs>
   <type>ext2</type>
   <fs-finetuning>
```

```
     <device-command>tune2fs -i 0 {device}</device-command>
    </fs-finetuning>
   </fs>
  </bylabel>
</fstab>
<install-recommends/>
<finetuning>
   <rm>/var/cache/apt/archives/*.deb</rm>
   <mkdir>/mnt/shared</mkdir>
   <command>echo "host0   /mnt/shared   9p
trans=virtio,version=9p2000.L   0   0"&gt;&gt;/etc/fstab</command>
</finetuning>
<pkg-list>
  <pkg>linux-image-arm64</pkg>
  <pkg>initramfs-tools</pkg>
  <pkg>openssh-server</pkg>
  <pkg>less</pkg>
  <pkg>bash</pkg>
  <pkg>vim-nox</pkg>
  <pkg>wget</pkg>
  <pkg>ntpdate</pkg>
  <pkg>busybox</pkg>
</pkg-list>
<project-finetuning>
  <losetup img="sdcard.img">
```

```
  <copy_from_partition part="1" artifact="vmlinuz">/vmlinuz-*-
arm64</copy_from_partition>
  <copy_from_partition part="1" artifact="initrd">/initrd.img-*-
arm64</copy_from_partition>
 </losetup>
 <img_convert fmt="qcow2"
dst="sdcard.qcow2">sdcard.img</img_convert>
 <set_packer packer="tarxz">sdcard.qcow2</set_packer>
</project-finetuning>
</target>
</ns0:RootFileSystem>
```

## 9.5 Recipe Explanation

This XML recipe describes a build configuration for an ARM64 (AArch64) system using the ELBE framework. The target system includes essential software, custom partitions, and specific virtualization configurations for QEMU.

**<finetuning>: System Configuration and Optimization**

This section is used to fine-tune the system's configuration after the initial setup, including file removals, directory creation, and system commands for mount configurations.

- **<rm>: Remove Files**

  Removes all .deb package files stored in /var/cache/apt/archives/. These files are no longer needed after installation and removing them helps free up disk space by clearing cached package files.

- **<mkdir>: Creating a Directory**

Creates a new directory at /mnt/shared, which can be used for mounting 9p filesystem to share data between the host and the qemu guest

- **<command>: Executing System Commands**

  echo "host0 /mnt/shared 9p trans=virtio,version=9p2000.L 0 0">>/etc/fstab

Appends a line to the **/etc/fstab** file, which is used to define filesystems and mount points. The line adds an entry to mount the shared directory host0 using the 9p protocol, with virtio transport and version 9p2000.L. This configuration ensures that the shared directory is mounted automatically during boot.

**<pkg-list>: Required Software Packages**

**Core System Packages**

- linux-image-arm64: ARM64 Linux kernel.
- initramfs-tools: Tools for creating the initial RAM disk.
- openssh-server: Enables remote access via SSH.
- Utilities: less, bash, vim-nox, wget, ntpdate, busybox.

**<project-finetuning>: Project-Level System Configuration**

This section defines additional fine-tuning steps for the project, specifically related to handling disk images, file conversions, and packaging. It includes operations such as setting up disk images, extracting kernel files, converting formats, and preparing the final packaged output.

**<losetup>: Set up a Loopback Device**

This sets up a loopback device for the disk image sdcard.img, enabling the system to interact with the contents of the image as though it were a physical device. This is useful for extracting or manipulating files within the image before finalizing it.

**<copy_from_partition>: Copying Files from a Partition**

- <copy_from_partition part="1" artifact="vmlinuz">/vmlinuz-*-arm64</copy_from_partition>
- <copy_from_partition part="1" artifact="initrd">/initrd.img-*-arm64</copy_from_partition>

This command copies the kernel file vmlinuz-*-arm64 initrd.img-*-arm64 from partition 1 of the disk image (sdcard.img). The * wildcard indicates that any specific version of the kernel matching this pattern will be copied.

**Kernel and Initrd for QEMU**

The kernel (vmlinuz-*-arm64) and the initrd image (initrd.img-*-arm64) are essential for booting the system, especially when running it through QEMU. These files must be passed as command-line arguments along with the disk image (sdcard.img) during QEMU launch.

Although these files are part of the installation process, using them in a QEMU virtual environment outside the original build requires extracting them from the partition where they were installed. By copying them out using ELBE's <copy_from_partition> directive, Krishna ensures they are available independently for later use.

**<img_convert>: Convert Disk Image Format**

<img_convert fmt="qcow2" dst="sdcard.qcow2">sdcard.img</img_convert>

This command converts the sdcard.img file to the QCOW2 format (QEMU Copy-On-Write). QCOW2 is optimized for virtual machine usage, offering features such as compression, snapshots, and thin provisioning.

**<set_packer>: Packaging the Disk Image**

<set_packer packer="tarxz">sdcard.qcow2</set_packer>

After conversion, this command compresses the QCOW2 image into a .tar.xz archive using the tarxz method. This makes the image suitable for distribution or integration into automated workflows.

## Downloading the Files as Part of the elbe control get_files Command

After extracting the necessary files (kernel and initramdisk), they are later downloaded as part of the elbe control get_files command. This step ensures that the kernel and initrd images are available externally for future use, including for launching the QEMU virtual environment with the appropriate configuration.

### Summary

This XML configuration builds an ARM64 virtual machine running Debian Trixie. It features:

- A dual-partition setup with a bootable VFAT boot partition and an EXT2 root filesystem.
- A QEMU-based virtual environment with kernel and initrd configurations.
- Pre-installed essential tools and a shared directory for host-guest interaction.
- Disk image customization, including conversion to QCOW2 and compression for distribution.

## Delivering the Solution

Krishna repeats the above process with a separate XML configuration for the **ARM32** image, ensuring both lightweight and high-performance scenarios are covered. After rigorous testing in QEMU, he validates that both images meet Datarion Pulse's performance and functionality requirements.

## Summary

This chapter demonstrated how ELBE can be used to build fully emulated ARM64 environments for QEMU without relying on physical hardware. By combining a custom Debian Trixie image, extracted kernel and initrd artifacts, and QEMU's virt machine model, engineers can reliably test ARM-based edge workloads in a reproducible and portable setup. The approach enables rapid development, debugging, and validation of ARM software across both high-performance and lightweight edge scenarios, making it well suited for CI pipelines and pre-hardware development phases.

### Further Reading and Resources

For advanced image customization and multi-architecture workflows, the ELBE documentation provides detailed guidance on filesystem layouts, artifact extraction, and automation.The QEMU System Emulation documentation covers ARM virt machine options, device models, and performance tuning techniques. Readers interested in ARM-specific boot processes can refer to the Linux Kernel and ARM64 documentation for deeper insight into kernel, initrd, and virtual platform behavior.

# Raspberry Pi

Up to this point, we've explored ELBE, built Docker containers, and created both x86 and ARM virtual machines. Now, we're entering the heart of this book: Raspberry Pi recipes. These chapters guide you through advanced topics such as SquashFS for compressed filesystems, encryption for secure deployments, and even running large language models (LLMs) on constrained hardware.

The first recipe chapter include detailed explanations to help you understand the structure and logic behind the setup. However, to maintain focus and avoid unnecessary repetition, subsequent chapters omit boilerplate XML declarations and recurring configuration blocks. This approach saves space, streamlines the reading experience, and respects your time and patience.

# 10 Raspberry Pi Basic Image

**Abstract:** This chapter introduces a foundational bootable image for Raspberry Pi using ELBE on Trixie. It includes company introduction, requirements, step-by-step implementation, the raspberrypi-trixie.xml recipe, and thorough explanation. This establishes a clean, reproducible starting point for further customization.

## 10.1 Company Introduction

**Itheris Labs** is a cutting-edge technology firm specializing in IoT solutions and embedded systems development. Renowned for delivering robust software and hardware integration, the company is frequently tasked with creating custom operating systems for specialized hardware platforms. Among these platforms, single-board computers such as the Raspberry Pi play a central role in their projects, enabling rapid prototyping and deployment of tailored embedded solutions.

## 10.2 Customer Requirements

**EvolvHome**, a smart home solutions startup, aims to develop the next generation of home automation devices using Raspberry Pi hardware. To support their product development, they require a custom Debian-based operating system tailored specifically for Raspberry Pi platform. The image must include support for GPIO pins, Wi-Fi, and Bluetooth, along with lightweight tools for Python-based development and remote device management.

To accelerate their development timeline, EvolvHome approaches Itheris Labs to create this custom image.

### Company Response

Leo, a seasoned embedded systems engineer at Itheris Labs, is excited to take on the challenge. He knows that ELBE can be used to create a highly customized Debian image for Raspberry Pi, and he plans to leverage its capabilities to build a robust and flexible operating system. This image will serve as the foundation for EvolvHome's smart home automation products, enabling rapid prototyping and deployment across their hardware lineup.

## 10.3 Implementation

To prepare the Raspberry Pi build environment, Leo uses the ELBE InitVM and submits the build directly with the XML configuration file.

### Submitting and Building the Image

```
$ elbe initvm submit raspberrypi-trixie.xml --output rpi-downloads
```

This command automatically creates a ELBE project, uploads the raspberrypi-trixie.xml configuration and immediately starts building the custom Debian image inside the InitVM. Build progress is streamed to the console.

To prepare Raspberry Pi build environment, Leo begins by setting up the ELBE InitVM. Once the environment is ready, he proceeds with the following steps to create and build the custom Debian image.

### Downloading the Build Artifacts

After the build completes successfully, ELBE downloads all generated files into the rpi-downloads directory. The resulting artifact includes:

- image.tgz – the compressed Raspberry Pi disk image

### Extracting the Disk Image

Leo navigates to the rpi-downloads directory and extracts the disk image for testing:

```
$ cd rpi-downloads
$ tar xvf image.tgz
```

### Flashing it to the SD card

He inserts an SD card and flashes sdcard.img to it

```
$ sudo dcfldd if=sdcard.img of=/dev/sdX
```

Replace X with the correct device identifier for the SD card.

```
$ sync
```

The sync command ensures all buffered data is written to disk.

### Powering the Raspberry Pi

- Connect the serial cable between the Raspberry Pi and the PC.
- Insert the flashed SD card into Raspberry Pi.
- Power on the Raspberry Pi.

### Login

Open a serial console and provide login details

Login: **root**

Password: **RockPaperScissors**

## 10.4 Recipe raspberrypi-trixie.xml

```
<ns0:RootFileSystem
xmlns:ns0="https://www.linutronix.de/projects/Elbe"
xmlns:xsi="http://www.w3.org/2001/XMLSchema-instance"
created="2009-05-20T08:50:56" revision="6"
xsi:schemaLocation="https://www.linutronix.de/projects/Elbe
dbsfed.xsd">
<project>
<name>Raspberry Pi</name>
<version>1.0</version>
<description>Raspberry Pi Basic Bootable Image</description>
<buildtype>aarch64</buildtype>
<mirror>
<primary_host>ftp.de.debian.org</primary_host>
<primary_path>/debian</primary_path>
<primary_proto>http</primary_proto>
 <url-list>
 <url>
   <binary>https://deb.debian.org/debian-security trixie-security
main</binary>
   <source>https://deb.debian.org/debian-security trixie-security
main</source>
 </url>
 <url>
   <binary>https://deb.debian.org/debian trixie non-free-
firmware</binary>
```

```
   <source>https://deb.debian.org/debian trixie non-free-
firmware</source>
  </url>
  <url>
   <binary>https://deb.debian.org/debian-security trixie-security non-free-
firmware</binary>
   <source>https://deb.debian.org/debian-security trixie-security non-
free-firmware</source>
  </url>
  </url-list>
 </mirror>
 <suite>trixie</suite>
</project>
<target>
 <hostname>raspberry</hostname>
 <domain></domain>

<passwd_hashed>$6$bOQ4Sf4rSdI1IfRd$3Hai04jz2OYEW108SZWew
eGO/rGvO65ITthDDtDuaC/8Gpwek/xT4rUvKBkBHFIjTDd6.klFdNJ685k
xgabHh/</passwd_hashed>

 <console>serial0,115200</console>
 <package><tar><name>image.tgz</name></tar></package>
 <debootstrap>
 <variant>minbase</variant>
 </debootstrap>

<images>
```

```
<msdoshd>
  <name>sdcard.img</name>
  <size>7GB</size>
  <partition>
    <size>256MB</size>
    <label>firmware</label>
  </partition>
  <partition>
    <size>remain</size>
    <label>root</label>
    <bootable/>
  </partition>
</msdoshd>
</images>
<fstab>
<bylabel>
  <label>firmware</label>
  <mountpoint>/boot/firmware</mountpoint>
  <fs>
    <type>vfat</type>
  </fs>
</bylabel>
<bylabel>
  <label>root</label>
  <mountpoint>/</mountpoint>
  <fs>
  <type>ext4</type>
  <fs-finetuning>
```

```
    <device-command>tune2fs -O ^64bit,^metadata_csum -i 0
{device}</device-command>
  </fs-finetuning>
  </fs>

</bylabel>
</fstab>

<install-recommends/>

<pkg-list>
 <pkg>linux-image-arm64</pkg>
 <pkg>firmware-brcm80211</pkg>
 <pkg>raspi-firmware</pkg>
 <pkg>zstd</pkg>
 <pkg>apt-utils</pkg>
 <pkg>systemd</pkg>
 <pkg>vim-tiny</pkg>
 <pkg>busybox</pkg>
 <pkg>bash</pkg>
 <pkg>dialog</pkg>
 <pkg>openssh-server</pkg>
 <pkg>wpasupplicant</pkg>
 <pkg>iproute2</pkg>
 <pkg>net-tools</pkg>
 <pkg>iputils-ping</pkg>
 <pkg>iw</pkg>
 <pkg>ifupdown</pkg>
```

```
 <pkg>bluez</pkg>
 <pkg>bluez-tools</pkg>
 <pkg>rfkill</pkg>
</pkg-list>

<project-finetuning>
 <set_packer packer="tarxz">sdcard.img</set_packer>
</project-finetuning>
<finetuning>
 <file dst="/etc/systemd/network/25-wlan0.network" mode="644">
  [Match]
  Name=wlan0

  [Network]
  DHCP=yes
  </file>
  <file dst="/etc/resolv.conf" mode="600">
  nameserver 8.8.8.8
 </file>
 <file dst="/etc/wpa_supplicant/wpa_supplicant-wlan0.conf"
mode="600">
  ctrl_interface=DIR=/var/run/wpa_supplicant GROUP=netdev
  update_config=1

  network={
  ssid="YourSSID"
  psk="YourKey"
  }
```

```
 </file>

 <file dst="/etc/default/raspi-firmware" append="true" >
  ROOTPART="LABEL=root"
  KERNEL_ARCH="arm64"
 </file>

 <file dst="/etc/default/raspi-extra-cmdline" append="true">
  init=/usr/lib/systemd/systemd
 </file>
 <command>update-initramfs -u -k all</command>
 <command>systemctl enable
wpa_supplicant@wlan0.service</command>
 <command>systemctl enable systemd-networkd</command>
</finetuning>
</target>
</ns0:RootFileSystem>
```

## 10.5 Recipe Explanation

This XML recipe describes a build configuration for an ARM64 (AArch64) system using the ELBE framework. The target system includes essential software, custom partitions, and specific virtualization configurations for QEMU.

### <project>: Project Information

This section defines metadata for the image being built.

- **<name>:** RaspberryPi - Indicates the project is intended for Raspberry Pi hardware.
- **<version>:** 1.0 - Sets the version of the project.

- **<description>:** Raspberry Pi Basic Bootable Image - Describes the purpose of the image - creating a basic bootable system for Raspberry Pi.
- **<buildtype>:** aarch64 - Specifies the target architecture as ARM64 (64-bit ARM), suitable for newer Raspberry Pi models.

**<mirror>: Mirror Configuration**

This section configures the Debian package sources used during the build.

- **<primary_host>:** ftp.de.debian.org

  The main Debian mirror used to fetch packages.

- **<primary_path>:** /debian

  Path to the Debian repository on the mirror.

- **<primary_proto>:** http

  Protocol used to access the repository.

- **<url-list>:**

  Contains additional URLs for fetching binary and source packages, including:

  - **<binary>:** URLs for trixie-security and trixie non-free-firmware binary packages.
  - **<source>:** URLs for the corresponding source packages.

**<suite>: Debian Distribution**

**trixie**: Specifies that the base system for this project is built using Debian Trixie (Debian 13), ensuring compatibility with the latest stable Debian release.

**<target>: Target Configuration**

Defines the configuration of the target environment.

- **<hostname>:** raspberry- Sets the hostname of the target system to raspberry, which will be used for network identification when Raspberry Pi is running.

- **<domain>: (empty)** - No specific domain is set for the target environment. This field is often used for network organization but is optional.
- **<passwd_hashed>: -** Defines a pre-hashed password for the default user (typically root). The hash uses the **SHA-512 algorithm**, indicated by the $6$ prefix, ensuring secure password storage.
- **<console>:** serial0,115200 - Configures the system to use **serial communication** at 115200 baud. This is commonly used for debugging or login access on Raspberry Pi devices via the GPIO serial interface.

### How the Password Hash is Created

To securely define a user password in the ELBE XML configuration, a **SHA-512 hash** is generated using the openssl utility. This hash is then embedded in the <passwd_hashed> tag.

```
$ openssl passwd -6 -salt ANkqTWpA RockPaperScissors

$6$ANkqTWpA$.qy1Wf5S.g5lYioOvZVx.XKawLVAziaZox0j1n6tQnTPYj
oUem0jhcHVBQDt/SnA2fUbsklNiZ80lEpqncEq50
```

### Components of the Command:

- **openssl passwd**: This invokes the OpenSSL utility to create password hashes.
- **-6**: Specifies the use of the SHA-512 hashing algorithm.
- **-salt ANkqTWpA**: Adds a custom salt to the hash, enhancing security against rainbow table attacks.
- **RockPaperScissors**: The plaintext password being hashed.

### <package>: Package Configuration

Defines a package configuration for the build process.

- **<tar>:** Specifies that the rootfs should be compressed into a tarball package

- **<name>:** image.tgz - Indicates the name of the output tarball.

**<debootstrap>: Debootstrap Configuration**

Defines the base system installation method.

**<variant>:** Specifies the debootstrap variant to use for the installation. In this case, the minbase variant is used, which installs the minimum set of essential packages needed to set up a Debian-based system. This variant is useful when you want to build a minimal system without unnecessary components, providing a clean base environment to customize further.

**<images>: Disk Image Configuration**

Defines the configuration of the disk image, including its partitions and layout.

**<msdoshd>:**

Represents a disk image configuration using an MS-DOS-style partition table, typically used for creating bootable images. In this case, it defines the storage layout of an SD card image for the target system.

- **<name>:** sdcard.img - Specifies the name of the disk image file. This image represents the SD card to be used.
- **<size>:** 7GB - Sets the total size of the disk image to 7 GB, defining the overall storage capacity allocated for the SD card.

**<partition>:**

Defines the partitions within the disk image. Two partitions are specified:

**First Partition:**

- **<size>:** 256MB - Allocates 256 MB for the first partition, typically used for firmware, bootloaders, or initial boot files.
- **<label>:** firmware - Labels the partition as firmware, indicating that it will contain the firmware files required for the system to boot.

**Second Partition:**

- **<size>:** remain - Allocates the remaining space on the disk to this partition.
- **<label>:** root - Labels the partition as root, designating it as the root filesystem containing the operating system and system files.

**<bootable/>** - Marks the second partition as bootable, which is essential for booting the operating system from this partition on Raspberry Pi.

**<fstab>: Filesystem Configuration**

This section defines the mounting of filesystems for the target system and specifies details such as the filesystem type, mount points, and additional fine-tuning settings.

- **<bylabel>:**

  The **<bylabel>** tag is used to mount partitions based on their labels, which allows for easy identification of partitions without relying on device names (such as **/dev/sda**).

**First Partition:**

- **<label>: firmware -** Refers to the partition labeled firmware, created earlier in the disk image configuration.
- **<mountpoint>: /boot/firmware -** Specifies the mount point for the firmware partition. This is typically used to store boot-related files such as bootloaders and firmware.
- **<fs>:**
  - **<type>: vfat -** Indicates that the firmware partition uses the VFAT filesystem, which is widely supported across platforms and bootloaders.

**Second Partition:**

- **<label>: root -** Refers to the root partition that contains the operating system and system files.

- **<mountpoint>: /** - Sets the mount point to the root directory of the filesystem.
- **<fs>:**
  - **<type>: ext4** - Specifies the EXT4 filesystem, known for reliability and performance in Linux environments.
  - **<fs-finetuning>:**
    - **<device-command>:** Provides additional tuning using the tune2fs utility.

```
tune2fs -O ^64bit,^metadata_csum -i 0 {device}
```

This command disables the 64-bit filesystem support **(^64bit)** and the metadata checksum feature **(^metadata_csum)** while also setting the inode time interval **(-i 0)** to zero, effectively removing the need for periodic inode updates. This can be useful for embedded or resource-constrained systems where these features are not required.

**Note**: The tune2fs options shown disable certain modern EXT4 features specifically 64-bit support and metadata checksums and prevent periodic inode timestamp updates. While these adjustments help simplify the filesystem for prototyping and embedded use cases, they may reduce compatibility with future Linux kernels or advanced filesystem features. For production environments or edge cases, users should carefully evaluate these settings and consider adjusting them based on performance, reliability, and long-term support requirements.

### <pkg-list>: Required Software Packages

This section specifies the list of software packages that will be installed in the target environment. These packages are essential for both the core functionality of Raspberry Pi boot image and its interaction with various hardware and network components.

**Core System Packages:**

- **linux-image-arm64:** ARM64 Linux kernel for the target system. This is necessary for booting and running the system on ARM64 architecture.

- **firmware-brcm80211:** Firmware for Broadcom wireless network devices, ensuring support for Wi-Fi hardware.
- **raspi-firmware:** Raspberry Pi firmware required for booting and configuring the hardware and additionally initramfs and kernel installation hook scripts for handling the proper naming of the file.
- **zstd:** A compression tool offering fast compression and decompression, used for system file handling and optimizations.
- **apt-utils:** Utilities for managing packages with apt, including front-end tools such as apt for package installation and upgrades.

**Systemd and Networking Packages:**

- **systemd:** The system and service manager for Linux, responsible for managing system services and resources.

**Utilities:**

- **vim-tiny:** A lightweight version of the Vim text editor, available for quick file editing.
- **busybox:** A single executable providing many Unix utilities, typically used in embedded systems to minimize disk space usage.
- **bash:** The GNU Bourne Again Shell (bash), which serves as the default shell for executing commands interactively.

**Network and Communication Tools:**

- **dialog:** A tool for creating text-based user interfaces in shell scripts, used for interactive configurations.
- **openssh-server:** Provides Secure Shell (SSH) access to the target device, enabling remote login and file transfer.
- **wpasupplicant:** Software for managing wireless network connections using WPA (Wi-Fi Protected Access).

- **iproute2:** A collection of utilities for network configuration, including **ip** commands for managing IP addresses and routing.
- **net-tools:** Provides basic networking utilities such as **ifconfig, netstat, route,** and more.
- **iputils-ping:** A package that provides the **ping** utility for testing network connectivity.

**Hardware Support Packages:**

- **iw:** A command-line tool for configuring wireless devices, enabling management of Wi-Fi interfaces.
- **ifupdown:** A utility for managing network interfaces, allowing the system to bring interfaces up or down as needed.
- **bluez:** The official Linux Bluetooth protocol stack, enabling Bluetooth communication on the system.
- **bluez-tools:** Command-line tools for managing Bluetooth devices and services.
- **rfkill:** A tool for enabling or disabling wireless devices (e.g., Wi-Fi, Bluetooth), useful for managing power or privacy settings.

**<project-finetuning>: Project-Level Configuration and Optimization**

This section is used to apply final adjustments or optimizations at the project level before packaging the image for deployment. It typically includes actions related to compressing or packaging the final system image to make it more efficient and suitable for distribution.

**<set_packer packer="tarxz">sdcard.img</set_packer>:**

Specifies the compression method for the project image. In this case, the sdcard.img disk image will be compressed using the **tarxz** format, which combines the tar archiving tool with the xz compression algorithm.

- **packer="tarxz":** Indicates the use of the tarxz packing method, resulting in a .tar.xz archive. This format is widely used for its balance between compression ratio and speed, making it ideal for distributing system images.
- **sdcard.img:** The target file to be compressed. This disk image will be converted into a compressed .tar.xz file, reducing its size and making it easier to store or transfer.

### <finetuning>: System Configuration and Customization

The <finetuning> section is used to apply system-level adjustments after the initial setup. It allows for file creation, configuration changes, and command execution to tailor the system for specific use cases. Below are the components and their functions:

### File Configuration

- **/etc/systemd/network/25-wlan0.network:**

Configures the wlan0 network interface.

- **[Match]:** This section matches the network interface by its name **(wlan0).**
- **[Network]:** Specifies network settings for the **wlan0** interface.

**DHCP=yes:** Configures the interface to use DHCP for automatic IP address assignment.

- **/etc/wpa_supplicant/wpa_supplicant-wlan0.conf:**

Configures WPA settings for the wlan0 interface.

  - **ctrl_interface:** Directory for the control interface.
  - **update_config=1:** Allows runtime configuration updates.
  - **network:** Contains Wi-Fi network settings:
    - ssid="Something": Wi-Fi network name.
    - psk="newtofindpasswrd": Pre-shared key (password).

- **/etc/default/raspi-firmware:**

Contains Raspberry Pi firmware configuration.

  - **ROOTPART="LABEL=root":** Specifies the root partition label.
  - **KERNEL_ARCH="arm64":** Sets the system architecture.

- **/etc/default/raspi-extra-cmdline:**

Adds extra kernel parameters at boot time.

  - **init=/usr/lib/systemd/systemd:** Sets systemd as the init system.

**<command>: System Commands**

- **update-initramfs -u -k all:** Updates the initial RAM filesystem (initramfs) for all installed kernels. This ensures that the necessary modules are included in the RAM disk for booting.
- **systemctl enable wpa_supplicant@wlan0.service**: Enables Wi-Fi connectivity on boot for the wlan0 interface.
- **systemctl enable systemd-networkd:** Activates the systemd network service for managing interfaces.

## Hardware Compatibility

The image built using this recipe is compatible with Raspberry Pi 3B+, Zero 2 W, Pi 4, and Pi 5. With the release of Debian Trixie and updated kernel support, Raspberry Pi 5 is now fully supported without requiring manual kernel or firmware installation.

## Summary

This chapter demonstrated how ELBE can be used to create a minimal, fully bootable Debian Trixie image for Raspberry Pi hardware. By defining firmware layout, filesystem tuning, networking configuration, and hardware-specific packages in a single XML recipe, a reproducible and hardware-ready image was produced. The resulting system provides a clean foundation making it ideal for rapid prototyping and as a base for customized IoT and embedded deployments.

## Further Reading and Resources

For hardware details and boot behavior, the Raspberry Pi documentation explains firmware, kernel loading, and device-tree mechanisms in depth.

# Initramfs

**Initramfs (Initial RAM File System)** is a temporary root file system that is loaded into memory during the boot process, before the real root file system is mounted. It is essential for the early stages of booting a Linux system and plays a crucial role in initializing the system, such as loading necessary kernel modules, setting up devices, and mounting the real root file system.

**Basics of initramfs:**

- **Purpose**: The primary purpose of the initramfs is to provide a minimal environment that allows the kernel to mount the real root file system and begin the system initialization process. It includes necessary drivers, scripts, and tools to ensure the kernel has access to the hardware and can load the system from a storage device.

- **Structure**: Initramfs is essentially a compressed cpio archive file that contains the necessary files and directories that the kernel needs during early boot. This archive is unpacked into memory at boot, and the init process in the initramfs environment is responsible for booting the rest of the system.

## Overview of initramfs-tools

The **initramfs-tools** package is responsible for creating, configuring, and updating the initramfs image used during the boot process. The initramfs image is essentially a compressed archive (typically in cpio format) that contains a minimal file system and essential files to help the kernel initialize hardware and mount the real root file system.

When a Linux system boots, the kernel initially mounts this initramfs image in memory before switching to the real root file system. The tools within the initramfs-tools package help ensure that the initramfs contains the correct drivers, modules, and scripts required for booting, depending on the hardware and configuration.

## Key components of initramfs-tools

1. **initramfs-tools Package**: This package includes scripts and configuration files that manage the generation and handling of initramfs images. It works in conjunction with the kernel to build and configure initramfs based on the system's requirements.
2. **update-initramfs Command**: This command is used to create or update the initramfs image on the system. It typically runs automatically after kernel upgrades, but users can invoke it manually to regenerate the initramfs for various reasons (e.g., after adding new modules or updating kernel parameters).

   Key options for update-initramfs include:

   - **-u**: Update the existing initramfs image.
   - **-c**: Create a new initramfs image.
   - **-k**: Specify the kernel version for which to create/update the initramfs (e.g., update-initramfs -u -k all to update initramfs for all installed kernels).
3. **initramfs-tools Directory Structure**: The configuration and hooks provided by initramfs-tools are located in several key directories, and these allow customization of the initramfs image that will be generated.

## Relationship Between Kernel Package and initramfs-tools

When you install or upgrade a Linux kernel package (e.g., linux-image-<version>), it automatically triggers initramfs-tools to:

1. Generate a new initramfs image for that kernel version.
2. Install the initramfs image to /boot/ (e.g., /boot/initrd.img-<version>).

This is handled by package post-installation scripts included in the kernel package. These scripts call the update-initramfs tool, which is part of the initramfs-tools package.

- **Key Files and Directories in initramfs-tools:**
- **/etc/initramfs-tools/**: This directory contains the main configuration files and scripts used by initramfs-tools to generate the initramfs.
- Key files:
    - **/etc/initramfs-tools/modules**: Lists kernel modules to be included in the initramfs.
    - **/etc/initramfs-tools/initramfs.conf**: This file contains configuration options for how the initramfs should be built, such as compression options and module loading behavior.
- **/etc/initramfs-tools/hooks/**: This directory contains "hooks" which are scripts that run at different points during the creation of the initramfs. Hooks are used to add files, settings, or scripts to the initramfs or modify its behavior. For example, hooks can add support for additional filesystems or hardware drivers.
- **/etc/initramfs-tools/conf.d/**: Contains additional configuration files for specific use cases, such as adding custom device support or handling different filesystems during the boot process.
- **/etc/initramfs-tools/scripts/**: This directory contains scripts that control the behavior of the initramfs at various stages.

1. **init-top/** Run very early to set up the initial environment before any devices are scanned.
2. **premount/** Used for checks or setup before trying to mount anything.
3. **local-top/** Prepare local storage (such as LVM, RAID, or decryption) before mounting the root file system.
4. **local-premount/** Final steps right before mounting the local root file system.

5. **local-bottom/** Actions to take after the root file system has been successfully mounted.

6. **init-bottom/** Final cleanup and hand-off to the real init system on the root file system

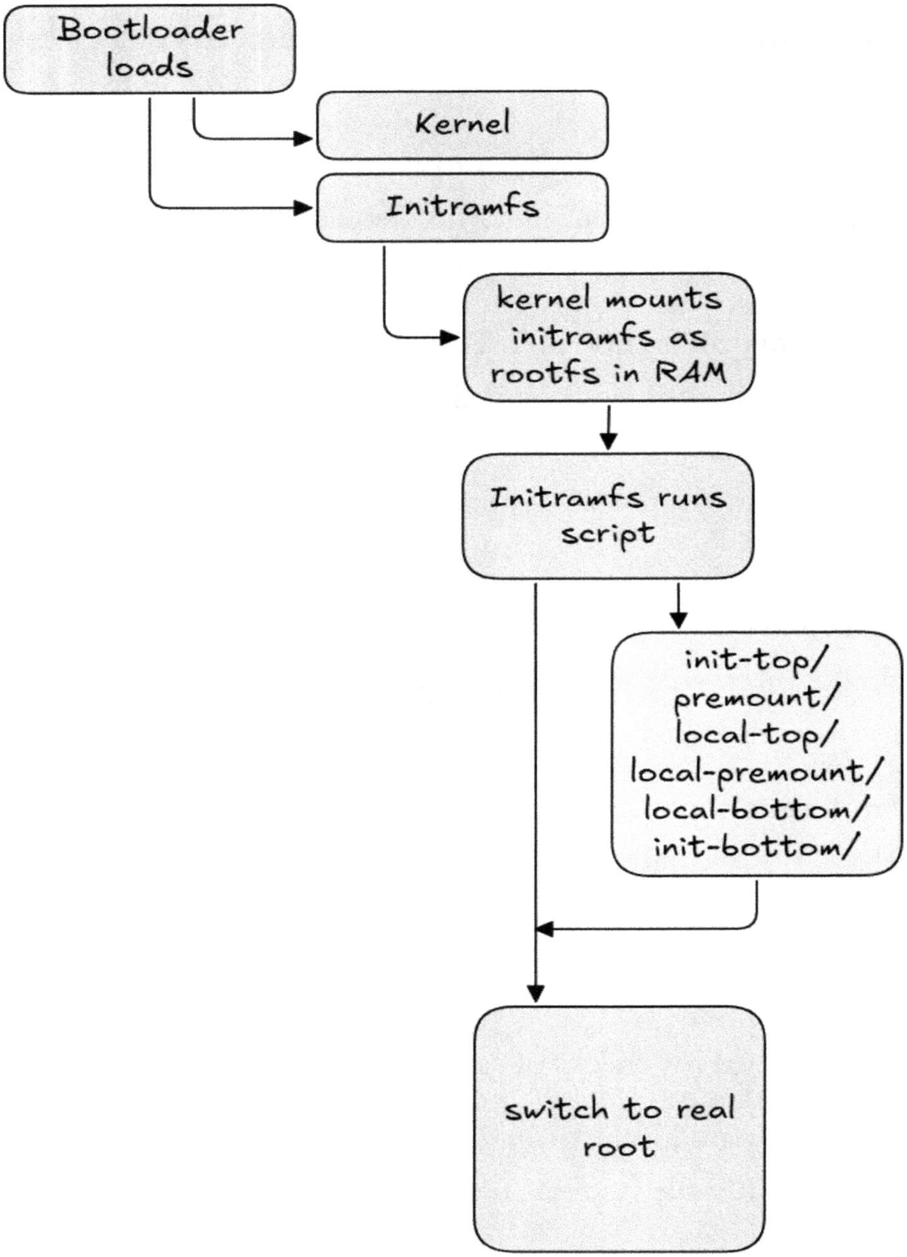


*Figure 27: Initramfs bootflow*

**initramfs-tools in Action:**

When a new kernel is installed or updated, update-initramfs is run to generate a new initramfs image that is compatible with the kernel. It will include necessary drivers, modules, and scripts.

The initramfs image is used by the kernel at boot time. The kernel loads this image into a tmpfs (RAM-based filesystem) and begins executing its initialization process by running /init, which includes loading necessary hardware drivers, modules, and setting up the system.

If the system requires specific hardware support (e.g., RAID, specific disk controllers, or network drivers), initramfs-tools ensures that the necessary modules are included in the initramfs image.

**Examples of Customizations:**

1. **Adding a Module**: To add a kernel module to your initramfs (e.g., mymodule), you would add mymodule to the /etc/initramfs-tools/modules file. After updating the initramfs with update-initramfs, the module is included in the initramfs image.
2. **Creating a Custom Hook**: If you want to include a custom file or make system modifications during the initramfs creation, you can create a hook script. For example, you might create a file /etc/initramfs-tools/hooks/myscript to copy configuration files or set specific environment variables in the initramfs.
3. **Using initramfs.conf for Configuration**: You can tweak the behavior of the initramfs-tools package using the /etc/initramfs-tools/initramfs.conf file. For example, you might choose a different compression method (e.g., gzip, bzip2, or lzma) to compress the initramfs image.

**Summary**

Initramfs provides an essential environment for booting the system, allowing the kernel to load necessary modules, set up storage devices, and transition to the real rootfile system. It involves various configuration files, scripts, and hooks that customize the behavior of the initramfs image to fit the needs of the system. The initramfs environment supports various filesystems, including traditional options such as ext4, advanced options such as Btrfs, and layered systems such as OverlayFS. ELBE recipes in this book make use of the initramfs-tools and its extensibility extensively, leveraging its modular design and scriptable phases to tailor the early boot environment to specific embedded system requirements.

# 11 Raspberry Pi Btrfs image

**Abstract:** This chapter advances filesystem choices by building a Raspberry Pi image with Btrfs for snapshots, compression, and robustness. It covers company needs, requirements, implementation details, the btrfs_rpi-trixie.xml recipe, and explanations of Btrfs integration in ELBE/boot setup.

## 11.1 Company Introduction

**Xaltra Innovations** is a dynamic tech company specializing in storage optimization and data reliability for IoT and edge devices. With deep expertise in designing secure and scalable storage systems, Xaltra is known for pushing the boundaries of what's possible on small-scale hardware such as Raspberry Pi. Their solutions often combine advanced filesystems with embedded Linux to deliver high-performance, fault-tolerant platforms for mission-critical applications.

## 11.2 Customer Requirements

**HyperFarm**, an agricultural IoT startup, is developing a Raspberry Pi-powered edge solution for monitoring and managing crop growth. Their device collects large amounts of sensor data including soil moisture, temperature, and sunlight exposure, which are stored locally before syncing with cloud servers.

However, HyperFarm faces two critical challenges:

1. **Data Integrity**: Frequent power fluctuations in rural areas pose a risk of data corruption during unexpected shutdowns.
2. **Resilient Root Filesystem**: They require a robust root filesystem that supports snapshots, allowing seamless rollback after updates or configuration changes.

To address these needs, HyperFarm approaches Xaltra Innovations to design a storage solution that ensures both reliability and flexibility on Raspberry Pi hardware.

**Company Response**

The team at **Xaltra Innovations** evaluates the requirements and identifies Btrfs as the optimal filesystem for this use case. With its features such as subvolumes, copy-on-write (CoW), checksums for data integrity, and snapshot functionality, Btrfs offers the resilience and modularity needed for HyperFarm's edge device.

Amar, a senior systems engineer at **Xaltra Innovations**, devises a solution: configure Raspberry Pi to use a Btrfs root filesystem. His plan includes:

- Mounting the main Btrfs volume with subvolid=5 as /btrfs, enabling access to all subvolumes.
- Defining the root filesystem as a subvolume @rootfs mounted at / using Raspberry Pi's cmdline.txt file.
- Creating a /btrfs/snaps directory to store snapshots of the root filesystem for quick rollback during system updates or failures.

## 11.3 Implementation

Amar sets up Raspberry Pi with the following steps:

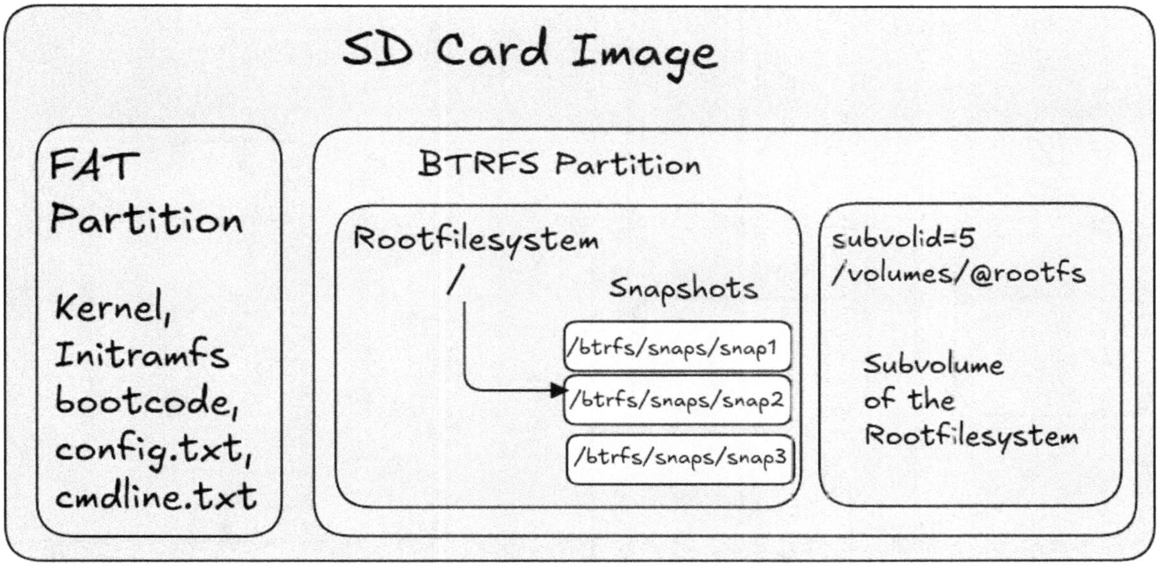


*Figure 28: SD card with BTRFS Partition*

1. **Partitioning and Formatting**: The SD card is partitioned, and the primary partition is formatted with the Btrfs filesystem to support advanced features such as snapshots and checksums.

2. **Subvolume Configuration**: Amar creates two subvolumes under /btrfs:

   @rootfs - serves as the root filesystem

   @snaps - stores snapshots for rollback and recovery

3. **Bootloader Adjustments**: Raspberry Pi's cmdline.txt is modified to mount the @rootfs subvolume as /. The main Btrfs volume (subvolid=5) is mounted at /btrfs to allow access to all subvolumes

4. **Snapshot Workflow**: Amar implements a script that regularly creates snapshots of the root filesystem and stores them in /btrfs/snaps. This enables HyperFarm to restore the system from /snaps in case of failure or misconfiguration.

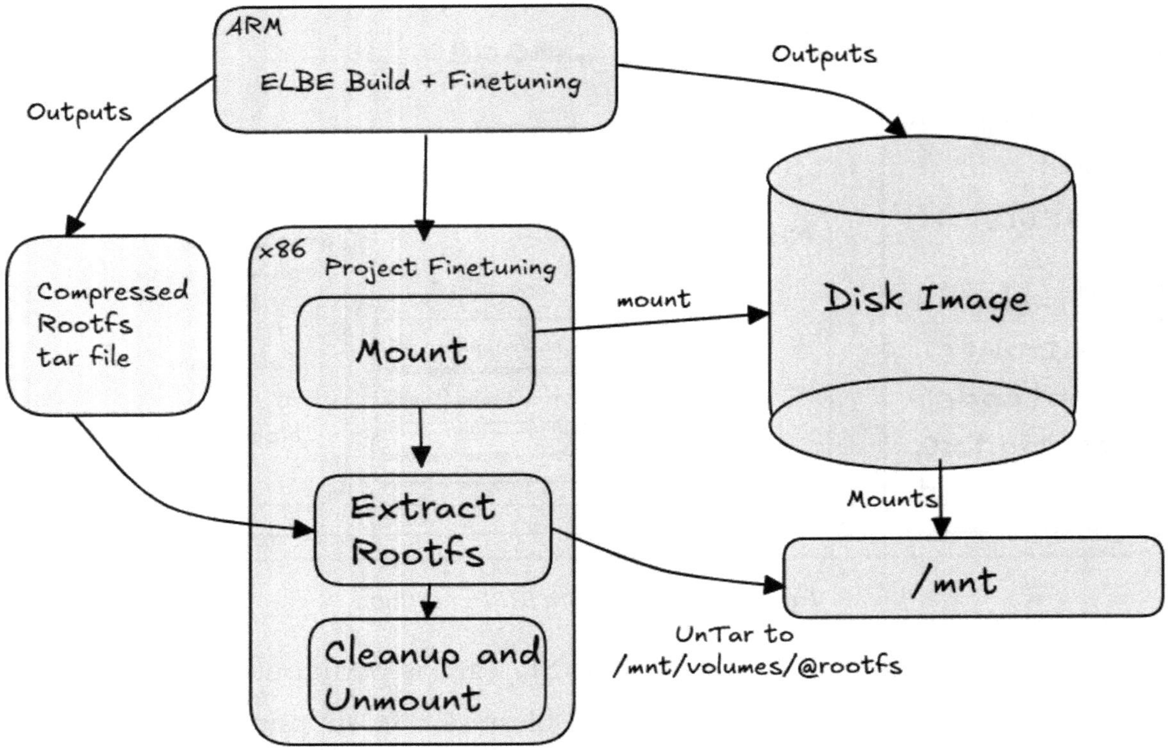


*Figure 29: BTRFS Build flow*

## Outcome

After thorough testing, the Btrfs-based solution performs reliably, providing HyperFarm with a resilient Raspberry Pi system. The device now ensures data integrity even during power outages, and administrators can restore previous system states quickly in seconds using snapshots. This flexibility allows HyperFarm to focus on innovation while trusting the reliability of their edge infrastructure.

The success of the project inspires Amar to explore further enhancements, such as automated snapshot rotation and offloading snapshots to cloud storage for long-term retention and disaster recovery.

The implementation is documented as follows.

```
$ elbe initvm submit  btrfs_rpi-trixie.xml --output rpi-downloads
```

After downloading the image, it is flashed to Raspberry Pi. The system is then accessed via the serial console for verification and configuration.

### Playing with Btrfs commands on Raspberry Pi

To verify the Btrfs mount configuration, Amar logs into Raspberry Pi via the serial console and runs:

```
root@rpi64:~# mount | grep btrfs
/dev/mmcblk0p2 on / type btrfs
(rw,relatime,ssd,space_cache,subvolid=256,subvol=volumes/@rootfs)
/dev/mmcblk0p2 on /btrfs type btrfs
(rw,relatime,ssd,space_cache,subvolid=5,subvol=/)
```

### Understanding the Mounts

**subvolid=5,subvol=/ (Top-level Filesystem)**:

- **subvolid=5**: The default subvolume ID in Btrfs, representing the top-level filesystem.
- **subvol=/**: Refers to the root of the Btrfs filesystem.
- **Mount point**: /btrfs - provides access to all subvolumes and the full Btrfs hierarchy.

**subvolid=256,subvol=/**volumes/@rootfs **(Active root filesystem)**:

- **subvolid=256**: A uniquely identified subvolume used as the system's root.
- **subvol=/**volumes/@rootfs : The subvolume configured to serve as the root filesystem.
- **Mount point**: / - this is the active root filesystem used by the operating system.

**Listing Subvolumes**

```
root@rpi64:~# btrfs subvolume list /btrfs
ID 256 gen 19 top level 5 path volumes/@rootfs
```

This shows the @rootfs subvolume with ID 256, located under /btrfs/volumes, and it is generation 19.

**Creating Snapshots**

```
root@rpi64:~#  btrfs subvolume snapshot /btrfs/volumes/\@rootfs/
/btrfs/snaps/snap1
Create a snapshot of '/btrfs/volumes/@rootfs/' in '/btrfs/snaps/snap1'
root@rpi64:~# btrfs subvolume snapshot /btrfs/volumes/\@rootfs/
/btrfs/snaps/snap2
 Create a snapshot of '/btrfs/volumes/@rootfs/' in '/btrfs/snaps/snap2'
```

The command creates a snapshot of the @rootfs subvolume in /btrfs/snaps/snap1 and /btrfs/snaps/snap2.

**Changing the boot entry**

To boot from a snapshot, Amar modifies Raspberry Pi's boot configuration:

**Edit /boot/firmware/cmdline.txt**

Before

```
rootflags=subvol=volumes/@rootfs init=/usr/lib/systemd/systemd
```

After

```
rootflags=subvol=snaps/snap1 init=/usr/lib/systemd/systemd
```

This change instructs the system to boot from the snap1 snapshot instead of the live root filesystem, enabling quick rollback and recovery.

### Rebooting and Verifying Snapshot Boot

```
root@rpi64:~# systemctl reboot
```

### Verify the change

```
root@rpi64:~# mount|grep btrfs
/dev/mmcblk0p2 on / type btrfs
(rw,relatime,ssd,space_cache,subvolid=256,subvol=snaps/snap1)
 /dev/mmcblk0p2 on /btrfs type btrfs
(rw,relatime,ssd,space_cache,subvolid=5,subvol=/)
```

This confirms that the system is now booting from the snap1 snapshot.

### Making the Snapshot Read-Only

To preserve the integrity of the snapshot, Amar marks it as read-only:

```
root@rpi64:~# btrfs property set -ts /btrfs/snaps/snap1 ro true
```

The command sets the read-only property on the snap1 subvolume, making it read-only.

### Exporting the Snapshot

Amar exports the snapshot for backup or transfer:

```
root@rpi64:~# btrfs send /btrfs/snaps/snap1/ >/btrfs/snap_data
At subvol /btrfs/snaps/snap1/
```

This command serializes the snapshot into a stream/file for later restoration

### Testing Snapshot Isolation

To test changes, Amar installs a package:

```
root@rpi64:~#  apt install can-utils
```

### Renaming the Snapshot

He renames the snapshot to reflect its new state:

```
root@rpi64:~#  mv /btrfs/snaps/snap1 /btrfs/snaps/snap3
```

### Restoring the Snapshot

To restore the original snapshot from the backup file:

```
root@rpi64:~# btrfs receive  /btrfs/snaps/ < /btrfs/snap_data
At subvol snap1
```

This recreates the original snap1 subvolume under /btrfs/snaps.

## 11.4 Recipe btrfs_rpi-trixie.xml

```
<?xml version="1.0"?>
<ns0:RootFileSystem
xmlns:ns0="https://www.linutronix.de/projects/Elbe"
xmlns:xsi="http://www.w3.org/2001/XMLSchema-instance"
created="2009-05-20T08:50:56" revision="6"
xsi:schemaLocation="https://www.linutronix.de/projects/Elbe
dbsfed.xsd">
<project>
<name>RaspberryPi-Btrfs</name>
<version>1.0</version>
```

```
<description>Raspberry Pi Btrfs image</description>
<buildtype>aarch64</buildtype>
<mirror>
 <primary_host>ftp.de.debian.org</primary_host>
 <primary_path>/debian</primary_path>
 <primary_proto>http</primary_proto>
 <url-list>
 <url>
   <binary>https://deb.debian.org/debian-security trixie-security
main</binary>
   <source>https://deb.debian.org/debian-security trixie-security
main</source>
 </url>
 <url>
   <binary>https://deb.debian.org/debian trixie non-free-
firmware</binary>
   <source>https://deb.debian.org/debian trixie non-free-
firmware</source>
 </url>
 <url>
   <binary>https://deb.debian.org/debian-security trixie-security non-free-
firmware</binary>
   <source>https://deb.debian.org/debian-security trixie-security non-
free-firmware</source>
 </url>
 </url-list>
</mirror>
<suite>trixie</suite>
</project>
```

```
<target>
<hostname>rpi5</hostname>
<domain/>
<passwd_hashed>$6$bOQ4Sf4rSdl1IfRd$3Hai04jz2OYEW108SZWew
eGO/rGvO65ITthDDtDuaC/8Gpwek/xT4rUvKBkBHFIjTDd6.klFdNJ685k
xgabHh/</passwd_hashed>
<console>serial0,115200</console>
<package>
  <tar>
    <name>rootfs.tgz</name>
  </tar>
</package>
<debootstrap>
  <variant>minbase</variant>
</debootstrap>
<images>
 <msdoshd>
 <name>sdcard.img</name>
 <size>8GB</size>
 <partition>
   <size>128MB</size>
   <label>firmware</label>
 </partition>
 <partition>
   <size>remain</size>
   <label>root</label>
   <bootable/>
 </partition>
 </msdoshd>
```

```
</images>
<fstab>
 <bylabel>
 <label>firmware</label>
 <mountpoint>/boot/firmware</mountpoint>
 <fs>
   <type>vfat</type>
 </fs>
 </bylabel>
 <bylabel>
 <label>root</label>
 <mountpoint>/</mountpoint>
 <fs>
   <type>btrfs</type>
   <fs-finetuning>
     <path-command>mkdir -p {path}/volumes/ </path-command>
     <path-command>btrfs subvolume create
{path}/volumes/@rootfs</path-command>
   </fs-finetuning>
 </fs>
 </bylabel>
</fstab>
<project-finetuning>
 <set_packer packer="none">sdcard.img</set_packer>
 <losetup img="sdcard.img">
 <command part="2" nomount="true">
   mount   ${ELBE_DEV} /mnt
 </command>
 <command part="2" nomount="true">
```

```
  tar -xvf ../rootfs.tgz -C /mnt/volumes/@rootfs
 </command>
 <command part="2" nomount="true">
  cd /mnt ; rm -rfv
bin,boot,dev,etc,home,initrd.img,initrd.img.old,lib,lost+found,media,mnt,
networkd,opt,proc,root,run,sbin,srv,sys,tmp,usr,var,vmlinuz,vmlinuz.old
 </command>
 <command part="2" nomount="true">
  cd / ; umount /mnt
 </command>
 </losetup>
</project-finetuning>
<install-recommends/>
<pkg-list>
  <pkg>linux-image-arm64</pkg>
  <pkg>firmware-brcm80211</pkg>
  <pkg>raspi-firmware</pkg>
  <pkg>zstd</pkg>
  <pkg>apt-utils</pkg>
  <pkg>systemd</pkg>
  <pkg>vim-tiny</pkg>
  <pkg>busybox</pkg>
  <pkg>bash</pkg>
  <pkg>openssh-server</pkg>
  <pkg>wpasupplicant</pkg>
  <pkg>iproute2</pkg>
  <pkg>net-tools</pkg>
  <pkg>iputils-ping</pkg>
  <pkg>iw</pkg>
```

```
  <pkg>ifupdown</pkg>
  <pkg>bluez</pkg>
  <pkg>bluez-tools</pkg>
  <pkg>rfkill</pkg>
  <pkg>avahi-daemon</pkg>
  <pkg>avahi-utils</pkg>
  <pkg>btrfs-progs</pkg>
  <pkg>btrbk</pkg>
  <pkg>rsync</pkg>
</pkg-list>
<finetuning>
  <file dst="/etc/systemd/network/25-wlan0.network" mode="644">
   [Match]
   Name=wlan0

   [Network]
   DHCP=yes
 </file>
 <file dst="/etc/wpa_supplicant/wpa_supplicant-wlan0.conf"
mode="600">
 ctrl_interface=DIR=/var/run/wpa_supplicant GROUP=netdev
 update_config=1
 country=US

 network={
 ssid=" SomeSSID "
 psk=" SomeKey "
 }
 </file>
```

```
<file dst="/etc/default/raspi-firmware" append="true">
  ROOTPART="LABEL=root"
  KERNEL_ARCH="arm64"
</file>
<file dst="/etc/default/raspi-extra-cmdline" append="true">
  rootflags=subvol=volumes/@rootfs init=/usr/lib/systemd/systemd
</file>
<file dst="/etc/btrbk/btrbk.conf">
  transaction_log /var/log/btrbk.log
  timestamp_format short
  snapshot_dir snaps
  snapshot_create always

  volume /
    subvolume /
    snapshot_preserve_min 7d
    snapshot_preserve 7d
</file>
<file dst="/etc/fstab" append="true">
  /dev/mmcblk0p2  /btrfs  btrfs  defaults,subvolid=5  0  0
</file>
<command>update-initramfs -u -k all</command>
<command>systemctl enable
wpa_supplicant@wlan0.service</command>
<command>systemctl enable systemd-networkd</command>
<command>systemctl enable avahi-daemon</command>
<command>update-initramfs -u -k all</command>
<command>mkdir /volumes</command>
<command>mkdir /snaps</command>
```

```
 <command>mkdir /btrfs</command>
</finetuning>
</target>
</ns0:RootFileSystem>
```

## 11.5 Recipe Explanation

**<fs-finetuning>: Filesystem customization**

This section sets up the Btrfs subvolume structure within the root partition:

**<path-command>**: mkdir -p {path}/volumes/

Creates the volumes/ directory inside the root mount point.

**<path-command>**: btrfs subvolume create {path}/volumes/@rootfs
Creates a Btrfs subvolume at volumes/@rootfs, which serves as the actual root filesystem (/).

**<losetup img="sdcard.img">: SD card Image Setup**

Defines how the sdcard.img image is prepared using loopback mounting:

<command part="2" nomount="true">

- mount ${ELBE_DEV} /mnt - Mounts the second partition from the image to /mnt.
- tar -xvf ../rootfs.tgz -C /mnt/volumes/@rootfs - Extracts the generated rootfs.tgz into /mnt/volumes/@rootfs.

**Why this matters:**

In Btrfs, the top-level / should not be mounted as the root filesystem. Instead, a subvolume such as @rootfs is used. This ensures that Raspberry Pi boots using the correct Btrfs subvolume structure.

**<finetuning>: System Configuration and Setup**

**dst="/etc/default/raspi-extra-cmdline" append="true"**

Appends kernel parameters to configure the boot process

```
rootflags=subvol=volumes/@rootfs init=/usr/lib/systemd/systemd
```

This ensures the system boots from the @rootfs subvolume and uses systemd as the init system.

**<fstab>: Filesystem Mount Entry**

**dst="/etc/fstab" append="true"**

Adds an entry to mount the top-level Btrfs volume:

```
/dev/mmcblk0p2 /btrfs btrfs defaults,subvolid=5 0 0
```

This mounts the second partition (/dev/mmcblk0p2) at /btrfs, exposing the full Btrfs hierarchy. subvolid=5 refers to the top-level subvolume, allowing access to all other subvolumes such as @rootfs and snapshots.

### Summary

This chapter presented the design and implementation of a Raspberry Pi image using a Btrfs root filesystem to enhance reliability and flexibility for IoT edge deployments. By integrating Btrfs into the ELBE build process, the system gains native support for subvolumes, snapshots, copy-on-write semantics, and checksumming, enabling robust protection against data corruption and safe rollback after updates or failures. The image is structured around a dedicated @rootfs subvolume mounted as the active root filesystem, while the Btrfs top-level subvolume is mounted at /btrfs to provide full access to snapshots and volume management. Practical examples demonstrated snapshot creation, snapshot-based booting, read-only enforcement, and snapshot export and restoration, illustrating how rapid recovery can be achieved on Raspberry Pi hardware. This approach delivers a resilient and maintainable platform well suited for power-unstable environments and long-running edge devices.

## Further Reading and Resources

For a deeper understanding of Btrfs concepts such as subvolumes, snapshots, and send/receive workflows, the official Btrfs documentation provides comprehensive technical detail and best practices. Additional guidance on filesystem customization, image post-processing, and advanced finetuning can be found in the ELBE project documentation. Readers seeking insight into boot-time configuration and root filesystem selection on Raspberry Pi should consult the Raspberry Pi firmware and boot documentation.

# 12 Raspberry Pi OverlayFS & SquashFS Image

**Abstract:** Focusing on read-only root with writable overlays for reliability and atomic updates, this chapter details SquashFS + OverlayFS configurations for Raspberry Pi. It presents requirements, implementation, separate recipes (Squashfs-trixie.xml and Sdcard-trixie.xml), and explanations of how these enable efficient, fail-safe deployments.

## 12.1 Company Introduction

**Obscuron Hive** is an innovative tech company specializing in embedded systems, operating system optimizations, and custom software solutions for IoT devices. With a strong focus on reducing system overhead and maximizing resource efficiency, Obscuron Hive collaborates with clients across industries such as automation, smart homes, and remote monitoring systems. Their expertise lies in crafting lightweight; resilient operating environments tailored for constrained hardware platforms such as Raspberry Pi.

## 12.2 Customer Requirements

**SakuraFeng Labs**, a company focused on creating energy-efficient smart home devices, approaches **Obscuron Hive** with a challenge. They are developing a line of

Raspberry Pi-powered environmental monitoring units, and they need a highly efficient bootable image that allows for easy software updates and custom configurations without altering the base system.

The specific requirements are:

- **OverlayFS :** To enable dynamic, writable layers on top of a read-only root filesystem. This allows secure updates and configuration changes while preserving the original system image.
- **SquashFS :** To create a compressed, read-only root filesystem that is lightweight and optimized for storage. This helps reduce the overall image size and improves performance
- **Bootable Integration**: The image must boot seamlessly with both layers functioning together. This ensures flexibility for updates and configuration changes in field deployments.

**Company Response**

Claire, a senior embedded systems engineer at Obscuron Hive, is assigned to create the solution for SakuraFeng Labs. After reviewing the requirements, she decides to use OverlayFS and SquashFS together to build an image that meets the need for efficiency, flexibility, and updatability.

- SquashFS will serve as the compressed, read-only base filesystem. It will contain the operating system and essential software, optimize storage usage and ensure consistency.
- OverlayFS will be layered on top of the SquashFS, providing a writable space for configuration changes, updates, and data storage. This approach allows modifications without altering the original system image.

Claire plans to use ELBE to build Raspberry Pi image, integrating both technologies into a bootable and maintainable system suitable for field deployment.

## 12.3 Implementation

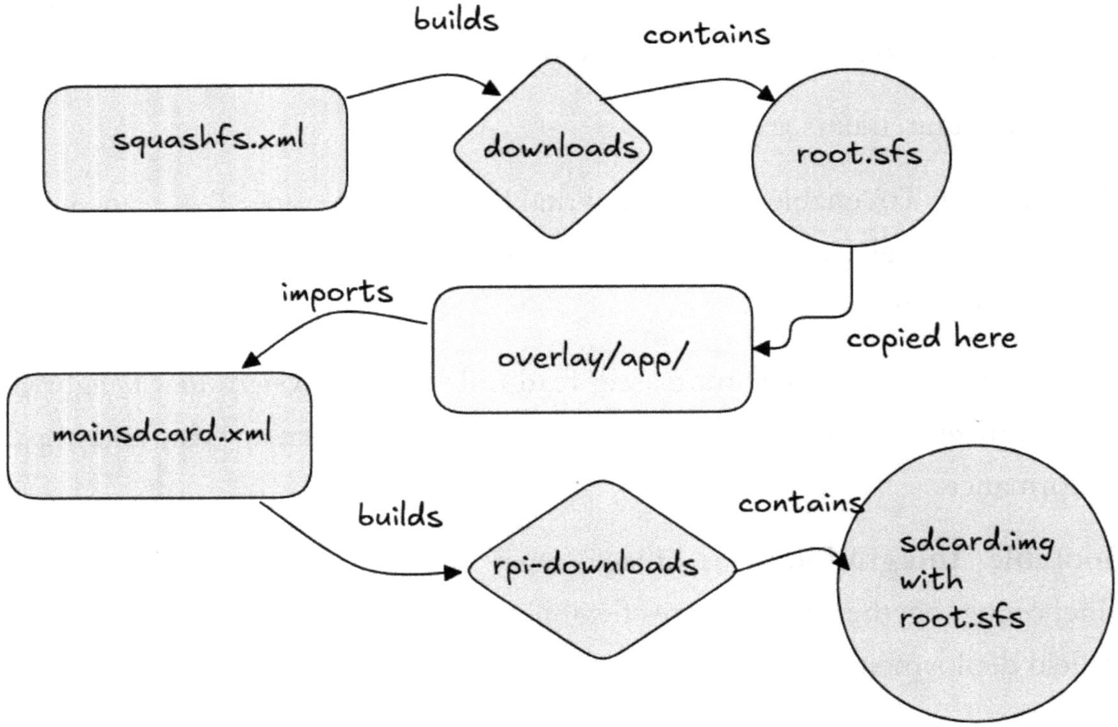


*Figure 30: Build workflow*

The build process follows a clear, two-stage flow:

1. **Creating the SquashFS Image**

   The first step involves building a compressed, read-only SquashFS image using the squashfs-trixie.xml recipe with ELBE.

2. **Integrating with the Main SD card Build**

   Once the SquashFS image is generated, it is downloaded and integrated into the overlay directory of the main SD card image build.

3. **Final Image Assembly**

   The main build recipe (sdcard.xml) uses the SquashFS image to assemble the final bootable SD card image for Raspberry Pi, combining both read-only and writable layers.

### Preparing Raspberry Pi Build Environment with ELBE

Claire begins by setting up the ELBE InitVM environment and executing the following steps:

### Step 1: Build the SquashFS Image

```
$ elbe initvm submit  squashfs-trixie.xml --output downloads
```

After the build completes, Claire retrieves the generated files and saves them to the downloads folder.

### Step 2: Copy SquashFS to Overlay Directory

```
$ mkdir -p overlays/app
$ cp downloads/root. squashfs overlays/app/
```

This prepares the SquashFS image for integration into the main SD card build.

### Step 3: Build the SD card Image

```
$ elbe initvm submit  sdcard.xml --output downloads
```

After downloading the final image, it is flashed to Raspberry Pi. Claire then logs in via the serial console to verify the system.

## 12.4 Recipe Squashfs-trixie.xml

```
<?xml version="1.0"?>
<ns0:RootFileSystem
xmlns:ns0="https://www.linutronix.de/projects/Elbe"
xmlns:xsi="http://www.w3.org/2001/XMLSchema-instance"
created="2009-05-20T08:50:56" revision="6"
```

```
xsi:schemaLocation="https://www.linutronix.de/projects/Elbe
dbsfed.xsd">
<project>
<name>RaspberryPi-Squashfs</name>
<version>1.0</version>
<description>Raspberry Pi squashfs image</description>
<buildtype>aarch64</buildtype>
<mirror>
 <primary_host>ftp.de.debian.org</primary_host>
 <primary_path>/debian</primary_path>
 <primary_proto>http</primary_proto>
 <url-list>
  <url>
   <binary>https://deb.debian.org/debian-security trixie-security
main</binary>
   <source>https://deb.debian.org/debian-security trixie-security
main</source>
  </url>
  <url>
    <binary>https://deb.debian.org/debian trixie non-free-
firmware</binary>
    <source>https://deb.debian.org/debian trixie non-free-
firmware</source>
  </url>
  <url>
    <binary>https://deb.debian.org/debian-security trixie-security non-
free-firmware</binary>
    <source>https://deb.debian.org/debian-security trixie-security non-
free-firmware</source>
```

```
  </url>
 </url-list>
</mirror>
<suite>trixie</suite>
</project>
<target>
<hostname>rpi64</hostname>
<domain/>
<passwd_hashed>$6$bOQ4Sf4rSdI1IfRd$3Hai04jz2OYEW108SZWew
eGO/rGvO65ITthDDtDuaC/8Gpwek/xT4rUvKBkBHFIjTDd6.klFdNJ685k
xgabHh/</passwd_hashed>
<console>serial0,115200</console>
<package>
 <squashfs>
  <name>root.squashfs</name>
 </squashfs>
</package>
<debootstrap>
    <variant>minbase</variant>
</debootstrap>

<pkg-list>
 <pkg>linux-image-arm64</pkg>
 <pkg>firmware-brcm80211</pkg>
 <pkg>raspi-firmware</pkg>
 <pkg>zstd</pkg>
 <pkg>apt-utils</pkg>
 <pkg>systemd</pkg>
```

```
 <pkg>systemd-resolved</pkg>
 <pkg>systemd-timesyncd</pkg>
 <pkg>vim-tiny</pkg>
 <pkg>busybox</pkg>
 <pkg>bash</pkg>
 <pkg>openssh-server</pkg>
 <pkg>unzip</pkg>
 <pkg>i2c-tools</pkg>
 <pkg>can-utils</pkg>
 <pkg>usbutils</pkg>
 <pkg>pciutils</pkg>
 <pkg>mmc-utils</pkg>
 <pkg>iptables</pkg>
 <pkg>bridge-utils</pkg>
</pkg-list>
</target>
</ns0:RootFileSystem>
```

**Squashfs**

The <squashfs> tag in the recipe produces a SquashFS output file named root.squashfs.

## 12.5 Recipe Sdcard-trixie.xml

```
<?xml version="1.0"?>
<ns0:RootFileSystem
xmlns:ns0="https://www.linutronix.de/projects/Elbe"
xmlns:xsi="http://www.w3.org/2001/XMLSchema-instance"
created="2009-05-20T08:50:56" revision="6"
```

```
xsi:schemaLocation="https://www.linutronix.de/projects/Elbe
dbsfed.xsd">
 <project>
 <name> Raspberry Pi-Overlay</name>
 <version>1.0</version>
 <description>
   Raspberry Pi Overlay Image
  </description>
 <buildtype>aarch64</buildtype>
 <mirror>
   <primary_host>ftp.de.debian.org</primary_host>
   <primary_path>/debian</primary_path>
   <primary_proto>http</primary_proto>
   <url-list>
   <url>
     <binary>https://deb.debian.org/debian-security trixie-security
main</binary>
     <source>https://deb.debian.org/debian-security trixie-security
main</source>
   </url>
   <url>
     <binary>https://deb.debian.org/debian trixie non-free-
firmware</binary>
     <source>https://deb.debian.org/debian trixie non-free-
firmware</source>
   </url>
   <url>
     <binary>https://deb.debian.org/debian-security trixie-security non-
free-firmware</binary>
```

```
    <source>https://deb.debian.org/debian-security trixie-security non-
free-firmware</source>
   </url>
   </url-list>
 </mirror>
 <suite>trixie</suite>
 </project>
 <target>
 <hostname>rpi64</hostname>
 <domain/>

<passwd_hashed>$6$bOQ4Sf4rSdl1IfRd$3Hai04jz2OYEW108SZWew
eGO/rGvO65ITthDDtDuaC/8Gpwek/xT4rUvKBkBHFIjTDd6.klFdNJ685k
xgabHh/</passwd_hashed>
 <console>serial0,115200</console>
 <debootstrap>
   <variant>minbase</variant>
 </debootstrap>
 <!-- define an sdcard image -->
 <images>
   <msdoshd>
   <name>sdcard.img</name>
   <size>5GB</size>
   <partition>
     <size>128MB</size>
     <label>firmware</label>
   </partition>
   <partition>
```

```
    <size>remain</size>
    <label>root</label>
    <bootable/>
  </partition>
  </msdoshd>
</images>
<fstab>
<bylabel>
  <label>firmware</label>
  <mountpoint>/boot/firmware</mountpoint>
  <fs>
    <type>vfat</type>
  </fs>
</bylabel>
<bylabel>
  <label>root</label>
  <mountpoint>/</mountpoint>
  <fs>
    <type>ext4</type>
  </fs>
  </bylabel>
</fstab>
  <install-recommends/>
 <pkg-list>
  <pkg>linux-image-arm64</pkg>
  <pkg>firmware-brcm80211</pkg>
  <pkg>raspi-firmware</pkg>
```

```
  <pkg>zstd</pkg>
  <pkg>apt-utils</pkg>
  <pkg>systemd</pkg>
  <pkg>systemd-resolved</pkg>
  <pkg>systemd-timesyncd</pkg>
  <pkg>vim-tiny</pkg>
  <pkg>busybox</pkg>
  <pkg>bash</pkg>
  <pkg>openssh-server</pkg>
 </pkg-list>
 <finetuning>
 <command>echo 'ROOTPART="LABEL=root"' &gt;&gt;
/etc/default/raspi-firmware</command>
 <command>echo 'KERNEL_ARCH="arm64"' &gt;&gt; /etc/default/raspi-
firmware</command>
 <command>echo 'init=/usr/lib/systemd/systemd' &gt;&gt;
/etc/default/raspi-extra-cmdline</command>
 <command>systemctl enable systemd-networkd</command>
 <command>echo 'overlay' &gt;&gt;/etc/initramfs-tools/modules
</command>
 <command>echo 'squashfs' &gt;&gt;/etc/initramfs-tools/modules
</command>
 <file dst="/etc/initramfs-tools/scripts/init-bottom/overlayfs" mode="755">
  #!/bin/sh
  set -e

  lowerdir=/mnt/lower
  upperdir=/mnt/upper
```

```
  workdir=/mnt/work
  ext4dir=/mnt/ext4

  mkdir -p $ext4dir $lowerdir $upperdir $workdir

  modprobe overlay
  modprobe squashfs

  mount /dev/mmcblk0p2  /mnt/ext4
  mount -t squashfs -o loop /mnt/ext4/app/root. squashfs $lowerdir

  mount -t overlay overlay -o
lowerdir=$lowerdir,upperdir=$upperdir,workdir=$workdir /root

  umount $lowerdir
  rmdir $lowerdir $upperdir $workdir

  exit 0

 </file>
 <file dst="/etc/initramfs-tools/hooks/overlayfs" mode="755">
   #!/bin/sh
  set -e

  PREREQ=""

  prereqs() {
```

```
        echo "$PREREQ"
  }

  case "$1" in
  prereqs)
        prereqs
        exit 0
        ;;
  esac

  . /usr/share/initramfs-tools/hook-functions

  manual_add_modules overlay
  manual_add_modules squashfs

  copy_exec /bin/mount /bin
  copy_exec /bin/umount /bin

  exit 0
 </file>
 <command>update-initramfs -u -k all</command>
 <command>rm -rf /bin /boot /dev /etc /home /initrd.img /initrd.img.old
/lib /lost+found /media /mnt /networkd /opt /proc /root /run /sbin /srv /sys
/tmp /usr /var /vmlinuz /vmlinuz.old</command>
  </finetuning>
 </target>
 <archivedir>overlays/</archivedir>
</ns0:RootFileSystem>
```

**Boot Flow Overview**

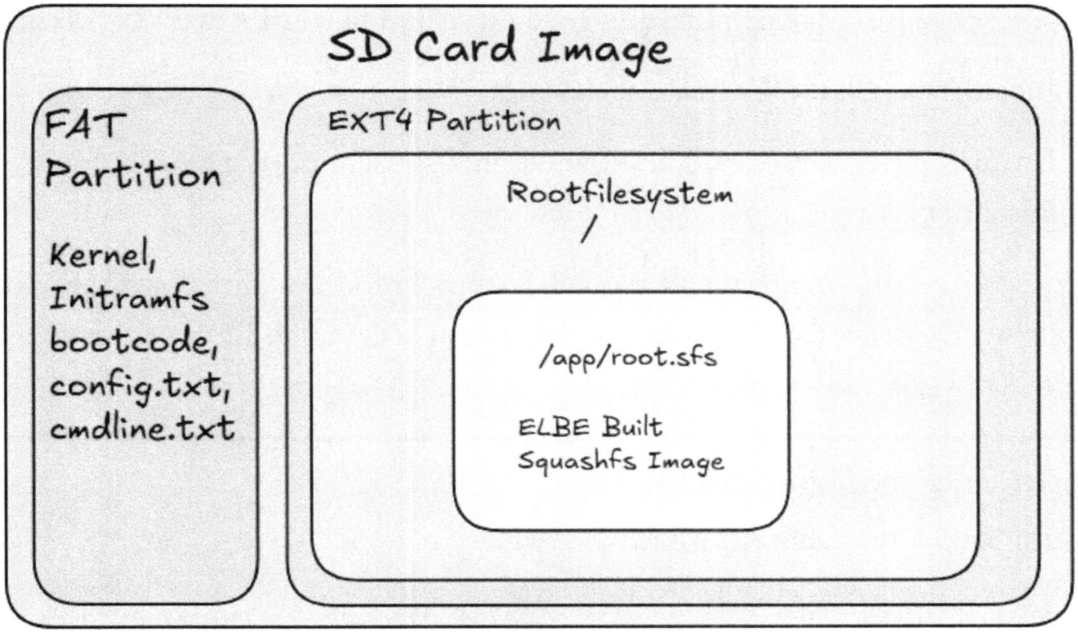


*Figure 31: SDCard with Squashfs*

## Partition Setup

The SD card has a root partition (/dev/mmcblk0p2) where a root. squashfs file resides. This file is the read-only root filesystem built separately using ELBE's squashfs-trixie.xml recipe.

## Initramfs Modules and Scripts

## /etc/initramfs-tools/modules

This file lists the kernel modules that should be explicitly included in the generated initramfs image. The modules overlay and squashfs are included in the initramfs via:

```
$ echo 'overlay' >> /etc/initramfs-tools/modules
$ echo 'squashfs' >> /etc/initramfs-tools/modules
```

These modules are essential for mounting the compressed filesystem and layering the writable overlay on top of it.

### /etc/initramfs-tools/hooks/overlayfs

This hook script runs during initramfs generation and performs two key tasks:

- Includes necessary binaries such as mount and umount.
- Ensures the required modules (overlay and squashfs) are manually added to the initramfs.

This ensures that the **overlay** and **squashfs** kernel modules are present and **loaded early during boot** — essential for mounting the compressed filesystem and layering the writable overlay on top of it.

```
manual_add_modules overlay
manual_add_modules squashfs
copy_exec /bin/mount /bin
copy_exec /bin/umount /bin
```

Together, the modules file and the hook ensure:

- The required modules are present in the initramfs.
- The system has the tools needed to mount and manage the layered filesystem during early boot.

## Mount Logic in Initramfs

### /etc/initramfs-tools/scripts/init-bottom/overlayfs

This script defines the logic for mounting the layered filesystem:

- Mounts the root partition /dev/mmcblk0p2 at /mnt/ext4.
- Mounts the root. squashfs file from that partition to /mnt/lower using a loop device.
- Creates upperdir and workdir for the writable OverlayFS layers.
- Mounts the OverlayFS filesystem at /root.

## Root Switch

After the overlay is mounted at /root, the temporary directories (lower, upper, and work) are unmounted and cleaned up. Control is then handed over to the real root filesystem. Since /root becomes the new root, the system continues booting from there, ensuring a clean and efficient boot process.

## Summary

This chapter explored the design and implementation of a Raspberry Pi image based on a read-only SquashFS root filesystem combined with a writable OverlayFS layer to achieve reliability, efficiency, and atomic system updates. By separating the immutable base system from writable runtime data, the solution enables safe configuration changes and field updates without modifying the original image. Using ELBE, the build process is split into two stages: first generating a compressed SquashFS root filesystem and then integrating it into a bootable SD card image that assembles the OverlayFS stack during early boot via initramfs. The boot flow ensures that SquashFS provides a lightweight and consistent base, while OverlayFS supplies a writable upper layer for system state and configuration. This approach results in a robust deployment model that minimizes storage usage, simplifies rollback, and significantly reduces the risk of filesystem corruption in embedded and power-constrained environments.

## Further Reading and Resources

For deeper insight into SquashFS internals, compression options, and performance trade-offs, the official SquashFS documentation provides comprehensive technical coverage. OverlayFS behavior, limitations, and best practices are detailed in the Linux kernel documentation, which is particularly useful for understanding layered filesystem semantics and update strategies. Additional guidance on early-boot customization, initramfs hooks, and filesystem mounting logic can be found in the Debian initramfs-tools documentation, while the ELBE project documentation offers further examples of multi-stage image builds and advanced filesystem integration for embedded Linux systems.

# 13 Encrypted Filesystem for Raspberry Pi

**Abstract:** Addressing security-critical use cases, this chapter guides building a Raspberry Pi image with full-disk encryption (likely LUKS/dm-crypt). It includes company context, requirements, implementation, the encryption_rpi-trixie.xml recipe, and detailed walkthroughs of initramfs and boot-time decryption setup.

## 13.1 Company Introduction

**Myriadex Shield** is a cybersecurity-focused technology company specializing in secure solutions for edge devices. Its mission is to ensure data security and privacy on small, resource-constrained hardware platforms such as Raspberry Pi. Myriadex Shield delivers advanced encryption and secure storage technologies for industries ranging from healthcare to industrial automation, where protecting sensitive data is critical.

## 13.2 Customer Requirements

**Quantara Lifecode**, a healthcare startup, is developing a portable patient monitoring system powered by Raspberry Pi. This device collects and stores sensitive medical data, including vital signs and diagnostic reports, before transmitting it securely to cloud the servers.

Quantara Lifecode faces a critical challenges:

1. **Data Security**: To comply with strict healthcare data protection regulations, the local storage on Raspberry Pi must be encrypted to prevent unauthorized access in case the device is lost or stolen.
2. **Ease of Use**: The encryption system must integrate seamlessly into Raspberry Pi without significantly affecting its performance.

To address these challenges, Quantara Lifecode turns to Myriadex Shield for a robust solution that secures the local storage with encryption.

**Company Response**

**Shinobu**, a seasoned security engineer at Myriadex Shield, proposes implementing an encrypted filesystem using **Cryptsetup with LUKS (Linux Unified Key Setup)**. LUKS provides strong encryption, ease of use, and compatibility with Raspberry Pi's lightweight hardware, making it an ideal choice for securing sensitive healthcare data.

## 13.3 Implementation

The build process aims to create a bootable image consisting of two partitions:

- **FAT Partition**
  Contains the kernel, initramfs, bootloader files, and configuration files such as config.txt and cmdline.txt. The initramfs also includes the disk encryption key required to unlock the encrypted partition during boot.
- **Encrypted Partition**
  Holds the root filesystem inside an **EXT4-formatted drive**, encrypted using **LUKS (Linux Unified Key Setup)**. This ensures that sensitive data remains secure even if the SD card is removed or the device is lost.

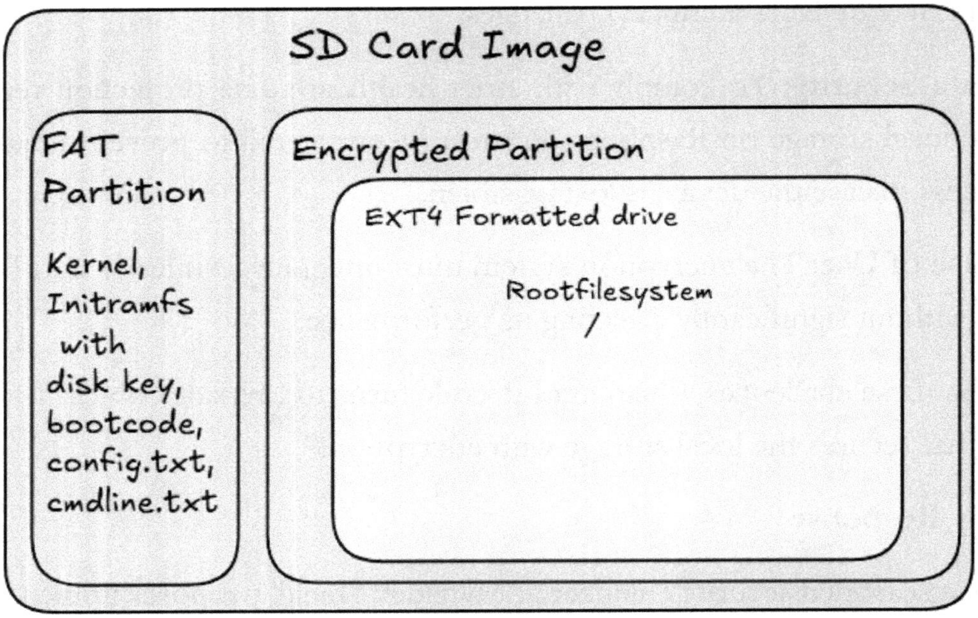


*Figure 32: SDCard with encrypted filesystem*

## Build Time Process

During the build process, the following steps occur:

- Key Generation
  A 32-byte random key is generated and saved as a keyfile. This key will be used for encryption.

- Encrypting the Partition
  The target partition is encrypted using LUKS2 with modern ciphers. This ensures strong security and compliance with data protection standards.

- Opening and Mapping
  The encrypted partition is opened using cryptsetup, which maps it to a device under /dev/mapper (e.g., /dev/mapper/encrypted_root).

- Formatting and Mounting
  The mapped device is formatted with the EXT4 filesystem, mounted at /mnt, and prepared for root filesystem extraction.

- Extracting Root Filesystem
  The compressed root filesystem tarball is extracted onto the mounted encrypted partition.
- Unmounting and Closing
  After setup, the partition is unmounted and closed, completing the secure image creation process.

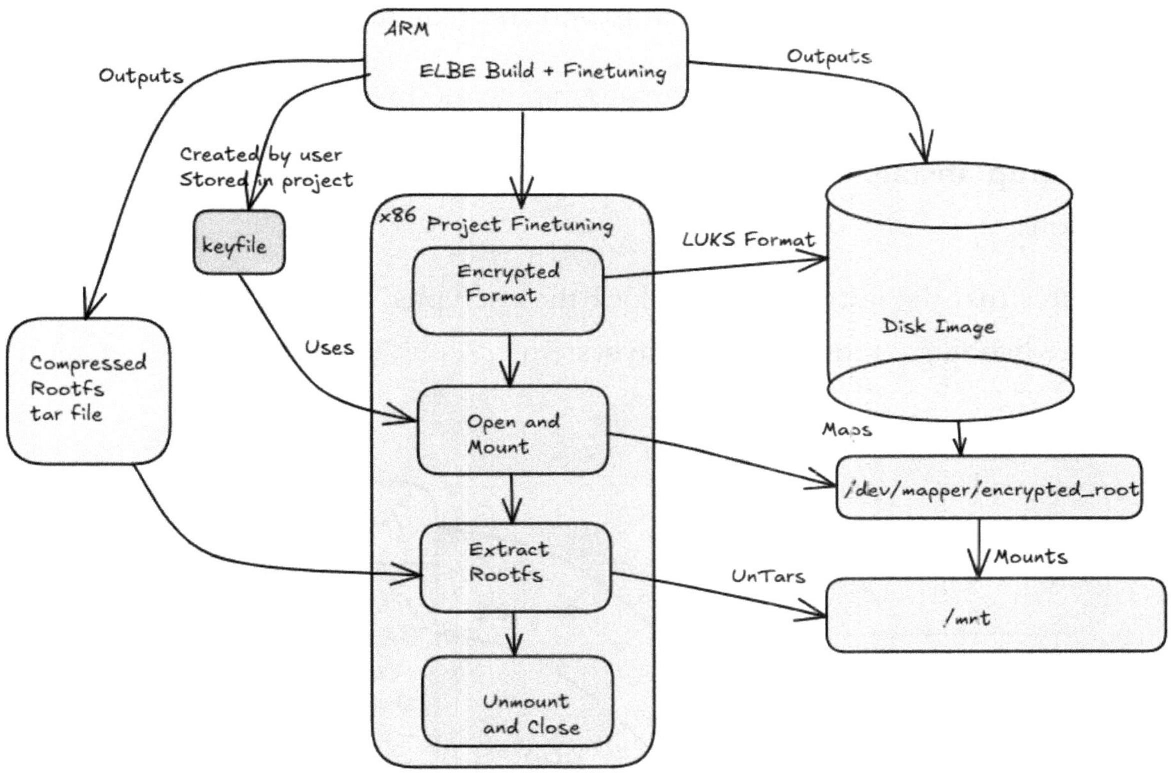


*Figure 33: Build flow of encrypted filesystem recipe*

## Initramfs Build

As part of the build process, the system creates an initramfs image. This initramfs must be capable of **decrypting the encrypted root partition** and mounting the filesystem during early boot. To achieve this, the image includes:

- All necessary **kernel modules** (e.g., dm_crypt, aes, sha256).

- Required **user-space tools** (e.g., cryptsetup, luksformat, cryptdisks_start, cryptdisks_stop).
- The **decryption keyfile** stored at /etc/cryptsetup/keyfile.

The process involves:

- **update-initramfs script**: Triggers the build and ensures hooks are executed.
- **Hook scripts**: Copy essential binaries and add required modules.
- **Module loader scripts**: Ensure cryptographic modules are available in initramfs.
- **cryptsetup install script**: Adds cryptsetup utilities for unlocking encrypted partitions.

This ensures that the initramfs can unlock the encrypted root partition and mount it as / before handing control to the main system.

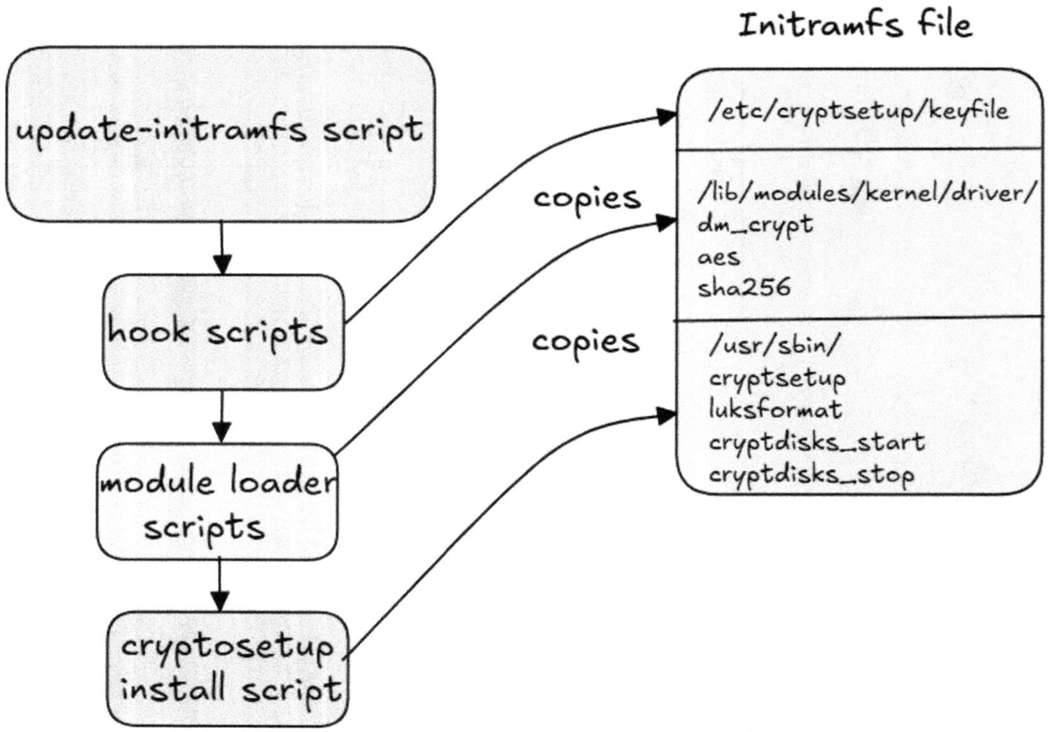


*Figure 34: Initramfs build flow*

## Boot Time

At boot, the system uses **cryptsetup** to open the encrypted partition using the same keyfile generated during build time. This process maps the encrypted partition to a device under /dev/mapper (for example, /dev/mapper/e_root). The mapped device is then mounted as the root (/) filesystem.

The **initramfs bootscript** runs through its stages (init-top, init-premount, local-top, local-premount, local-block, local-bottom, init-bottom) and executes the hook script responsible for unlocking the encrypted partition. Once the partition is opened and mapped, the initramfs mounts it and hands control over to the main init system.

Kernel parameters such as:

```
ROOTPART="/dev/mapper/e_root"
CRYPTDEVICE="/dev/mmcblk0p2:e_root"
```

are passed via cmdline.txt and /etc/default/raspi-firmware to ensure the init system uses the decrypted root device during system startup.

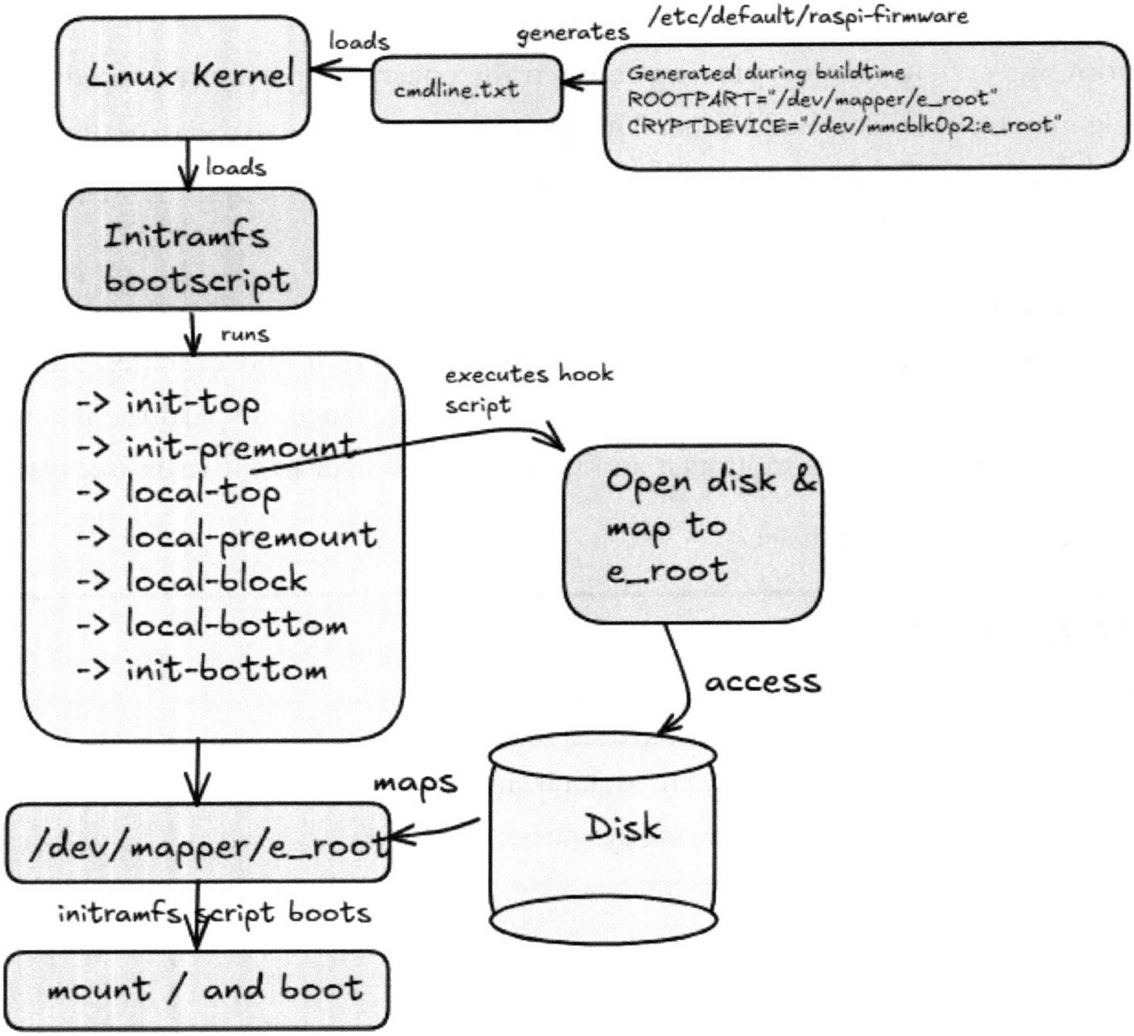


*Figure 35: Boot flow of encrypted fs recipe*

The documentation of the implementation is as follows.

### Creating Keyfile

```
$ openssl rand -hex 32 > keyfile
$ cat keyfile
b876f8a83819316128f752033fa8fb2afeaf43d9d910da951d509872af091
d60
```

The above command generates a random 32-byte (256-bit) key in hexadecimal format and saves it to a file named keyfile.

- **openssl rand**: Generates cryptographically secure random data.
- **-hex**: Outputs the data in hexadecimal format..
- **32**: Specifies the number of bytes to generate (32 bytes = 256 bits).
- **>**: Redirects the output to the file keyfile.

Since each byte is represented by two hexadecimal characters, the resulting file contains 64 hex characters, representing 256 bits of random data.

**Copy to overlay layer**

```
$ mkdir -p overlays/etc/cryptsetup/
$ cp keyfile overlays/etc/cryptsetup/keyfile
```

In ELBE, the overlays directory is used to inject custom files or configurations into the final root filesystem image. These commands:

- Create the necessary directory structure for placing Cryptsetup-related configuration files.
- Copy the keyfile into overlays/etc/cryptsetup/.

As a result, the key will be included in the final system image at /etc/cryptsetup/keyfile, ensuring it is available during early boot for the decryption process.

**Install cryptsetup in InitVM**

The cryptsetup operation during build time is performed within the InitVM but outside the QEMU ARM emulator. This approach is necessary because ELBE does not natively support building encrypted filesystems with cryptsetup. Instead, encryption is manually integrated during the project fine-tuning phase.

```
$ elbe initvm attach/ssh
username:root
Password:root
# apt install cryptsetup
# Ctrl + 5 # This key stroke will exit from the initvm shell
```

**Build the SD card**

Execute the following command to build the encrypted Raspberry Pi image:

```
$ elbe initvm submit   encryption_rpi-trixie.xml   --output downloads
```

This workflow ensures that the final Raspberry Pi image includes all necessary components for the encrypted filesystem with Cryptsetup preconfigured and ready to use.

## 13.4 Recipe encryption_rpi-trixie.xml

```
<?xml version="1.0"?>
<ns0:RootFileSystem
xmlns:ns0="https://www.linutronix.de/projects/Elbe"
xmlns:xsi="http://www.w3.org/2001/XMLSchema-instance"
created="2009-05-20T08:50:56" revision="6"
xsi:schemaLocation="https://www.linutronix.de/projects/Elbe
dbsfed.xsd">
<project>
<name>RaspberryPi-Encrypt</name>
<version>1.0</version>
<description>Raspberry Pi Encrypted image</description>
<buildtype>aarch64</buildtype>
```

```
<mirror>
 <primary_host>ftp.de.debian.org</primary_host>
 <primary_path>/debian</primary_path>
 <primary_proto>http</primary_proto>
 <url-list>
 <url>
   <binary>https://deb.debian.org/debian-security trixie-security main</binary>
   <source>https://deb.debian.org/debian-security trixie-security main</source>
 </url>
 <url>
   <binary>https://deb.debian.org/debian trixie non-free-firmware</binary>
   <source>https://deb.debian.org/debian trixie non-free-firmware</source>
 </url>
 <url>
   <binary>https://deb.debian.org/debian-security trixie-security non-free-firmware</binary>
   <source>https://deb.debian.org/debian-security trixie-security non-free-firmware</source>
 </url>
 </url-list>
</mirror>
<suite>trixie</suite>
</project>
```

```
<target>
<hostname>rpi64</hostname>
<domain/>
<passwd_hashed>$6$bOQ4Sf4rSdl1IfRd$3Hai04jz2OYEW108SZWew
eGO/rGvO65ITthDDtDuaC/8Gpwek/xT4rUvKBkBHFIjTDd6.klFdNJ685k
xgabHh/</passwd_hashed>
<console>serial0,115200</console>
<package>
  <tar>
   <name>rootfs.tgz</name>
  </tar>
</package>
<debootstrap>
  <variant>minbase</variant>
</debootstrap>

<images>
 <msdoshd>
 <name>sdcard.img</name>
 <size>4GB</size>
 <partition>
   <size>128MB</size>
   <label>firmware</label>
 </partition>
 <partition>
   <size>remain</size>
   <label>root</label>
```

```
    <bootable/>
  </partition>
  </msdoshd>
</images>
<fstab>
  <bylabel>
   <label>firmware</label>
   <mountpoint>/boot/firmware</mountpoint>
   <fs>
     <type>vfat</type>
   </fs>
  </bylabel>
  <bylabel>
   <label>root</label>
   <mountpoint>/</mountpoint>
   <fs>
     <type>ext4</type>
   </fs>
  </bylabel>
</fstab>
<project-finetuning>
  <set_packer packer="none">sdcard.img</set_packer>
  <losetup img="sdcard.img">
  <command part="2" nomount="true">
    cryptsetup luksFormat  --type luks2  --cipher xchacha20,aes-
adiantum-plain64 --hash sha256  --iter-time 1000 --key-size 256 --pbkdf
pbkdf2  --key-file keyfile ${ELBE_DEV}
```

```
</command>

<command part="2" nomount="true">
  cryptsetup open ${ELBE_DEV} encrypted_root --key-file keyfile
</command>

<command part="2" nomount="true">
  mkfs.ext4 /dev/mapper/encrypted_root
</command>
<command part="2" nomount="true">
  mount   /dev/mapper/encrypted_root /mnt
</command>
<command part="2" nomount="true">
  pwd
</command>
<command part="2" nomount="true">
  tar -xvf ../rootfs.tgz -C /mnt
</command>
<command part="2" nomount="true">
  umount /mnt
</command>
<command part="2" nomount="true">
  cryptsetup luksClose  encrypted_root
</command>
</losetup>
</project-finetuning>
```

```
<install-recommends/>
<pkg-list>
 <pkg>linux-image-arm64</pkg>
 <pkg>cryptsetup-initramfs</pkg>
 <pkg>firmware-brcm80211</pkg>
 <pkg>raspi-firmware</pkg>
 <pkg>zstd</pkg>
 <pkg>apt-utils</pkg>
 <pkg>systemd</pkg>
 <pkg>systemd-resolved</pkg>
 <pkg>systemd-timesyncd</pkg>
 <pkg>vim-tiny</pkg>
 <pkg>cryptsetup</pkg>
 <pkg>busybox</pkg>
 <pkg>bash</pkg>
 <pkg>dialog</pkg>
 <pkg>openssh-server</pkg>
 <pkg>wpasupplicant</pkg>
 <pkg>iproute2</pkg>
 <pkg>net-tools</pkg>
 <pkg>iputils-ping</pkg>
 <pkg>iw</pkg>
 <pkg>ifupdown</pkg>
 <pkg>bluez</pkg>
 <pkg>bluez-tools</pkg>
 <pkg>rfkill</pkg>
```

```
</pkg-list>
<finetuning>
 <file dst="/etc/initramfs-tools/scripts/local-top/cryptroot" mode="755">
  #!/bin/sh

  PREREQ=""

  prereqs() {
        echo "$PREREQ"
  }

  case "$1" in
    prereqs)
          prereqs
          exit 0
    ;;
  esac

  echo "Running decryptfs script in init-bottom..." &gt; /dev/.decrypt_log
  modprobe ext4
  ROOT_DEV="/dev/mmcblk0p2"
  MAPPER_NAME="encrypted_root"
  KEY_FILE="/etc/cryptsetup/keyfile"
  echo $PWD
  cryptsetup open --type luks2 "$ROOT_DEV" "$MAPPER_NAME" --
key-file "$KEY_FILE"
```

```
 exit 0
</file>
<file dst="/etc/initramfs-tools/hooks/add-keyfile" mode="755">
 #!/bin/sh

 PREREQ=""

 prereqs() {
        echo "$PREREQ"
 }

 case "$1" in
   prereqs)
         prereqs
         exit 0
   ;;
 esac

 if [ -e /etc/cryptsetup/keyfile ]; then
  mkdir -p  "${DESTDIR}/etc/cryptsetup/"
  cp /etc/cryptsetup/keyfile "${DESTDIR}/etc/cryptsetup/keyfile"
  chmod 600 "${DESTDIR}/etc/cryptsetup/keyfile"
 fi

</file>
<file dst="/etc/initramfs-tools/modules" mode="755">
```

```
   dm_crypt
   aes
   sha256
  </file>
  <file dst="/etc/crypttab" mode="755">
   encrypted_root /dev/mmcblk0p2 /etc/cryptsetup/keyfile luks
  </file>
  <file dst="/etc/initramfs-tools/conf.d/cryptsetup" mode="755">
   CRYPTSETUP=y
  </file>
  <file dst="/etc/systemd/network/25-wlan0.network" mode="644">
   [Match]
   Name=wlan0

   [Network]
   DHCP=yes

  </file>
  <file dst="/etc/wpa_supplicant/wpa_supplicant-wlan0.conf"
mode="600">
   ctrl_interface=DIR=/var/run/wpa_supplicant GROUP=netdev
   update_config=1
   country=US

   network={
   ssid="SomeSSID"
   psk=" SomeKey"
```

```
  }
 </file>
 <file dst="/etc/default/raspi-firmware" append="true">
  ROOTPART="/dev/mapper/encrypted_root"
  CRYPTDEVICE="/dev/mmcblk0p2:encrypted_root"
  KERNEL_ARCH="arm64"
 </file>
 <file dst="/etc/default/raspi-extra-cmdline" append="true">
  init=/usr/lib/systemd/systemd
 </file>
 <command>update-initramfs -u -k all</command>
 <command>systemctl enable
wpa_supplicant@wlan0.service</command>
 <t2b_cp path="/etc/cryptsetup/keyfile">keyfile</t2b_cp>
</finetuning>
</target>
<archivedir>overlays/</archivedir>
</ns0:RootFileSystem>
```

## 13.5 Recipe Explanation

### In project-finetuning

```
$ cryptsetup luksFormat  --type luks2  --cipher xchacha20,aes-adiantum-
plain64 --hash sha256  --iter-time 1000 --key-size 256 --pbkdf pbkdf2  --
key-file keyfile ${ELBE_DEV}
```

**cryptsetup luksFormat**

Initializes the block device with LUKS encryption, erasing existing data and preparing it for secure use.

**--type luks2**

Uses the modern LUKS2 format, which offers improved metadata handling and flexibility compared to LUKS1.

**--cipher xchacha20,aes-adiantum-plain64**

Specifies encryption ciphers: Sets the encryption cipher.

- xchacha20: High-performance stream cipher suitable for CPUs without AES acceleration.
- aes-adiantum-plain64: Optimized for embedded systems such as ARM boards.

**--hash sha256**

Hash function for key derivation, ensuring strong security

**--iter-time 1000**

Key derivation runs for ~1000 ms, making brute-force attacks more expensive.

**--key-size 256**

Sets encryption key size to 256 bits for strong security.

**--pbkdf pbkdf2**

Specifies the Password-Based Key Derivation Function (PBKDF) to be used. PBKDF2 is a standard and widely supported method, though newer options such as Argon2 may be more secure in some contexts.

**--key-file keyfile**

Uses the generated keyfile instead of prompting for a password.

**${ELBE_DEV}**

Represents the target block device (e.g., /dev/mmcblk0p2

```
$ cryptsetup open ${ELBE_DEV} encrypted_root –key-file keyfile
```

Unlocks the encrypted device ${ELBE_DEV} using the key stored in keyfile.Maps the decrypted content to a new virtual block device at /dev/mapper/encrypted_root, making it accessible for formatting and file operations.

```
$ mkfs.ext4 /dev/mapper/encrypted_root
```

Creates an ext4 filesystem on the decrypted (mapped) device

```
$ mount   /dev/mapper/encrypted_root /mnt
```

Mounts the newly created ext4 filesystem at /mnt.

```
$ tar -xvf ../rootfs.tgz -C /mnt
$ umount /mnt
```

Extracts the prebuilt root filesystem archive (rootfs.tgz) into the mounted target directory. Once the extraction is complete, the partition is unmounted to ensure all data is properly written and the filesystem is safely closed.

**Note:** While rootfs.tgz is originally produced as an output of the build process via the <tar><name>rootfs.tgz</name></tar> directive, it also plays a key role in preparing the encrypted filesystem specifically, it is used to populate the partition after formatting and mounting, before the volume is closed again

```
$ cryptsetup luksClose  encrypted_root
```

Closes the encrypted mapping created earlier, this securely detaches /dev/mapper/encrypted_root

## Initramfs and Boot Configuration

### /etc/initramfs-tools/conf.d/cryptsetup

```
<file dst="/etc/initramfs-tools/conf.d/cryptsetup" mode="755">
CRYPTSETUP=y
</file>
```

Setting **CRYPTSETUP=y** instructs the initramfs to include cryptsetup during boot. This enables the system to decrypt encrypted partitions (such as the root filesystem) before mounting them.

### /etc/default/raspi-firmware

```
<file dst="/etc/default/raspi-firmware" append="true" >
        ROOTPART="/dev/mapper/encrypted_root"
        CRYPTDEVICE="/dev/mmcblk0p2:encrypted_root"
        KERNEL_ARCH="arm64"
</file>
```

This configuration appends critical boot parameters:

### ROOTPART="/dev/mapper/encrypted_root":

Specifies the decrypted root filesystem device created by cryptsetup open.

### CRYPTDEVICE="/dev/mmcblk0p2:encrypted_root":

Tells initramfs which encrypted block device to unlock. The format is <device>:<mapped_name>.

### /etc/initramfs-tools/hooks/add-keyfile

```
if [ -e /etc/cryptsetup/keyfile ]; then
   mkdir -p  "${DESTDIR}/etc/cryptsetup/"
```

```
    cp /etc/cryptsetup/keyfile "${DESTDIR}/etc/cryptsetup/keyfile"
    chmod 600 "${DESTDIR}/etc/cryptsetup/keyfile"
fi
```

This hook ensures the keyfile is included in the initramfs image for use during early boot.

**<t2b_cp path="/etc/cryptsetup/keyfile">keyfile</t2b_cp>**

The keyfile is initially passed to the InitVM build process via the overlay folder, where it becomes part of the root filesystem and gets packaged into rootfs.tgz. However, after this step, the keyfile is no longer directly accessible in the build environment. Since the actual encryption of the disk occurs later during the **project-finetuning phase**, the keyfile needs to be available at that point. To ensure this, it is copied from the target image back into the build directory using t2b_cp during the rootfs.tgz creation process.

**/etc/initramfs-tools/modules:**

```
<file dst="/etc/initramfs-tools/modules" mode="755">
  dm_crypt
  aes
  sha256
</file>
```

These are names of kernel modules that are necessary for disk encryption:

- **dm_crypt**: Core module for device-mapper-based encryption (used by LUKS).
- **aes**: Provides AES encryption algorithm.
- **sha256**: Provides SHA-256 hashing for key derivation.

Including these modules ensures initramfs can unlock encrypted partitions during early boot.

## Summary

This chapter addressed security-critical edge deployments by demonstrating how to build a Raspberry Pi image with full-disk encryption using LUKS and dm-crypt. Framed around a real-world healthcare use case, it showed how Myriadex Shield designed a secure storage solution for sensitive medical data collected by Quantara Lifecode's patient monitoring devices. Using ELBE, the implementation created a dual-partition image consisting of an unencrypted FAT boot partition and an encrypted EXT4 root filesystem, with encryption integrated during the project finetuning phase. The chapter provided a detailed walkthrough of key generation, LUKS2 configuration, encrypted partition setup, and root filesystem population, followed by an in-depth explanation of initramfs customization to support early-boot decryption. By embedding cryptsetup tools, kernel modules, and a keyfile into initramfs and configuring the Raspberry Pi boot parameters accordingly, the system reliably unlocks and mounts the encrypted root filesystem at boot. The resulting image delivers strong data protection with minimal performance overhead, making it suitable for regulatory-compliant, security-sensitive Raspberry Pi deployments.

## Further Reading and Resources

Readers seeking deeper insight into disk encryption concepts and best practices can consult the official cryptsetup and LUKS documentation, which explains LUKS2 metadata, cipher selection, key derivation functions, and security trade-offs in detail. The Linux kernel documentation on dm-crypt and device-mapper provides valuable background on the underlying encryption mechanisms used during boot. For early-boot customization and initramfs behavior, the Debian initramfs-tools documentation offers comprehensive guidance on hooks, scripts, and module inclusion. Additional context on Raspberry Pi boot configuration, kernel parameters, and firmware behavior can be found in the Raspberry Pi documentation, while the ELBE project documentation covers advanced image customization workflows and project-finetuning techniques relevant to encrypted filesystem builds.

# 14 Podman

**Abstract:** This chapter explores container runtime integration with Podman (rootless alternative to Docker) on Raspberry Pi. It covers company requirements, implementation, the podman-trixie.xml recipe plus an rpi.xml variant, and explanations of configuration for secure, daemonless container support in embedded contexts.

## 14.1 Company Introduction

**Rootfx** is a trailblazer in IoT and edge computing, known for delivering cutting-edge solutions tailored for compact devices such as Raspberry Pi. Their expertise lies in modular, scalable systems that meet the specific needs of industries ranging from agriculture to urban infrastructure.

## 14.2 Customer Requirements

Hyperfarms, a forward-thinking hydroponics startup, is developing IoT farming systems to monitor nutrient levels, weather conditions, and crop growth across distributed farms.

Their deployment involves Raspberry Pi devices installed in remote field locations with strict constraints on resources. To achieve their goals, Hyperfarms needs:

- A lightweight container runtime compatible with Raspberry Pi.
- A container image capable of processing real-time sensor and running region-specific machine learning models.
- Compatibility with low-resource environments where power and memory usage must be minimized.

### Company Response

Rootfx assigns Sumona to design the solution. She uses ELBE to build a custom Podman-ready image for Raspberry Pi, ensuring:

- **Lightweight and Secure Design**: A Debian base optimized for Podman.
- **Dynamic Configurability**: Region-specific overlays for hardware and sensor variations
- **Ease of Deployment**: Compatibility with both Podman and Docker runtimes.

### Why Podman Was Chosen

The decision to use Podman over Docker was strategic

1. **Daemonless Operation**: No central daemon, reducing overhead on resource-constrained devices.
2. **Rootless Containers**: Enhances security by allowing non-root users to run containers.
3. **Systemd Integration**: Simplifies container management as system services.

### Outcome

The Podman-ready image, provides Hyperfarms with:

- **Seamless Deployment**: Lightweight, secure containers running efficiently on Raspberry Pi.

- **Improved Security**: Rootless operation reduces vulnerabilities in remote environments.

Hyperfarm rolls out its solution across hundreds of farms, enhancing crop health monitoring and yielding significant improvements in efficiency.

## 14.3 Implementation

The building of a container-based Raspberry Pi image is carried out in two phases. In the first round, the container itself is built using the ELBE. The container is a root filesystem in a tarball format (.tgz), which can be imported using the docker or podman command line interfaces. In the second build phase, the compressed container image file is copied to the overlay folder of the Raspberry Pi XML recipe. The recipe is configured to import the content, which is under the folder overlay, using the command elbe chg_archive preprocess.xml overlays. It can also be done using the xml tag archivedir, and point to the path overlays, as done in the previous recipe.

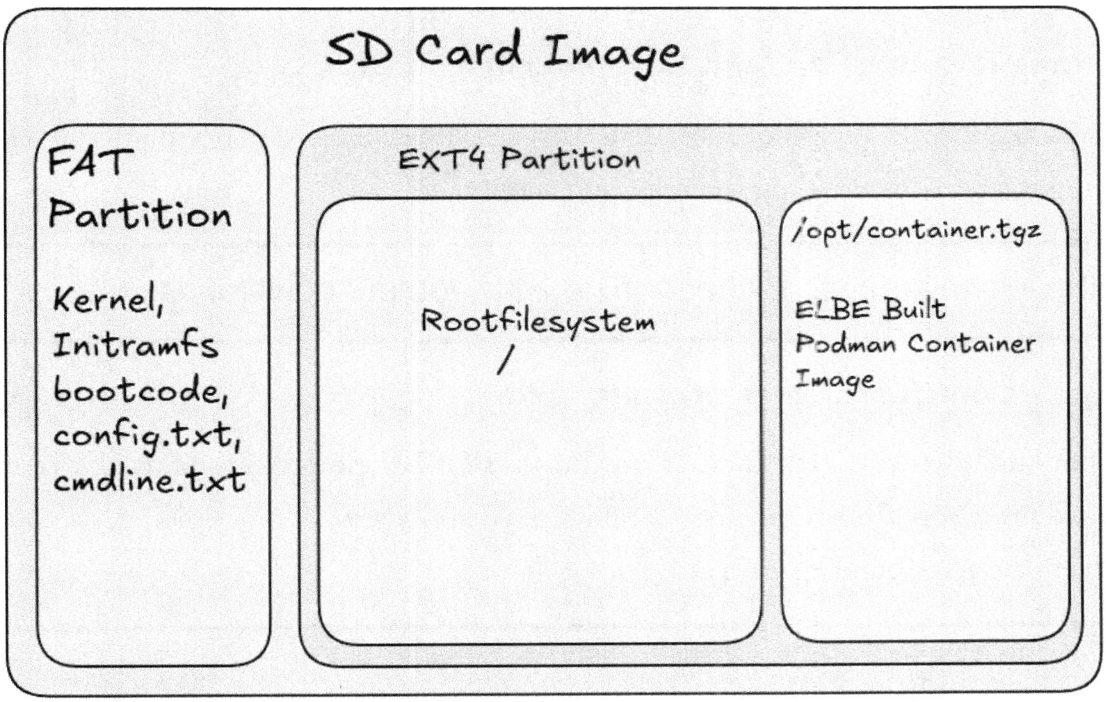


*Figure 36: SD card with Podman Container*

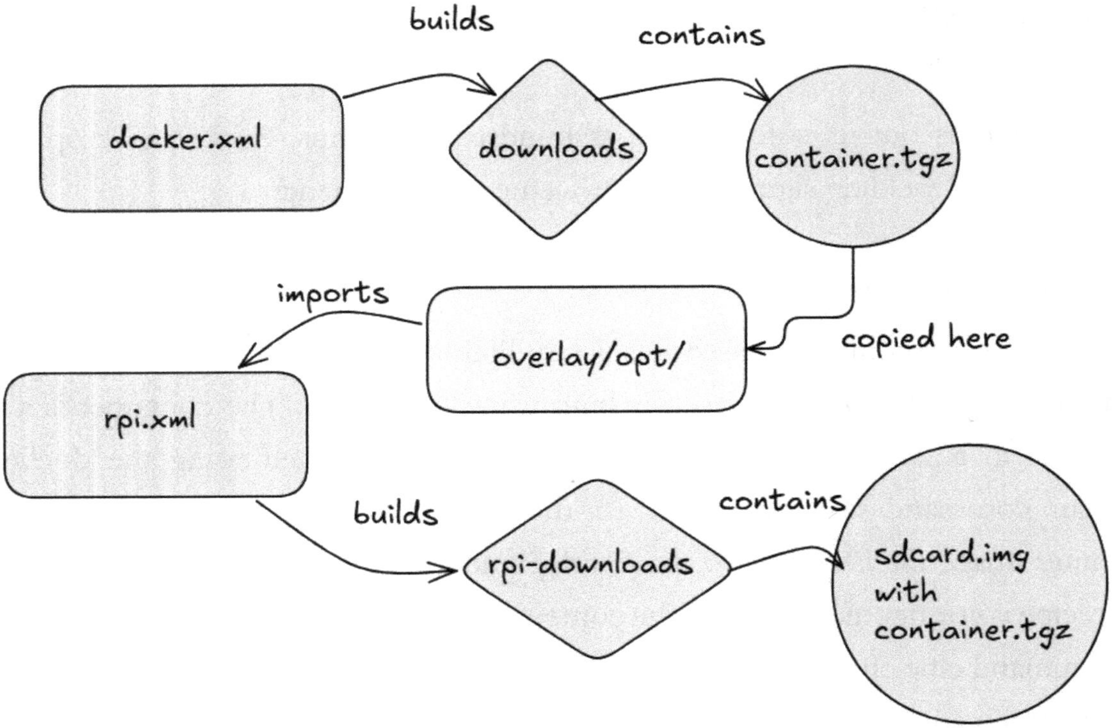


*Figure 37: Podman recipe build workflow*

## Preparing Raspberry Pi Build Environment with ELBE

Sumona begins by creating an ELBE project, uploading the podman.xml recipe, building it, and downloading the resulting output:

```
$ elbe initvm submit   podman-trixie.xml  --output downloads
```

## Copying Container archive to overlay folder

The container.tgz file generated from the first ELBE project contains the minimal userland necessary for running the containerized application. It is copied to the overlay folder of the next build rpi.xml

```
$ mkdir -p overlays/opt
$ cp rpi-downloads/container.tgz overlays/opt/
```

### Creating Raspberry Pi Image with Embedded Container

```
$ elbe initvm submit   rpi.xml  --output  rpi-downloads
```

After downloading the image, it is flashed to Raspberry Pi and logged in and in serial console

### Running Podman Commands

Import the container tarball and run it

```
$ podman  import /opt/container.tgz container
$ podman run -it --user $(id -u):$(id -g) -w /workspace -v $
"$PWD:/workspace" --hostname container container bash
```

Pull and run a Python image

```
$ podman pull python:3.11
$ podman run -it python:3.11
```

## 14.4 Recipe podman-trixie.xml

```
<ns0:RootFileSystem
xmlns:ns0="https://www.linutronix.de/projects/Elbe"
xmlns:xsi="http://www.w3.org/2001/XMLSchema-instance"
created="2009-05-20T08:50:56" revision="6"
xsi:schemaLocation="https://www.linutronix.de/projects/Elbe
dbsfed.xsd">
<project>
 <name>RaspberryPi-Container</name>
 <version>1.0</version>
```

```
 <description>
    RaspberryPi  Container
 </description>
 <buildtype>aarch64</buildtype>
 <mirror>
  <primary_host>deb.debian.org</primary_host>
  <primary_path>/debian</primary_path>
  <primary_proto>http</primary_proto>
  <url-list>
   <url>
    <binary>https://deb.debian.org/debian-security trixie-security
main</binary>
    <source>https://deb.debian.org/debian-security trixie-security
main</source>
   </url>
  </url-list>
 </mirror>
 <suite>trixie</suite>
</project>
<target>
<hostname>crossbuildenv</hostname>
<domain>arm64</domain>

<passwd_hashed>$6$bOQ4Sf4rSdI1IfRd$3Hai04jz2OYEW108SZWew
eGO/rGvO65ITthDDtDuaC/8Gpwek/xT4rUvKBkBHFIjTDd6.kIFdNJ685k
xgabHh/</passwd_hashed>
```

```
<debootstrap>
    <variant>minbase</variant>
</debootstrap>
<package>
  <tar>
    <name>container.tgz</name>
  </tar>
</package>
<finetuning>
  <mkdir>/workspace</mkdir>
  <adduser
passwd_hashed="$6$bOQ4Sf4rSdI1IfRd$3Hai04jz2OYEW108SZWew
eGO/rGvO65ITthDDtDuaC/8Gpwek/xT4rUvKBkBHFIjTDd6.klFdNJ685k
xgabHh/" shell="/bin/bash" uid="1000"
create_group="true">u1</adduser>
</finetuning>

<pkg-list>
 <pkg>bash</pkg>
 <pkg>bc</pkg>
 <pkg>bison</pkg>
 <pkg>flex</pkg>
</pkg-list>
</target>
</ns0:RootFileSystem>
```

## 14.5 Recipe rpi.xml

```
<?xml version="1.0"?>
<ns0:RootFileSystem
xmlns:ns0="https://www.linutronix.de/projects/Elbe"
xmlns:xsi="http://www.w3.org/2001/XMLSchema-instance"
created="2009-05-20T08:50:56" revision="6"
xsi:schemaLocation="https://www.linutronix.de/projects/Elbe
dbsfed.xsd">
 <project>
 <name>RaspberryPi-DockerInside</name>
 <version>1.0</version>
 <description>
  Raspberry Pi Boot image with Docker Inside
 </description>
 <buildtype>aarch64</buildtype>
 <mirror>
  <primary_host>ftp.de.debian.org</primary_host>
  <primary_path>/debian</primary_path>
  <primary_proto>http</primary_proto>
  <url-list>
   <url>
    <binary>https://deb.debian.org/debian-security bookworm-security
main</binary>
    <source>https://deb.debian.org/debian-security bookworm-security
main</source>
   </url>
   <url>
```

```
    <binary>https://deb.debian.org/debian bookworm non-free-
firmware</binary>
    <source>https://deb.debian.org/debian bookworm non-free-
firmware</source>
   </url>
   <url>
    <binary>https://deb.debian.org/debian-security bookworm-security
non-free-firmware</binary>
    <source>https://deb.debian.org/debian-security bookworm-security
non-free-firmware</source>
   </url>
   </url-list>
  </mirror>
  <suite>bookworm</suite>
  </project>
  <target>
  <hostname>rpi64</hostname>
  <domain/>

<passwd_hashed>$6$bOQ4Sf4rSdI1IfRd$3Hai04jz2OYEW108SZWew
eGO/rGvO65ITthDDtDuaC/8Gpwek/xT4rUvKBkBHFIjTDd6.kIFdNJ685k
xgabHh/</passwd_hashed>
  <console>serial0,115200</console>
  <package>
   <tar>
    <name>image.tgz</name>
   </tar>
```

```
</package>
<debootstrap>
  <variant>minbase</variant>
</debootstrap>
<images>
<msdoshd>
  <name>sdcard.img</name>
  <size>7GB</size>
  <partition>
    <size>256MB</size>
    <label>firmware</label>
  </partition>
  <partition>
    <size>remain</size>
    <label>root</label>
    <bootable/>
  </partition>
</msdoshd>
</images>
<fstab>
 <bylabel>
  <label>firmware</label>
  <mountpoint>/boot/firmware</mountpoint>
  <fs>
    <type>vfat</type>
  </fs>
```

```
  </bylabel>
  <bylabel>
   <label>root</label>
   <mountpoint>/</mountpoint>
   <fs>
     <type>ext4</type>
     <fs-finetuning>
       <device-command>tune2fs -O ^64bit,^metadata_csum -i 0
{device}</device-command>
     </fs-finetuning>
   </fs>
  </bylabel>
 </fstab>
 <install-recommends/>
 <pkg-list>
  <pkg>linux-image-arm64</pkg>
  <pkg>kmod</pkg>
  <pkg>initramfs-tools</pkg>
  <pkg>firmware-brcm80211</pkg>
  <pkg>raspi-firmware</pkg>
  <pkg>zstd</pkg>
  <pkg>apt-utils</pkg>
  <pkg>systemd</pkg>
  <pkg>systemd-networkd</pkg>
  <pkg>vim-tiny</pkg>
  <pkg>busybox</pkg>
  <pkg>bash</pkg>
```

```
  <pkg>dialog</pkg>
  <pkg>openssh-server</pkg>
  <pkg>wpasupplicant</pkg>
  <pkg>iproute2</pkg>
  <pkg>net-tools</pkg>
  <pkg>iputils-ping</pkg>
  <pkg>iw</pkg>
  <pkg>ifupdown</pkg>
  <pkg>bluez</pkg>
  <pkg>bluez-tools</pkg>
  <pkg>rfkill</pkg>
  <pkg>podman</pkg>
  <pkg>iptables</pkg>
  <pkg>ca-certificates</pkg>
</pkg-list>
<project-finetuning>
  <set_packer packer="tarxz">sdcard.img</set_packer>
</project-finetuning>
<finetuning>
 <file dst="/etc/systemd/network/25-wlan0.network" mode="644">
   [Match]
   Name=wlan0

   [Network]
   DHCP=yes


     </file>
```

```
  <file dst="/etc/wpa_supplicant/wpa_supplicant-wlan0.conf"
mode="600">
    ctrl_interface=DIR=/var/run/wpa_supplicant GROUP=netdev
    update_config=1
    country=US

    network={
      ssid=" SomeSSID"
      psk=" SomeKey"
    }
  </file>
  <file dst="/etc/default/raspi-firmware" append="true">
    ROOTPART="LABEL=root"
    KERNEL_ARCH="arm64"
  </file>
  <file dst="/etc/default/raspi-extra-cmdline" append="true">
    init=/usr/lib/systemd/systemd
  </file>
  <command>update-initramfs -u -k all</command>
  <command>rpi-eeprom-update</command>
  <command>systemctl enable
wpa_supplicant@wlan0.service</command>
  <command>systemctl enable systemd-networkd</command>
 </finetuning>
 </target>
</ns0:RootFileSystem>
```

**XML Description**

Both XML recipes follow ELBE's schema to ensure predictable and reproducible builds for the base container image and the full Raspberry Pi bootable image with an integrated Podman runtime. The first recipe creates a minimal container image packaged as a .tgz tarball, which can be imported using Podman or Docker. This tarball is then copied into the overlay directory of the second recipe, which builds a Raspberry Pi image and embeds the container under /opt/container.tgz. The integration process uses either the elbe chg_archive preprocess.xml overlays command or the <archivedir> tag to include overlay content. This approach provides a modular, secure, and efficient workflow for deploying containerized applications on resource-constrained Raspberry Pi devices without repeating structural details already covered in earlier examples.

## Summary

This chapter explored the integration of Podman as a lightweight, secure container runtime for Raspberry Pi–based edge deployments. Using a real-world IoT farming scenario, it demonstrated how Rootfx designed a Podman-ready system image to meet Hyperfarms' requirements for low resource usage, strong security, and flexible deployment across remote environments. The implementation followed a two-stage ELBE workflow in which a minimal container image was first built as a tarball and then embedded into a Raspberry Pi bootable image via overlays. By selecting Podman for its daemonless architecture, rootless container support, and native systemd integration, the resulting system enables secure container execution without the overhead of a central daemon. The chapter detailed how container images are imported, executed, and managed directly on the device, providing a modular and efficient foundation for running sensor processing and machine learning workloads on resource-constrained Raspberry Pi hardware.

## 15 Further Reading and Resources

Readers interested in Podman's architecture and security model can consult the official Podman documentation, which covers rootless containers, systemd integration, and compatibility with Docker workflows. Additional background on container standards and image formats is available through the Open Container Initiative (OCI) specifications, which underpin Podman and other modern runtimes. For optimizing container performance on ARM and embedded platforms, the Debian and Raspberry Pi documentation offer guidance on resource management and kernel configuration.

# 15 Raspberry Pi Custom Kernel

**Abstract:** For performance or hardware-specific needs, this chapter teaches building images with a custom-compiled Linux kernel. It details requirements, implementation, multiple recipes (raspberrypi.xml, raspberrypi-kernel.xml), and explanations of kernel patching, configuration, and integration into ELBE builds.

## 15.1 Company Introduction

**Crythonis Vectra** is a cutting-edge embedded solutions company specializing in optimizing Linux-based environments for single-board computers. Their team of experts designs custom firmware and operating systems for industrial automation, robotics, and edge computing applications.

## 15.2 Customer Requirements

**Nimbusyn FlowTech**, a drone analytics company, is developing a fleet of Raspberry Pi 5-powered drones for real-time environmental monitoring. These drones require a highly optimized Linux image with strict performance and security requirements.

Their key requirements include:

- **A stable and lightweight Debian-based root filesystem** to maintain compatibility with existing tools.

- **Two approaches for evaluation**
    1. **A stock Raspberry Pi kernel** from Raspberry Pi OS archive for quick deployment and standard support.
    2. **A fully custom kernel** with only necessary modules to enhance performance and security.

**Company Response**

**Ria**, a senior embedded engineer at **Crythonis Vectra**, takes on the challenge and decides to create two separate Raspberry Pi 5 images:

1. **Stock Kernel Approach**
    - **Ria** sources the **prebuilt Raspberry Pi kernel** from the official Raspberry Pi OS archive.
    - She pairs it with a clean **Debian root filesystem**, ensuring quick setup and compatibility.
    - This approach offers **out-of-the-box stability and mainstream driver support**.
2. **Custom Kernel Approach**
    - Compiles a minimal, performance-tuned Linux kernel with essential drivers only.
    - Uses a Debian root filesystem with tailored optimizations for security and speed.

**Note:** At the time of writing, Debian Trixie had not yet been released, and official Raspberry Pi 5 support was limited. Now that Trixie is available with native Raspberry Pi 5 support, the stock kernel approach may suffice for many users. Nevertheless, the custom kernel method remains valuable for performance tuning, security hardening, and as a reference for future hardware that may not yet be fully supported.

## 15.3 Implementation

The documentation of the implementation is as follows.

```
$ elbe initvm submit   raspberrypi.xml  --output  rpi-downloads
```

## 15.4 Recipe raspberrypi.xml

```
<ns0:RootFileSystem
xmlns:ns0="https://www.linutronix.de/projects/Elbe"
xmlns:xsi="http://www.w3.org/2001/XMLSchema-instance"
created="2009-05-20T08:50:56" revision="6"
xsi:schemaLocation="https://www.linutronix.de/projects/Elbe
dbsfed.xsd">
<project>
 <name>rpi-image</name>
 <version>1.0</version>
 <description>
    Raspberry Pi 5 Boot image
 </description>
 <buildtype>aarch64</buildtype>
 <mirror>
  <primary_host>ftp.de.debian.org</primary_host>
  <primary_path>/debian</primary_path>
  <primary_proto>http</primary_proto>
  <url-list>
   <url>
      <binary>https://deb.debian.org/debian-security bookworm-security
main</binary>
```

```
      <source>https://deb.debian.org/debian-security bookworm-security main</source>
   </url>
   <url>
      <binary>https://deb.debian.org/debian bookworm non-free-firmware</binary>
      <source>https://deb.debian.org/debian bookworm non-free-firmware</source>
   </url>
   <url>
      <binary>https://deb.debian.org/debian-security bookworm-security non-free-firmware</binary>
      <source>https://deb.debian.org/debian-security bookworm-security non-free-firmware</source>
   </url>
   <url>
      <binary>https://archive.raspberrypi.org/debian bookworm main</binary>
      <source>https://archive.raspberrypi.org/debian bookworm main</source>
      <raw-key>
            -----BEGIN PGP PUBLIC KEY BLOCK-----
            Version: GnuPG v1.4.12 (GNU/Linux)
mQENBE/d7o8BCACrwqQacGJfn3tnMzGui6mv2lLxYbsOuy/+U4rqMmGEuo3h9m92
m++/7s3K3L0zWopdhMVcgg6Nt9gcjzqN1c0gy55L/g==
            =mNSj
```

```
            -----END PGP PUBLIC KEY BLOCK-----
      </raw-key>
    </url>

  </url-list>
 </mirror>

    <suite>bookworm</suite>
</project>
<target>
 <hostname>rpi64</hostname>
 <domain></domain>

<passwd_hashed>$6$bOQ4Sf4rSdl1IfRd$3Hai04jz2OYEW108SZWew
eGO/rGvO65ITthDDtDuaC/8Gpwek/xT4rUvKBkBHFIjTDd6.klFdNJ685k
xgabHh/</passwd_hashed>
 <console>serial0,115200</console>
 <package>
    <tar>
       <name>image.tgz</name>
    </tar>
 </package>
 <debootstrap >
    <variant >minbase</variant>
 </debootstrap>

 <images>
```

```
 <msdoshd>
 <name>sdcard.img</name>
 <size>3GB</size>
 <partition>
    <size>556MB</size>
    <label>firmware</label>
 </partition>
 <partition>
    <size>remain</size>
    <label>root</label>
    <bootable/>
 </partition>
 </msdoshd>
</images>
<fstab>
 <bylabel>
  <label>firmware</label>
  <mountpoint>/boot/firmware</mountpoint>
  <fs>
     <type>vfat</type>
  </fs>
 </bylabel>
 <bylabel>
   <label>root</label>
   <mountpoint>/</mountpoint>
   <fs>
      <type>ext4</type>
```

```
        <fs-finetuning>
            <device-command>tune2fs -O ^64bit,^metadata_csum -i 0
{device}</device-command>
        </fs-finetuning>
    </fs>

  </bylabel>
 </fstab>
<install-recommends/>
<pkg-list>
   <pkg>linux-image-6.6.51+rpt-rpi-v8</pkg>
   <pkg>kmod</pkg>
   <pkg>linux-base</pkg>
   <pkg>zstd</pkg>
   <pkg>apt-utils</pkg>
   <pkg>systemd</pkg>
   <pkg>systemd-resolved</pkg>
   <pkg>systemd-timesyncd</pkg>
   <pkg>vim-tiny</pkg>
   <pkg>busybox</pkg>
   <pkg>bash</pkg>
   <pkg>dialog</pkg>
   <pkg>openssh-server</pkg>
   <pkg>wpasupplicant</pkg>
   <pkg>iproute2</pkg>
   <pkg>net-tools</pkg>
   <pkg>iputils-ping</pkg>
```

```
    <pkg>iw</pkg>
    <pkg>ifupdown</pkg>
    <pkg>bluez</pkg>
    <pkg>bluez-tools</pkg>
    <pkg>rfkill</pkg>
    <pkg>avahi-daemon</pkg>
    <pkg>avahi-utils</pkg>
    <pkg>wireless-tools</pkg>
    <pkg>pciutils</pkg>
    <pkg>usbutils</pkg>

    <pkg>raspberrypi-archive-keyring</pkg>
    <pkg>raspi-config</pkg>
    <pkg>raspi-firmware</pkg>
    <pkg>raspi-gpio</pkg>
    <pkg>raspi-utils-core</pkg>
    <pkg>raspi-utils-dt</pkg>
    <pkg>raspi-utils-eeprom</pkg>
    <pkg>raspi-utils-otp</pkg>
    <pkg>raspi-utils</pkg>
    <pkg>firmware-realtek</pkg>
    <pkg>raspberrypi-net-mods</pkg>
    <pkg>raspberrypi-sys-mods</pkg>
    <pkg>raspberrypi-ui-mods</pkg>
    <pkg>firmware-brcm80211</pkg>
    <pkg>initramfs-tools-core</pkg>
    <pkg>initramfs-tools</pkg>
</pkg-list>
```

```
<project-finetuning>
   <set_packer packer="tarxz">sdcard.img</set_packer>
</project-finetuning>
<finetuning>
 <file dst="/etc/systemd/network/25-wlan0.network" mode="644">
    [Match]
    Name=wlan0

    [Network]
    DHCP=yes

  </file>
 <file dst="/etc/wpa_supplicant/wpa_supplicant-wlan0.conf"
mode="600">
  ctrl_interface=DIR=/var/run/wpa_supplicant GROUP=netdev
  update_config=1
  country=US

  network={
     ssid=" SomeSSID"
     psk=" SomeKey"
  }
 </file>
 <file dst="/etc/default/raspi-firmware" append="true" >
 ROOTPART="LABEL=root"
 KERNEL_ARCH="arm64"
 </file>
 <file dst="/boot/firmware/cmdline.txt" mode="755">
```

```
 earlyprintk console=ttyAMA0,115200 console=tty1
root=/dev/mmcblk0p2 rootfstype=ext4 fsck.repair=yes rootwait
cfg80211.ieee80211_regdom=GB
 </file>
 <file dst="/boot/firmware/config.txt" mode="755">
  enable_uart=1
  arm_64bit=1
  dtoverlay=disable-bt
  dtoverlay=uart0
  dtparam=uart0
  auto_initramfs=1
  kernel=vmlinuz-6.6.51+rpt-rpi-v8
 </file>

 <file dst="/etc/default/raspi-extra-cmdline" append="true">
 init=/usr/lib/systemd/systemd
 </file>

 <command>update-initramfs -u -k all</command>
 <command>systemctl enable
wpa_supplicant@wlan0.service</command>
 <command>systemctl enable systemd-networkd</command>
 <command>systemctl enable systemd-resolved</command>
 <command>systemctl enable systemd-timesyncd</command>
 <command>systemctl enable avahi-daemon</command>
</finetuning>
</target>
</ns0:RootFileSystem>
```

## 15.5 Recipe Explanation

The key points requiring explanation are:

- raw-key
- stock kernel

### Raw-key

By default, ELBE requires mirror repositories to be GPG-signed to ensure the authenticity and integrity of all packages. This verification is handled by debootstrap, which first looks for the InRelease file in the repository root. InRelease combines and signs metadata from Release and Release.gpg and is preferred when available. If not found, debootstrap falls back to using separate Release and Release.gpg files.

In the case of Raspberry Pi official Debian repository (https://archive.raspberrypi.org/debian/), neither InRelease nor Release is provided. Instead, the GPG key is available as raspberrypi.gpg.key. To enable ELBE to authenticate packages from this repository, the contents of raspberrypi.gpg.key must be copied verbatim into the <raw-key> block.

Note: For testing purposes, you can use the <option>trusted=yes</option> tag to disable authentication. However, this should never be used in production environments.

### Raspberry Pi stock kernel

To build a bootable image, you must specify the appropriate kernel package. Without it, ELBE can still generate the image successfully, but it will not be bootable.

For standard Debian systems, the kernel package name is typically linux-image-arm64, which is a meta-package pointing to the latest kernel. For Raspberry Pi repository, the equivalent is raspberrypi-kernel. This package corresponds to a specific kernel version, even though newer versions may exist in the repository.

To identify the latest available kernel package, use the following commands:

```
$ wget
https://archive.raspberrypi.org/debian/dists/bookworm/main/binary-
arm64/Packages.gz
```

Extract the packages with name linux-image

```
$ zgrep linux-image  Packages.gz
```

This will list all available kernel packages in the repository. Choose the latest version for your build.

**A Raspberry Pi custom kernel Implementation:**

**Compiler installation**

Install the cross-compiler and required build tools

```
$ sudo apt install crossbuild-essential-arm64 bc bison flex libssl-dev
make libc6-dev libncurses5-dev
```

**Fetch Kernel Source**

```
$ git clone --depth=1 https://github.com/raspberrypi/linux
```

**Configure and compile**

Navigate to the kernel source directory and configure for Raspberry Pi 5:

```
$ cd linux
$ KERNEL=kernel_2712
$ make ARCH=arm64 CROSS_COMPILE=aarch64-linux-gnu-
bcm2712_defconfig
```

```
$ make -j4 ARCH=arm64 CROSS_COMPILE=aarch64-linux-gnu-
Image modules dtbs
```

**Create Debian Package.**

```
$ make ARCH=arm64 CROSS_COMPILE=aarch64-linux-gnu- -
j4  LOCALVERSION=-v8 KDEB_PKGVERSION=1-1 deb-pkg
```

This generates Debian packages in the parent directory, including:

**linux-image-6.6.78-v8-16k-v8_1-1_arm64.deb.**

```
$ dpkg --info linux-image-6.6.78-v8-16k-v8_1-1_arm64.deb
 new Debian package, version 2.0.
 size 30366664 bytes: control archive=56792 bytes.
    372 bytes,    12 lines      control
  231110 bytes,  2225 lines      md5sums
     304 bytes,    12 lines   *  postinst
     300 bytes,    12 lines   *  postrm
     302 bytes,    12 lines   *  preinst
     298 bytes,    12 lines   *  prerm
 Package: linux-image-6.6.78-v8-16k-v8
```

**Custom Kernel Integration with ELBE**

Ria begins by ensuring a clean state for the new project:

```
$ elbe initvm stop
$ elbe initvm start
```

**Best Practice**: Stopping the InitVM before starting a new build ensures a clean environment, avoiding conflicts, leftover data from previous builds, or time synchronization issues.

### Creating the ELBE Project

With the environment ready, Ria initializes a new project:

```
$ ID=$(elbe control create_project)
```

### Preprocessing and Configuring the Project

```
$ elbe preprocess  raspberrypi-kernel.xml
$ elbe control set_xml $ID preprocess.xml
```

Ria uploads the tailored XML configuration file for Raspberry Pi 5 image, which includes network capabilities, file-sharing support, and development tools

### Uploading Custom Kernel Package

```
$ elbe prjrepo upload_pkg  $ID ~/build/linux-image-6.6.66-v8-16k-2712_1-1_arm64.deb
```

This command uploads the custom kernel Debian package built earlier into the ELBE project repository.

### Building and Retrieving the Image

```
$ elbe control build $ID
$ elbe control wait_busy $ID
$ elbe control get_files $ID --output downloads
```

After the build completes, Ria retrieves all generated files into the downloads directory.

**Note:** The prjrepo command is not the recommended method for using custom Debian packages. Instead, create a Debian repository using reprepro (see Chapter 5.2.3), add your packages to that repository, and reference it via its web URI in the mirror list.

## 15.6 Recipe raspberrypi-kernel.xml

```
<ns0:RootFileSystem
xmlns:ns0="https://www.linutronix.de/projects/Elbe"
xmlns:xsi="http://www.w3.org/2001/XMLSchema-instance"
created="2009-05-20T08:50:56" revision="6"
xsi:schemaLocation="https://www.linutronix.de/projects/Elbe
dbsfed.xsd">
<project>
<name>rpi-image</name>
<version>1.0</version>
<description>
   Raspberry Pi Boot image
</description>
<buildtype>aarch64</buildtype>
<mirror>
 <primary_host>ftp.de.debian.org</primary_host>
 <primary_path>/debian</primary_path>
 <primary_proto>http</primary_proto>
 <url-list>
  <url>
   <binary>https://deb.debian.org/debian-security trixie-security
main</binary>
```

```
    <source>https://deb.debian.org/debian-security trixie-security
main</source>
  </url>
  <url>
    <binary>https://deb.debian.org/debian trixie non-free-
firmware</binary>
    <source>https://deb.debian.org/debian trixie non-free-
firmware</source>
  </url>
  <url>
    <binary>https://deb.debian.org/debian-security trixie-security non-
free-firmware</binary>
    <source>https://deb.debian.org/debian-security trixie-security non-
free-firmware</source>
  </url>
 </url-list>
</mirror>
<suite>trixie</suite>
</project>
<target>
<hostname>rpi64</hostname>
<domain></domain>
<passwd_hashed>$6$bOQ4Sf4rSdI1IfRd$3Hai04jz2OYEW108SZWew
eGO/rGvO65ITthDDtDuaC/8Gpwek/xT4rUvKBkBHFIjTDd6.klFdNJ685k
xgabHh/</passwd_hashed>
<console>serial0,115200</console>
<package>
```

```
  <tar>
   <name>image.tgz</name>
  </tar>
</package>
 <debootstrap>
  <variant>minbase</variant>
  <include>gpgv</include>
 </debootstrap>

<images>
 <msdoshd>
  <name>sdcard.img</name>
  <size>2GB</size>
  <partition>
    <size>556MB</size>
    <label>firmware</label>
  </partition>
  <partition>
   <size>remain</size>
    <label>root</label>
    <bootable/>
  </partition>
 </msdoshd>
</images>
<fstab>
 <bylabel>
```

```
  <label>firmware</label>
  <mountpoint>/boot/firmware</mountpoint>
  <fs>
     <type>vfat</type>
  </fs>
 </bylabel>
 <bylabel>
  <label>root</label>
  <mountpoint>/</mountpoint>
  <fs>
    <type>ext4</type>
    <fs-finetuning>
      <device-command>tune2fs -O ^64bit,^metadata_csum -i 0
{device}</device-command>
    </fs-finetuning>
  </fs>

 </bylabel>
</fstab>
<install-recommends/>
<pkg-list>
 <pkg>linux-image-6.6.78-v8-16k-v8</pkg>
 <pkg>kmod</pkg>
 <pkg>initramfs-tools</pkg>
 <pkg>linux-base</pkg>
```

```
<pkg>firmware-brcm80211</pkg>
<pkg>firmware-misc-nonfree</pkg>
<pkg>firmware-atheros</pkg>
<pkg>firmware-libertas</pkg>
<pkg>firmware-linux-free</pkg>
<pkg>firmware-misc-nonfree</pkg>
<pkg>firmware-realtek</pkg>
<pkg>raspi-firmware</pkg>
<pkg>zstd</pkg>
<pkg>apt-utils</pkg>
<pkg>systemd</pkg>
<pkg>systemd-resolved</pkg>
<pkg>systemd-timesyncd</pkg>
<pkg>vim-tiny</pkg>
<pkg>busybox</pkg>
<pkg>bash</pkg>
<pkg>dialog</pkg>
<pkg>openssh-server</pkg>
<pkg>wpasupplicant</pkg>
<pkg>iproute2</pkg>
<pkg>net-tools</pkg>
<pkg>iputils-ping</pkg>
<pkg>iw</pkg>
<pkg>ifupdown</pkg>
<pkg>bluez</pkg>
<pkg>bluez-tools</pkg>
```

```
 <pkg>rfkill</pkg>
 <pkg>avahi-daemon</pkg>
 <pkg>avahi-utils</pkg>

</pkg-list>
<project-finetuning>
   <set_packer packer="tarxz">sdcard.img</set_packer>
</project-finetuning>
<finetuning>

 <command>echo 'ROOTPART="LABEL=root"' &gt;&gt;
/etc/default/raspi-firmware</command>
 <command>echo 'KERNEL_ARCH="arm64"' &gt;&gt; /etc/default/raspi-
firmware</command>
 <command>echo 'init=/usr/lib/systemd/systemd' &gt;&gt;
/etc/default/raspi-extra-cmdline</command>
 <command>mkdir -p /boot/firmware</command>
 <command>cp /usr/lib/raspi-firmware/* /boot/firmware/</command>
 <command>cp -a /usr/lib/linux-image-6.6.78-v8-16k-v8/overlays/
/boot/firmware</command>
 <command>cp -a /usr/lib/linux-image-6.6.78-v8-16k-v8/broadcom/*
/boot/firmware</command>
 <command>cp  /boot/vmlinuz-6.6.78-v8-16k-v8
/boot/firmware</command>
 <command>mkinitramfs -o /boot/initrd.img-6.6.78-v8-16k-v8 6.6.78-v8-
16k-v8</command>
```

```
<file dst="/etc/systemd/network/25-wlan0.network" mode="644">
   [Match]
   Name=wlan0

   [Network]
   DHCP=yes

</file>
<file dst="/etc/wpa_supplicant/wpa_supplicant-wlan0.conf"
mode="600">
 ctrl_interface=DIR=/var/run/wpa_supplicant GROUP=netdev
 update_config=1
 country=US

 network={
    ssid=" SomeSSID"
    psk=" SomeKey"
 }
    </file>
le dst="/etc/default/raspi-firmware" append="true" >
 ROOTPART="LABEL=root"
 KERNEL_ARCH="arm64"
    </file>

<file dst="/etc/default/raspi-extra-cmdline" append="true">
  init=/usr/lib/systemd/systemd
```

```
 </file>

 <command>update-initramfs -u -k all</command>
 <command>systemctl enable
wpa_supplicant@wlan0.service</command>
 <command>systemctl enable systemd-networkd</command>
 <command>systemctl enable avahi-daemon</command>
 <file dst="/boot/firmware/cmdline.txt" mode="755">
    earlyprintk console=ttyAMA0,115200 console=tty1
root=/dev/mmcblk0p2 rootfstype=ext4 fsck.repair=yes rootwait
cfg80211.ieee80211_regdom=GB  init=/usr/lib/systemd/systemd
 </file>
 <file dst="/boot/firmware/config.txt" mode="755">
   enable_uart=1
   arm_64bit=1
   dtoverlay=disable-bt
   dtoverlay=uart0
   dtparam=uart0
   kernel=vmlinuz-6.6.78-v8-16k-v8
   initramfs initrd.img-6.6.78-v8-16k-v8
 </file>

</finetuning>
</target>
<archivedir>overlays/</archivedir>
</ns0:RootFileSystem>
```

## 15.7 Recipe Explanation

The key points of the recipe are the following commands.

```
<command>mkdir -p /boot/firmware</command>
<command>cp /usr/lib/raspi-firmware/* /boot/firmware/</command>
<command>cp -a /usr/lib/linux-image-6.6.78-v8-16k-v8/overlays
/boot/firmware</command>
<command>cp -a /usr/lib/linux-image-6.6.78-v8-16k-v8/broadcom/*
/boot/firmware</command>
<command>cp  /boot/vmlinuz-6.6.78-v8-16k-v8
/boot/firmware</command>
<command>mkinitramfs -o /boot/initrd.img-6.6.78-v8-16k-v8 6.6.78-v8-
16k-v8</command>
```

**Kernel and Initramfs**

This sequence copies the necessary boot files to the boot partition and creates an initramfs in the same location. Unlike previous recipes, these steps are performed manually because:

- Standard Debian kernel packages and Raspberry Pi stock kernel packages include **hook scripts** that automatically trigger initramfs updates and bootloader configuration during installation.
- These hooks are typically located in /etc/kernel/postinst.d/ and /etc/initramfs-tools/hooks/ and are executed by initramfs-tools when the kernel is installed or updated.
- Custom kernel .deb packages often lack these post-installation scripts. As a result, the system does not automatically regenerate the initramfs or copy boot files, which can lead to boot failures.

By manually running these commands, you ensure that the initramfs is properly generated and all required boot files are placed in the correct location, making the image bootable.

## Summary

This chapter demonstrated how to build Raspberry Pi images with both stock and custom-compiled Linux kernels to meet performance, security, and hardware-specific requirements in advanced embedded deployments. Using a drone analytics use case, it compared a fast, stable approach based on the official Raspberry Pi kernel with a fully customized kernel tailored to include only essential drivers and features. The chapter explained how ELBE integrates kernel selection into reproducible image builds, including handling unsigned repositories, selecting appropriate kernel packages, and configuring firmware and boot parameters. It then walked through the complete custom kernel workflow, from cross-compiling and packaging the kernel as a Debian package to integrating it into an ELBE project and manually installing boot files and initramfs when standard kernel hooks are unavailable. Together, these approaches provide a flexible framework for balancing rapid deployment against deep system optimization, making the chapter a practical reference for performance tuning, security hardening, and future hardware enablement on Raspberry Pi platforms.

## Further Reading and Resources

For a deeper understanding of Linux kernel configuration, compilation, and packaging, the official Linux kernel documentation and the Debian kernel handbook provide comprehensive guidance on build options, module management, and initramfs integration. The Raspberry Pi documentation offers detailed explanations of firmware behavior, boot flow, device-tree overlays, and kernel requirements specific to Raspberry Pi hardware. Readers interested in security and performance tuning can consult kernel hardening guides and documentation on minimizing kernel attack surfaces. Finally, the ELBE project documentation and Debian installer resources provide additional context on reproducible image builds, custom package integration, and best practices for maintaining long-term kernel support in embedded Linux systems.

# 16 LLM Dev Machine on Trixie Raspberry Pi 5

**Abstract:** Targeting modern AI workloads, this chapter constructs a Raspberry Pi 5 development machine optimized for large language models (LLM) on Debian Trixie. It includes company scenarios, requirements, implementation, the raspberrypi-llm-trixie.xml recipe, and explanations of package selections, drivers, and optimizations for compute-intensive tasks.

## 16.1 Company Introduction

**Xenostrate Ascension** is a forward-thinking startup dedicated to democratizing AI and machine learning. Its mission is to make powerful AI tools accessible to individuals and small-scale developers by leveraging affordable hardware like the Raspberry Pi 5.

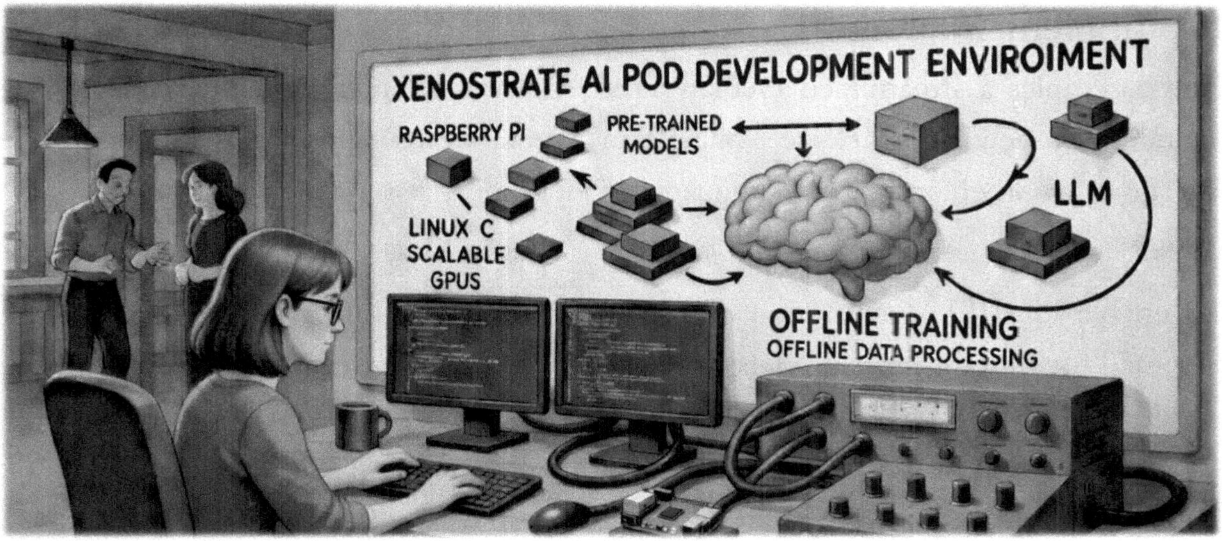


## 16.2 Customer Requirements

**The Xenostrate Ascension** engineering team was approached with a request to create a standalone machine learning development setup using the new Raspberry Pi 5. The goal was to enable offline experimentation with large language models (LLMs) without relying on cloud services.

### Key requirements

- A compact development environment for LLM experimentation.
- The ability to run AI models directly on Raspberry Pi 5's ARM architecture.
- A seamless setup that combines development tools, libraries, and pre-trained models into a single cohesive image.
- Scalability, with options to easily extend the setup as needed.

### Company Response

The task is assigned to Kira, a software engineer at Xenostrate Ascension with expertise in embedded systems and AI environments. Kira decides to build a custom Debian-based operating system image optimized for running AI applications directly on the Raspberry Pi 5.

## 16.3 Implementation

Kira assembles a streamlined Debian Trixie image tailored for Raspberry Pi 5. She includes the new **llm** package available in Trixie, which provides a command-line interface for interacting with language models ideal for prototyping and prompt testing.

To enable local LLM execution and API serving, Kira integrates **Ollama**, a tool designed for running large models offline. Ollama is configured as a **systemd service** under a dedicated system user, ensuring it starts automatically on boot. To simplify system interaction, **Cockpit** is added as a lightweight web interface.

### Creating the ELBE Project

```
$ ID=$(elbe control create_project)
$ elbe control set_xml raspberrypi-llm-trixie.xml
$ elbe prjrepo upload_pkg $ID ~/build/linux-image-6.6.66-v8-16k-
2712_1-1_arm64.deb
```

```
$ elbe control build $ID
$ elbe control wait_busy $ID
$ elbe control get_files $ID --output download
```

**Note:** The prjrepo command is not the recommended method for using custom Debian packages. Instead, create a Debian repository using reprepro (see Chapter 5.2.3), add your packages to that repository, and reference it via its web URI in the mirror list.

After extensive testing, Kira finalizes a polished, lightweight development image for the Raspberry Pi 5. The result is a fully self-contained AI development environment that empowers users to process data, fine-tune models, and experiment with LLMs all entirely offline. The image supports both command-line workflows and web-based access.

### Web-Based LLM Access with Ollama, LLM Tools, and Cockpit

The image combines three key components:

- **Ollama**: Installed as a background service running under a dedicated system user, configured to launch automatically on boot. It provides an API layer for serving and querying large language models locally, eliminating the need for cloud connectivity.
- **llm CLI Tool**: Offers direct interaction with models from the terminal, enabling prompt testing, automation, and rapid prototyping.
- **Cockpit**: Configured to expose a web dashboard at https://<device-ip>:9090. Users can access model logs, control Ollama services, and potentially integrate custom panels for browser-based LLM interaction.

This setup makes managing and experimenting with local models intuitive and visually driven, especially for users less comfortable with the terminal.

## 16.4 Recipe raspberrypi-llm-trixie.xml

```
<ns0:RootFileSystem
xmlns:ns0="https://www.linutronix.de/projects/Elbe"
xmlns:xsi="http://www.w3.org/2001/XMLSchema-instance"
created="2009-05-20T08:50:56" revision="6"
xsi:schemaLocation="https://www.linutronix.de/projects/Elbe
dbsfed.xsd">
<project>
 <name>raspberrypi5-custom_kernel-trixie</name>
 <version>1.0</version>
 <description>
    Raspberry Pi 5 Boot image for LLMs
 </description>
 <buildtype>aarch64</buildtype>
 <mirror>
  <primary_host>ftp.de.debian.org</primary_host>
  <primary_path>/debian</primary_path>
  <primary_proto>http</primary_proto>
  <url-list>
   <url>
    <binary>https://deb.debian.org/debian-security trixie-security
main</binary>
    <source>https://deb.debian.org/debian-security trixie-security
main</source>
   </url>
   <url>
```

```
    <binary>https://deb.debian.org/debian trixie non-free-
firmware</binary>
    <source>https://deb.debian.org/debian trixie non-free-
firmware</source>
   </url>
   <url>
    <binary>https://deb.debian.org/debian trixie contrib</binary>
    <source>https://deb.debian.org/debian trixie contrib</source>
   </url>
   <url>
     <binary>https://deb.debian.org/debian-security trixie-security non-
free-firmware</binary>
     <source>https://deb.debian.org/debian-security trixie-security non-
free-firmware</source>
   </url>
  </url-list>
 </mirror>
 <suite>trixie</suite>
</project>
<target>
 <hostname>rpi64</hostname>
 <domain></domain>

<passwd_hashed>$6$bOQ4Sf4rSdI1IfRd$3Hai04jz2OYEW108SZWew
eGO/rGvO65ITthDDtDuaC/8Gpwek/xT4rUvKBkBHFIjTDd6.kIFdNJ685k
xgabHh/</passwd_hashed>
 <console>serial0,115200</console>
 <package>
```

```
  <tar>
    <name>image.tgz</name>
  </tar>
</package>
<debootstrap>
  <variant>minbase</variant>
  <include>gpgv</include>
</debootstrap>

<images>
<msdoshd>
<name>sdcard.img</name>
<size>6GB</size>
<partition>
  <size>256MB</size>
  <label>firmware</label>
</partition>
<partition>
  <size>remain</size>
  <label>root</label>
  <bootable/>
</partition>
</msdoshd>
</images>
<fstab>
 <bylabel>
```

```
    <label>firmware</label>
    <mountpoint>/boot/firmware</mountpoint>
    <fs>
      <type>vfat</type>
    </fs>
  </bylabel>
  <bylabel>
    <label>root</label>
    <mountpoint>/</mountpoint>
    <fs>
      <type>ext4</type>
      <fs-finetuning>
        <device-command>tune2fs -O ^64bit,^metadata_csum -i 0
{device}</device-command>
      </fs-finetuning>
    </fs>

  </bylabel>
 </fstab>
 <install-recommends/>
 <pkg-list>
  <pkg>linux-image-6.6.78-v8-16k-v8</pkg>
  <pkg>initramfs-tools</pkg>
  <pkg>firmware-brcm80211</pkg>
  <pkg>firmware-misc-nonfree</pkg>
  <pkg>firmware-atheros</pkg>
```

```
<pkg>firmware-libertas</pkg>
<pkg>firmware-linux-free</pkg>
<pkg>firmware-misc-nonfree</pkg>
<pkg>firmware-realtek</pkg>
<pkg>raspi-firmware</pkg>
<pkg>zstd</pkg>
<pkg>apt-utils</pkg>
<pkg>systemd</pkg>
<pkg>systemd-resolved</pkg>
<pkg>systemd-timesyncd</pkg>
<pkg>vim-tiny</pkg>
<pkg>busybox</pkg>
<pkg>bash</pkg>
<pkg>dialog</pkg>
<pkg>openssh-server</pkg>
<pkg>wpasupplicant</pkg>
<pkg>iproute2</pkg>
<pkg>net-tools</pkg>
<pkg>iputils-ping</pkg>
<pkg>iw</pkg>
<pkg>ifupdown</pkg>
<pkg>bluez</pkg>
<pkg>bluez-tools</pkg>
<pkg>rfkill</pkg>
<pkg>network-manager</pkg>
<pkg>curl</pkg>
```

```
  <pkg>ca-certificates</pkg>
  <pkg>cockpit</pkg>
  <pkg>llm</pkg>
 </pkg-list>
 <project-finetuning>
  <set_packer packer="tarxz">sdcard.img</set_packer>
 </project-finetuning>
 <finetuning>
  <adduser
passwd_hashed="$6$bOQ4Sf4rSdI1IfRd$3Hai04jz2OYEW108SZWew
eGO/rGvO65ITthDDtDuaC/8Gpwek/xT4rUvKBkBHFIjTDd6.klFdNJ685k
xgabHh/" shell="/bin/bash" >pi</adduser>

  <command>ln -s /lib/firmware/brcm/brcmfmac43455-sdio.bin
/lib/firmware/brcm/brcmfmac43455-sdio.raspberrypi,5-model-
b.bin</command>
  <command>mkdir -p /boot/firmware</command>
  <command>cp -a /usr/lib/raspi-firmware/* /boot/firmware/</command>
  <command>cp -a /usr/lib/linux-image-6.6.78-v8-16k-v8/overlays/
/boot/firmware</command>
  <command>cp -a /usr/lib/linux-image-6.6.78-v8-16k-v8/broadcom/*
/boot/firmware</command>
  <command>cp  /boot/vmlinuz-6.6.78-v8-16k-v8
/boot/firmware</command>
  <command>mkinitramfs -o /boot/initrd.img-6.6.78-v8-16k-v8 6.6.78-v8-
16k-v8</command>
```

```
<file dst="/etc/NetworkManager/system-
connections/wifi.nmconnection" mode="600" >
[connection]
id=wifi
type=wifi
autoconnect=true

[wifi]
mode=infrastructure
ssid="YourSSID"

[wifi-security]
key-mgmt=wpa-psk
psk=YourPSK

[ipv4]
method=auto

[ipv6]
method=ignore

</file>
<file dst="/etc/cockpit/disallowed-users" >

</file>
<file dst="/etc/resolv.conf" >
```

```
  nameserver 8.8.8.8
</file>
<file dst="/etc/systemd/system/ollama.service" >
  [Unit]
  Description=Ollama Service
  After=network-online.target

  [Service]
  ExecStart=/usr/bin/ollama serve
  User=ollama
  Group=ollama
  Restart=always
  RestartSec=3
  Environment="PATH=$PATH"

  [Install]
  WantedBy=default.target
</file>

<command>systemctl enable NetworkManager</command>
<command>systemctl enable systemd-networkd</command>
<command>curl -fsSL https://ollama.com/install.sh|sh</command>
<command>systemctl daemon-reload</command>
<command>systemctl enable ollama.service</command>

<command>update-initramfs -u -k all</command>
```

```
  <file dst="/boot/firmware/cmdline.txt" mode="755">
  earlyprintk console=ttyAMA0,115200 console=tty1
root=/dev/mmcblk0p2 rootfstype=ext4 fsck.repair=yes rootwait
cfg80211.ieee80211_regdom=GB  init=/usr/lib/systemd/systemd

  </file>
  <file dst="/boot/firmware/config.txt" mode="755">
     enable_uart=1
     arm_64bit=1
     dtoverlay=disable-bt
     dtoverlay=uart0
     dtparam=uart0
     kernel=vmlinuz-6.6.78-v8-16k-v8
     initramfs initrd.img-6.6.78-v8-16k-v8
  </file>
 </finetuning>
</target>
</ns0:RootFileSystem>
```

## 16.5 Recipe Explanation

```
<include>gpgv</include>
```

- This explicitly includes the gpgv package in the bootstrapped rootfs.
- Starting with Debian Trixie, gpgv is required by debootstrap to verify signatures on the Release files of the Debian archive.
- Including it ensures the debootstrap process completes successfully and securely.

## Summary

This chapter presented the construction of a self-contained large language model (LLM) development machine for Raspberry Pi 5 using Debian Trixie, targeting offline and resource-aware AI experimentation. Through the Xenostrate Ascension use case, it showed how a compact yet capable AI environment can be built on affordable ARM hardware by combining a carefully selected kernel, firmware, and userland with modern AI tooling. The implementation leveraged ELBE to produce a reproducible system image that integrates the Trixie llm command-line tool, the Ollama runtime for local model execution and API serving, and Cockpit as a lightweight web-based management interface. By configuring Ollama as a systemd service and optimizing package selection and boot components for compute-intensive workloads, the resulting image delivers a seamless development experience that supports both terminal-driven workflows and browser-based interaction, enabling scalable, cloud-independent LLM experimentation directly on the Raspberry Pi 5.

## Further Reading and Resources

Readers interested in running AI workloads on ARM-based systems can explore the Debian Trixie release notes and package documentation for details on the llm tool and recent improvements to ARM64 performance. The Ollama documentation provides deeper insight into local model execution, API usage, and service configuration for offline environments. For understanding Raspberry Pi 5–specific kernel, firmware, and boot optimizations, the official Raspberry Pi documentation offers authoritative guidance on hardware enablement and performance tuning. Additional background on reproducible system image generation and advanced finetuning techniques can be found in the ELBE project documentation, which complements the workflows demonstrated in this chapter.

# 17 Additional Recipe

**Abstract:** This supplementary chapter presents a community-inspired recipe: an Ubuntu-based ROS2 setup for Raspberry Pi 5. It highlights the flexibility of ELBE beyond pure Debian, enabling robotics and advanced application stacks.

## 17.1 Ubuntu ROS2 Raspberry Pi 5

```
<ns0:RootFileSystem
xmlns:ns0="https://www.linutronix.de/projects/Elbe"
xmlns:xsi="http://www.w3.org/2001/XMLSchema-instance"
created="2009-05-20T08:50:56" revision="6"
xsi:schemaLocation="https://www.linutronix.de/projects/Elbe
dbsfed.xsd">
<project>
<name>RaspberryPi-Ubuntu</name>
<version>1.0</version>
<description>
   Raspberry Pi Ubuntu image
</description>
<buildtype>aarch64</buildtype>
 <mirror>
 <primary_host>ports.ubuntu.com/</primary_host>
 <primary_path>/ubuntu-ports</primary_path>
 <primary_proto>http</primary_proto>
 <host>https://archive.ubuntu.com/ubuntu</host>
 <url-list>
```

```
 <url>
  <binary>https://ports.ubuntu.com/ubuntu-ports jammy
restricted</binary>
  <source>https://ports.ubuntu.com/ubuntu-ports jammy
restricted</source>
 </url>
  <url>
   <binary>https://ports.ubuntu.com/ubuntu-ports jammy main universe
multiverse</binary>
   <source>https://ports.ubuntu.com/ubuntu-ports jammy main universe
multiverse</source>
  </url>
  <url>
   <binary>https://ports.ubuntu.com/ubuntu-ports jammy-updates main
universe multiverse</binary>
   <source>https://ports.ubuntu.com/ubuntu-ports jammy-updates main
universe multiverse</source>
  </url>
  <url>
   <binary>https://ports.ubuntu.com/ubuntu-ports jammy-security main
universe multiverse</binary>
   <source>https://ports.ubuntu.com/ubuntu-ports jammy-security main
universe multiverse</source>
  </url>

 </url-list>
```

```
</mirror>
<suite>jammy</suite>

</project>
<target>
<hostname>rpi4-ubuntu</hostname>
<domain></domain>
<passwd_hashed>$6$bOQ4Sf4rSdI1IfRd$3Hai04jz2OYEW108SZWew
eGO/rGvO65ITthDDtDuaC/8Gpwek/xT4rUvKBkBHFIjTDd6.kIFdNJ685k
xgabHh/</passwd_hashed>
<console>serial0,115200</console>
<package>
<tar>
   <name>rootfs.tgz</name>
</tar>
</package>
<debootstrap>
 <variant>minbase</variant>
 <include>gpgv,curl</include>

</debootstrap>

<images>
 <msdoshd>
 <name>sdcard.img</name>
 <size>15GB</size>
```

```
 <partition>
    <size>256MB</size>
    <label>firmware</label>
 </partition>
 <partition>
    <size>remain</size>
    <label>root</label>
    <bootable/>
 </partition>
 </msdoshd>
</images>
<fstab>
 <bylabel>
  <label>firmware</label>
  <mountpoint>/boot/firmware</mountpoint>
  <fs>
     <type>vfat</type>
  </fs>
 </bylabel>
 <bylabel>
    <label>root</label>
    <mountpoint>/</mountpoint>
    <fs>
 <type>ext4</type>
 <fs-finetuning>
     <device-command>tune2fs -O ^64bit,^metadata_csum -i 0
{device}</device-command>
```

```
 </fs-finetuning>
    </fs>
 </bylabel>
</fstab>
<project-finetuning>
   <set_packer packer="none">sdcard.img</set_packer>
</project-finetuning>
<install-recommends/>
<pkg-list>
 <pkg>linux-raspi</pkg>
 <pkg>linux-firmware-raspi</pkg>
 <pkg>linux-firmware</pkg>
 <pkg>u-boot-rpi</pkg>
 <pkg>u-boot-tools</pkg>
 <pkg>rpi-eeprom</pkg>
 <pkg>libraspberrypi-bin</pkg>
 <pkg>zstd</pkg>
 <pkg>apt-utils</pkg>
 <pkg>systemd</pkg>
 <pkg>systemd-timesyncd</pkg>
 <pkg>vim-tiny</pkg>
 <pkg>busybox</pkg>
 <pkg>bash</pkg>
 <pkg>openssh-server</pkg>
 <pkg>initramfs-tools</pkg>
```

```
 <pkg>curl</pkg>
 <pkg>gnupg2</pkg>
 <pkg>lsb-release</pkg>
 <pkg>software-properties-common</pkg>
 <pkg>build-essential</pkg>

 <pkg>python3-argcomplete</pkg>
 <pkg>python3-pip</pkg>
 <pkg>git</pkg>
 <pkg>cmake</pkg>


 <pkg>python3-empy</pkg>
 <pkg>python3-numpy</pkg>

</pkg-list>
<finetuning>

 <command>echo 'ROOTPART="LABEL=root"' &gt;&gt;
/etc/default/raspi-firmware</command>
 <command>echo 'KERNEL_ARCH="arm64"' &gt;&gt; /etc/default/raspi-
firmware</command>
 <command>echo 'init=/usr/lib/systemd/systemd' &gt;&gt;
/etc/default/raspi-extra-cmdline</command>
 <command>mkdir -p /boot/firmware</command>
 <command>cp /usr/lib/linux-firmware-raspi/*
/boot/firmware</command>
```

```
 <command>cp -a /lib/firmware/5.15.0-1087-raspi/device-tree/overlays
/boot/firmware</command>
 <command>cp -a /lib/firmware/5.15.0-1087-raspi/device-
tree/broadcom/*  /boot/firmware</command>
 <command>cp  /boot/vmlinuz-5.15.0-1087-raspi
/boot/firmware</command>
 <command>cp  /boot/initrd.img-5.15.0-1087-raspi
/boot/firmware</command>
 <file dst="/boot/firmware/cmdline.txt" mode="755">
    console=serial0,115200 console=tty1 root=/dev/sdb2 rootfstype=ext4
fsck.repair=yes rootwait quiet splash plymouth.ignore-serial-consoles
cfg80211.ieee80211_regdom=GB
 </file>
 <file dst="/boot/firmware/config.txt" mode="755">
    enable_uart=1
    arm_64bit=1
    kernel=vmlinuz-5.15.0-1087-raspi
    initramfs initrd.img-5.15.0-1087-raspi
 </file>

 <command>curl -sSL
https://raw.githubusercontent.com/ros/rosdistro/master/ros.key -o
/usr/share/keyrings/ros-archive-keyring.gpg</command>
 <command>echo "deb [arch=arm64 signed-by=/usr/share/keyrings/ros-
archive-keyring.gpg] https://packages.ros.org/ros2/ubuntu jammy main"
| tee /etc/apt/sources.list.d/ros2.list</command>
 <command>apt update</command>
```

```
 <command>apt search ros-humble-desktop</command>
 <command>apt install -y ros-humble-desktop</command>
 <command>update-initramfs -u -k all</command>

</finetuning>
</target>
</ns0:RootFileSystem>
```

# 18 Conclusion

**Abstract:** The closing chapter reflects on the journey: summarizing built systems, distilling best practices for reproducible embedded development with ELBE, exploring future directions (e.g., emerging hardware, security trends), and offering final encouragement to readers to experiment, contribute, and deploy confidently.

## 18.1 What We Built Together

This book started with the foundations of Linux, Debian, and Raspberry Pi platform, and gradually moved toward building complete embedded Linux systems using ELBE. You learned how Debian works under the hood, how ELBE structures system builds, and how to turn requirements into reproducible images.

Through practical examples, you created real-world Raspberry Pi systems, which work with different filesystems, encryption, containers, custom kernels, and even an LLM development machine. These examples demonstrate how embedded Linux development can be approached as a structured, repeatable process rather than a collection of manual steps.

## 18.2 Best Practices

Keep these principles in mind as you continue working with ELBE:

- Version control all build descriptions
- Avoid shipping manually created golden images
- Automate image builds
- Treat OS images as code
- Document system requirements clearly in XML

## 18.3 Future Directions

Possible next steps include Secure Boot, OTA updates, A/B partitioning, SBOM generation, and deeper CI/CD integration. These topics build naturally on the foundation established in this book and enable more advanced, production-ready systems.

## 18.4 Final Thoughts

Embedded Linux is no longer about simply making a system boot. It is about **maintainability, security, and reproducibility**.

By adopting ELBE and a build-system mindset, you gain a solid foundation for building embedded Linux systems that can grow from simple experiments into reliable, real-world products.

# 19 Glossary

**APT** (Advanced Package Tool) : Debian's package management system for installing, updating, and removing software packages.

**Archive** : In ELBE, a base64-encoded collection of files (e.g., configuration overrides or custom scripts) that can be integrated into the target root filesystem during build.

**Bootloader** : Software (e.g., U-Boot or Raspberry Pi firmware) that initializes hardware and loads the Linux kernel.

**BusyBox** : A lightweight, single-binary tool providing many standard Unix utilities (e.g., ls, cp, grep) in a minimal footprint, ideal for resource-constrained embedded root filesystems.

**Chroot** : A Linux system call that changes the apparent root directory for a process, used in build environments to isolate filesystem views.

**Cross-compilation** (or Cross-toolchain) : Compiling code on one architecture (e.g., x86 host) to run on another (e.g., ARM on Raspberry Pi).

**Debian** : A popular Linux distribution that serves as the base for many embedded systems, known for its package management and stability.

**Debootstrap** : A Debian tool used to create a base Debian system by downloading and installing core packages into a directory; ELBE uses it (or similar) to bootstrap the target root filesystem.

**Deterministic / Reproducible Build** : A build process that produces identical output (bit-for-bit) given the same inputs, crucial for reliability, security auditing, and long-term maintenance in embedded systems.

**Device Tree** (or DTB / Flattened Device Tree) : A binary file (compiled from DTS source) that describes hardware components to the Linux kernel at boot time, essential for ARM-based platforms like Raspberry Pi.

**ELBE** (Embedded Linux Build Environment) : A tool for creating reproducible Debian-based root filesystems from XML descriptions, emphasizing determinism and maintainability.

**Filesystem Hierarchy Standard (FHS)** : The standard layout for directories in a Linux root filesystem (e.g., /bin, /etc, /usr).

**Finetuning** : In ELBE, a section in the project XML for custom post-build modifications to the root filesystem (e.g., scripts to adjust configs, add users, or remove packages).

**Initramfs** (or Initial RAM Filesystem) : A temporary root filesystem loaded into memory during boot to prepare the real root filesystem.

**Initvm** : In ELBE, the initial virtual machine (built with QEMU/KVM) that provides a native build environment for creating reproducible root filesystems.

**Kernel** (Linux Kernel) : The core of the operating system, managing hardware, processes, memory, and system calls.

**Overlay** (or Overlay Filesystem) : A mechanism to layer modifications on top of a base filesystem without altering the original (used in ELBE for customizations).

**pbuilder** : A Debian tool for building packages in a clean, isolated chroot environment; ELBE uses it to compile custom or source packages and integrate them into the target system.

**Project XML** (or ELBE XML) : The central configuration file for an ELBE project, defining the target architecture, packages, archive, finetuning, and other build parameters.

**QEMU** : An open-source emulator and virtualizer used in ELBE (often with KVM acceleration) to run a native build environment for cross-architecture targets.

**Raspberry Pi** : A family of small, affordable single-board computers popular for embedded prototyping and development.

**RFS** (Root Filesystem) : The directory structure mounted as / on a running Linux system, containing binaries, libraries, configuration files, and applications.

**Root Filesystem** : See **RFS** (often abbreviated RFS in embedded contexts).

**SDK** (Software Development Kit) : A set of tools, libraries, and documentation for developing applications for a specific platform or system.

**SquashFS** : A compressed read-only filesystem often used for embedded root filesystems.

**Toolchain** : A set of compiler, linker, debugger, and other tools for building software (often cross-toolchains in embedded work).

**U-Boot** : A popular open-source bootloader for embedded systems, supporting many architectures including ARM.

**Virtualization** : Running multiple operating systems or isolated environments on one host

www.ingramcontent.com/pod-product-compliance
Lightning Source LLC
Chambersburg PA
CBHW061200240926
51846CB00006B/1069
* 9 7 8 3 9 8 2 8 3 4 4 0 5 *